LANGUAGE AND LITERACY SERIES
Dorothy S. Strickland and Celia Genishi, SERIES EDITORS

(Continued)

Exploring Blue Highways: Literacy Reform,
School Change, and the Creation of Learning Communities
JOBETH ALLEN, MARILYNN CARY, and
LISA DELGADO, Coordinators

Envisioning Literature:
Literary Understanding and Literature Instruction
JUDITH A. LANGER

Teaching Writing as Reflective Practice
GEORGE HILLOCKS, JR.

Talking Their Way into Science: Hearing Children's
Questions and Theories, Responding with Curricula
KAREN GALLAS

Whole Language Across the Curriculum: Grades 1, 2, 3
SHIRLEY C. RAINES, Editor

No Quick Fix: Rethinking Literacy Programs in
America's Elementary Schools
RICHARD L. ALLINGTON and SEAN A. WALMSLEY, Editors

Nonfiction for the Classroom: Milton Meltzer on
Writing, History, and Social Responsibility
E. WENDY SAUL, Editor

When Children Write:
Critical Re-Visions of the Writing Workshop
TIMOTHY LENSMIRE

Dramatizing Literature in Whole Language Classrooms,
SECOND EDITION
JOHN WARREN STEWIG and CAROL BUEGE

The Languages of Learning: How Children Talk, Write,
Dance, Draw, and Sing Their Understanding of the World
KAREN GALLAS

Partners in Learning:
Teachers and Children in Reading Recovery
CAROL A. LYONS, GAY SU PINNELL, and DIANE E. DEFORD

Social Worlds of Children Learning to Write in an
Urban Primary School
ANNE HAAS DYSON

The Politics of Workplace Literacy: A Case Study
SHERYL GREENWOOD GOWEN

Inside/Outside: Teacher Research and Knowledge
MARILYN COCHRAN-SMITH and SUSAN L. LYTLE

Literacy Events in a Community of Young Writers
YETTA M. GOODMAN and SANDRA WILDE, Editors

Whole Language Plus:
Essays on Literacy in the United States and New Zealand
COURTNEY B. CAZDEN

Process Reading and Writing: A Literature-Based Approach
JOAN T. FEELEY, DOROTHY S. STRICKLAND, and
SHELLEY B. WEPNER, Editors

The Child as Critic: Teaching Literature in Elementary and
Middle Schools, THIRD EDITION
GLENNA DAVIS SLOAN

Literacy for a Diverse Society:
Perspectives, Practices, and Policies
ELFRIEDA H. HIEBERT, Editor

The Complete Theory-to-Practice Handbook of Adult
Literacy: Curriculum Design and Teaching Approaches
RENA SOIFER, MARTHA IRWIN, BARBARA CRUMRINE,
EMO HONZAKI, BLAIR SIMMONS, and DEBORAH YOUNG

The Administration
and
Supervision
of
Reading Programs

Third Edition

EDITED BY

Shelley B. Wepner
Dorothy S. Strickland
AND
Joan T. Feeley

FOREWORD BY **Jack Cassidy**

TEACHERS
COLLEGE
PRESS

Teachers College, Columbia University
New York and London

Published by Teachers College Press, 1234 Amsterdam Avenue, New York, NY 10027

Library of Congress Cataloging-in-Publication Data

The administration and supervision of reading programs / edited by Shelley B. Wepner, Dorothy S. Strickland, Joan T. Feeley. — 3rd ed.
     p.   cm. — (Language and literacy series)
   Includes bibliographical references and index.
   ISBN 0-8077-4181-7 (pbk. : alk. paper)
     1. Reading—United States.   2. School management and organization—United States.
   3. School supervision—United States.   I. Wepner, Shelley B., 1951–   II. Feeley, Joan T.,
   1932–   III. Strickland, Dorothy S.   IV. Language and literacy series (New York, N.Y.)

   LB1050.2 .A36 2001
   428.4'071—dc21   2001040988

ISBN 0-8077-4181-7   (paper)

Printed on acid-free paper
Manufactured in the United States of America
09   08   07   06   05   04   03   8   7   6   5   4   3   2

11/22/04

Again, to our parents, our first role models and supervisors:
Carole and Bernard Markovitz
Evelyn and Leroy Salley Sr.
Theresa and Ed Stollmeyer

And to our families for giving us the opportunity
to continue the legacy of our parents:
Husband, Roy Wepner; and
daughters, Leslie and Meredith

In memory of husband, Maurice Strickland;
sons, Mark, Randy, and Michael; and
grandchildren, Chelsea, Rebecca, Cooper, Paige, and Hannah

In memory of husband, Bob Feeley;
children, John and Maura; and
grandchildren, Brian, Scott, Kelli, and Cristina

CONTENTS

PART III

Program Implementation and Evaluation

PART IV

Interconnections

FOREWORD

About 15 years ago, I was an external evaluator for a graduate reading program at a university in New Jersey. While there, I observed a class in the administration and supervision of reading programs taught by a young, intelligent, and diligent scholar named Shelley Wepner. Since I was a former reading supervisor and also taught a graduate course on the same subject, I was particularly attentive. Needless to say, I was impressed. In a conversation at the conclusion of the class, Shelley and I both bemoaned the fact that there was not a good basic text dealing with the supervision of reading programs. We challenged each other to write one. Over the next few years, I forgot our conversation. Luckily for reading educators nationwide, Shelley Wepner did not. With her two colleagues, Joan T. Feeley and Dorothy S. Strickland, Shelley produced the first edition of *The Administration and Supervision of Reading Programs* in 1989. In 1995, the second edition appeared. For both of these volumes, I had the honor of writing the foreword. More importantly, I now had a wonderful text to use in my graduate classes. The text formed the basis on which my whole course was organized, and my graduate students extolled the virtues of the text on a weekly basis.

Shelley and I have both moved on to other universities and other roles. This year I am serving as interim director of a doctoral program in educational leadership. Once again, I am turning to this text as I advise school administrators who are also doctoral candidates preparing dissertations on the administration of reading programs in their schools. It is not only reading educators who can profit from the chapters in this text.

That is why I am particularly pleased that there will now be a third edition of this book.

Like the previous editions, this text is organized into four major sections: overview, program development, program implementation and evaluation, and interconnections. Each of the sections is completely updated. Particularly impressive is the list of authors of the various chapters—a veritable Who's Who in reading education.

The first section of the book gives an overview of the components of an effective reading program as well as the roles of reading personnel. It is noteworthy that Rita Bean of the University of Pittsburgh is the author of the first chapter. She recently completed a four-year term as chair of the National Commission on the Role of the Reading Specialist, sponsored by the International Reading Association (IRA). Diana Quatroche, co-author of the second chapter (with Dr. Wepner), also served on that commission.

The second section of the book deals with the development of reading programs from the pre-elementary level to the college and adult levels. With the increased federal funding at the pre-K level, the chapter on pre-elementary programs is particularly relevant. Former IRA president Dorothy S. Strickland of Rutgers University gives some excellent and practical insights into what should be included in such programs. Another former IRA president, Richard T. Vacca of Kent State University, provides similar insights into adolescent literacy programs. He is also the founder of IRA's Adolescent Literacy Commission.

As in the previous editions, the third section of the book deals with all the necessary components of a school reading program—materials, observation, professional development, and assessment. All of the chapters in this section have been significantly revised with an increased emphasis on adolescent programs. Particularly relevant is the information about the standards movement, large-scale assessments, and the National Board of Professional Teaching Standards.

The last section of this volume deals with several types of interconnections: interconnections between reading, writing, and technology; reading interconnections with diverse populations and special needs students; interconnections with the community. Chapters in this section have been updated to include information about school and university partnerships and the federally sponsored America Reads program. Like the other chapters in this book, these are authored by cutting-edge leaders in the field.

I concluded my foreword in the last edition of this volume with a paragraph of thanks to Drs. Wepner, Feeley, and Strickland for providing my students and countless other graduate students with a valuable reference in helping them organize a school reading program. This edition will also provide relevant information and research to present and future graduate students. Furthermore, school administrators at all levels need to read this volume to better understand exactly how a reading program should be organized at both the district and school levels.

In short, Drs. Wepner, Strickland, and Feeley have done it again! They have provided us with a relevant, research-based, and readable reference on the organization of school reading programs, an often neglected area in reading education.

Jack Cassidy
Professor of Education
Texas A&M University–Corpus Christi
President of the International
Reading Association, 1982–83

ACKNOWLEDGMENTS

Time and again, as we went through yet another round of sending chapters back and forth to someone for something, however important or trivial, we would remark to each other that we were in the best of company. We found ourselves in awe of our authors' knowledge base and inspired by our authors' dedication to the writing process. As with any edited book, its value comes from both the individual and collective contributions of its authors. Authors need to be able to communicate a message that not only can stand on its own but also adds, with just the right measure, to the overall mission of the book. We acknowledge with great appreciation the contribution of each of our authors and the significant role each played in helping this third edition come together.

There also are people on the sidelines who contribute directly or indirectly to a publication. Particularly important to recognize is the work of graduate assistant Michelle Cotter, who did this and that, almost on a daily basis, to facilitate the process. With great humor and skill, Michelle demonstrated grace under pressure throughout her assistance, for which we are grateful. We also recognize Rebecca Brittain for her review and critique of parts of the book. Also significant was the work of our photographer, Kelly Jenkins, who took time away from her studies to capture the magic in classrooms. She worked tirelessly with administrators, teachers, and students to identify the perfect shot for each of the chapters in the book. We also sincerely acknowledge those in the photographs who allowed us to publish a slice of their classroom life within the professional community.

We recognize that this third edition would not exist without the kind and sincere support of Teachers College Press Editor Carol Collins. Without fail, Carol was responsive to our questions, encouraging with our plans, and tactfully helpful with our mission. From beginning to end, we benefitted from her sharp eye for the written message and her exceptional talent for editing, and quite naturally, we are deeply appreciative of her efforts.

On a more personal level, we acknowledge the understanding and support of our families, friends, and colleagues. They had an uncanny ability to look the other way when we were late for a social event, missed a deadline or a meeting, or simply were unavailable for the chitchat that makes life that much more full.

Finally, we thank you, the readership, for letting us know that a third edition was needed, and would be read.

INTRODUCTION:
LOOKING FORWARD, LOOKING BACK

Since the publication of the second edition of *The Administration and Supervision of Reading Programs*, dramatic changes have taken place in literacy education growing out of research findings, legislative changes, political initiatives, technological advances, student diversity, and recognition of the relationship between literacy and learning. High-stakes testing, standards-based education, accountability for both Pre-K–12 education and teacher education, and school choice have challenged us to reform administrative policies and instructional practices to communicate to the public that we are indeed using our creative juices to develop, maintain, and cultivate literacy. The type of school (public or private, charter or parochial) does not matter. The authors in this book believe that there must be leaders of literacy—reading specialists, supervisors, and administrators—who can set the agenda and provide incentives and resources for helping others to move in the same direction.

This third edition aims to help prospective and current leaders of literacy understand how to organize and supervise reading programs within the context of national, state, and local changes. Examples, observations, and research are used to make this text both practical and readable. As with previous editions, the book is divided into four parts; however, chapters have been overhauled to incorporate the many and varied changes in literacy education. Part I provides an overview of reading supervision by describing effective reading program components and the personnel for program implementation. Part II presents guidelines for developing

reading programs at the pre-elementary through university levels. The chapter on college and university reading programs is new to include a broader spectrum of responsibilities for reading personnel. Part III describes four critical areas for program implementation and evaluation: reading material selection and use, teacher observation, professional development, and assessment. Part IV explores five areas that must be interconnected with comprehensive reading program development: writing, technology, diverse student populations, the community, and special needs students.

What follows is a summary of the themes that recur across the four parts of the book. Related as connections and directions, they represent the key ideas presented by the authors. This introductory section serves two purposes: (1) to foreshadow overarching concepts and (2) to reflect back on authors' ideas. We encourage you to use this discussion to frame your thoughts for reading and then to return to it after you complete the book to reframe your thinking.

Connections

1. Administrators and supervisors are challenged to use standards-based education and high-stakes testing as an opportunity to create systemic reform within reading programs. On one hand, there now exist identifiable and prescriptive standards for students' literacy learning with accompanying large-scale assessment instruments that determine students' degree of success. On the other hand, there are teachers and administrators whose instructional and assessment practices are out of sync with state-regulated standards.

Those responsible for guiding the development of a comprehensive reading program need to convince both key personnel and the parent community that standards provide a focus for instruction, giving all students access to a rigorous curriculum. Leaders need to work with their colleagues to align the school or district's framework for curriculum, instruction, and assessment with standards. Such a framework needs a sound theoretical base, realistic instructional goals, and benchmarks for students' learning that are based on knowledge of the school and the community.

Embedded within the framework are connections between instruction and assessment for both reading and writing. Materials and resources, both traditional and electronic, must be considered in light of such modifications. Equally significant is the need to maintain congruence between revised instructional or assessment practices and programs for students with special needs. Teachers' professional development opportunities must be reviewed for their usefulness and contribution to teachers' competencies with changes in the reading program.

Any meaningful change in schools requires a time-consuming and painstaking process of rethinking and retooling. These reform efforts, ever so critical with today's standards, require leaders who have the knowledge and skill to guide such changes. This ability requires a deep knowledge and understanding of reading research, reading acquisition, reading instruction, and assessment. Leaders also need the ability to convince other stakeholders about the importance of a shared vision for reforming a reading program.

2. Administrators and supervisors are responsible for creating the culture and ethos for change. Administrators and supervisors can't expect to be expert in all disciplines, developmental levels, and areas of concern for which they are responsible. However, if they are to be credible and successful leaders of literacy, they need to have their own set of competencies. This entails having knowledge about the field, standards, assessment mandates, methodologies, and materials, and using such knowledge to promote change. It also means being aware of the conflicting demands and needs of different constituencies, and having sufficient intellectual and emotional stamina to work well with all people to get the most from them. Leaders of literacy also need to know enough about a school or district to establish and communicate realistic expectations, and to know when to call on the expertise of others.

A major responsibility of administrators and supervisors is to guide the change process so that it is perceived by teachers as supportive rather than burdensome. An ongoing program of professional development helps teachers keep current about reading and writing instruction, and to understand how standards-based assessment works in their classrooms. Resources must be provided, and teachers' voices must be valued in planning both the process and the content of professional development. Consideration should be given to how observations and portfolios help to assess and document accomplishments, and how action research helps to develop a problem-solving mindset for answering questions about instructional practices. Because teachers are an essential component of literacy achievement, administrators and supervisors need to do all that is humanly possible to promote teachers' investment in changing expectations.

3. Communication and collaboration among colleagues and with the community are essential. Dynamic reading programs emanate from strong leadership within the school as well as from sincere efforts by school personnel to reach out and involve the family and the community. Regular communication and collaboration with colleagues help educators to better understand and plan for the varied complexities of reading programs. This connection allows leaders of literacy to take stock of the successes and failures with students, and the conditions surrounding each. It also provides for better coordination within and across grade levels, and between regular and special programs.

Communication with the community helps parents understand the reading program and support changes in the way programs are reframed to meet standards. Collaboration with the community helps bring about important initiatives that extend a school's resources. Forming Professional Development Schools and other types of partnership networks between the pre-K–12 and higher education communities helps bridge the gap between theory and practice as higher education faculty and students work directly with pre-K–12 faculty and students. Intergenerational programs, where the community comes in to share books, or the children go to the community to visit others, promote the concept of using an entire village to support students' literacy and learning.

4. Reading, as both a cognitive and social act, continues to require a balanced approach to instruction. Recent scrutiny of literacy practices has challenged us to work even harder to make sure that learners are becoming readers in the best possible learning environments. With widespread acknowledgment of the need for a balanced reading program, leaders of literacy need to help teachers promote literacy by using a multitude of strategies, including phonics instruction, to help students make meaningful connections. Authentic, connected text from a wide variety of reading materials, including high-quality works of literature for children and adolescents, should be part of instruction to ensure valid learning experiences.

The goal is for students to become independent text readers. Even though a simple solution for bringing students to high levels of literacy does not exist, there will continue to be inroads to help students function in and out of school. Early intervention programs help identify children at risk for literacy failure and provide strategy training, immediate reinforcement, and corrective feedback. Pull-out and push-in programs help elementary and middle school students with special needs. These programs are especially effective when students have qualified teachers, are instructed with programs that are congruent with regular classroom programs, receive individualized help with materials at their instructional levels, are monitored and reinforced for their efforts, and are exposed to effective instructional practices. Secondary and post-secondary literacy programs equip students with the strategies they need to strengthen their learning within and across specific subjects and courses.

In sum, these four themes communicate that the quality of a reading program is determined by its leadership. Leaders administer with care and competence when they possess the necessary knowledge and skill to help schools set appropriate and realistic goals, when they create a culture that values teachers' professionalism and parents' contributions in support of students' literacy, and when they do everything in their power to provide a balanced, yet meaningful literacy program. Just as there is no best program for all learners at every level, there is no best way to supervise under all circumstances. A key to administering a program is to create a balance with one's goals, one's abilities, and one's realities.

Directions

This third edition of *The Administration and Supervision of Reading Programs*, written seven years after the publication of the second edition, contains a dozen directions that speak to major shifts in thinking about educating our youth. These directions account for areas of both rapid change and steady state. They are, in fact, a set of hypotheses about the next steps needed to build on existing opportunities and discoveries. Implicit in these directions is the recognition that leaders of literacy definitely will need to know more, be more, and help more as schools change their expectations for teachers and students.

1. Those in the position to initiate change—politicians, state boards of education, building- and district-level administrators, and school board members—will continue to learn about the importance of literacy for learning and, consequently, focus on ways to strengthen reading programs to support

students at every level. *Rita M. Bean* (Chapter 1) describes the elements that agents of change must consider as they develop effective reading programs.

2. Teachers, as an unmistakable influence on students' achievement in the classroom, will need to come to classrooms prepared to teach literacy and will need to actively seek professional development opportunities to expand their knowledge and upgrade their skills. They will not be able to do it all, and they will need qualified and regular assistance in their classrooms to address students' multiple needs. *Bill Harp* (Chapter 8) offers guidelines for observing and assisting teachers so that they are equipped to grow into their roles.

3. Leaders of literacy will need to work with teachers to help them combine their own knowledge and instructional standards for both reading and writing with local, state, and national standards for literacy learning. *Kathryn H. Au* (Chapter 4) demonstrates how to do this for elementary programs, and *Karen Bromley* (Chapter 11) shows how to include writing instruction to promote reading and learning across the pre-K–12 curriculum.

4. There will be a shift in reading specialists' method of delivery of instructional services in which push-in instruction will be used to complement pull-out instruction. *Shelley B. Wepner* and *Diana J. Quatroche* (Chapter 2) offer examples of how the roles and responsibilities of reading personnel are evolving.

5. The worlds of pre-K–12 education and of teacher education will continue to come together to help prepare teachers and to bring the best ideas to both environments. *JoAnne L. Vacca* and *Maryann Mraz* (Chapter 9) provide concrete examples of partnerships and initiatives between both worlds.

6. There will be growing use of early intervention and prevention programs that become part of regular classroom practice as their success in preventing reading failure continues to become more evident. *Dorothy S. Strickland* (Chapter 3) describes how to establish and assess a supportive language and literacy

curriculum for pre-elementary reading programs, and *Dixie Lee Spiegel* (Chapter 15) discusses how specific early intervention programs work for students with special needs.

7. The increased cultural, racial, ethnic, and linguistic diversity in the classroom will require teachers and leaders of literacy to adapt instruction and assessment to meet students' needs. *Junko Yokota* and *William Teale* (Chapter 13) discuss ways to create a classroom climate responsive to diverse student needs.

8. There will be an increased focus on helping adolescents and young adults achieve advanced levels of literacy so that they can function productively in the society in which they find themselves. *Richard T. Vacca* and *Christine A. McKeon* (Chapter 5) highlight characteristics of effective middle school and high school reading programs, and *Arlene D. Wartenberg* (Chapter 6) does the same for college and university reading programs to communicate the importance of contributing constructively at any level of learning.

9. Instructional materials and resources will continue to get more sophisticated, complicated, and precise. As *Diane Lapp, Douglas Fisher, James Flood, Kelly Goss-Moore,* and *Juel Moore* (Chapter 7) explain, the usefulness of instructional materials will be felt when they are packaged with assessment and monitoring tools, and when they include comprehensible and doable suggestions for use.

10. Electronic literacy will become a way of life as more and more teachers learn that they and their students cannot live without it for information and communication purposes. *Shelley B. Wepner* and *Lucinda C. Ray* (Chapter 12) argue that as the technology becomes more accessible, both physically and cognitively, schools will have to invest in the hardware and in their teachers.

11. Assessment, formal and informal, will continue to be a way of life, with greater focus given to understanding how to frame instruction around assessment tools. *Barbara A. Kapinus* (Chapter 10) offers specific ideas for using both large-scale and classroom assessment data to make decisions about instruction.

12. Community outreach efforts will become much more central to the life of the classroom, with parents serving as partners in children's literacy education. *Anthony D. Fredericks* (Chapter 14) describes ways to involve parents and the community in the life of the school.

In looking back to look ahead, we agree that "We've come a long way, baby," in what we know about literacy development and in how we shape our environments to capitalize on available personnel and resources. We also grudgingly accept that many of our efforts simply are just the beginning, and we invite you, the reader, to join us in using and reusing our authors' insights and ideas to reach for our next milestone in developing literacy for all.

Shelley B. Wepner
Dorothy S. Strickland

PART I

Overview

Part I sets the stage for this book by providing an overview of the components and personnel needed to administer an effective reading program. Chapter 1 provides specific guidelines for implementing three essential elements of a reading program—curriculum, instruction, and assessment. It addresses the concept of a balanced approach to reading, the impact of standards on curriculum and instruction, and the "how" of incorporating standards into program development.

Chapter 2 addresses the current status and use of reading personnel. It describes the independent and interdependent roles and responsibilities of reading specialists, reading supervisors, principals, and classroom teachers. It also looks at characteristics of personnel as leaders along four dimensions. In combination, these two chapters illustrate the necessity of having the right systems and people in place for successful reading program development.

CHAPTER ONE

Developing an Effective Reading Program

Rita M. Bean

Developing a comprehensive schoolwide reading program is an awesome and often controversial task. During the past decade, reading education has been the focus not only of teachers, parents, and students, but of legislators, politicians, citizens' groups, and the media. The cry for greater expectations of teachers and increased literacy performance of students has never been greater. Time and time again, we read or hear that the reading test scores of American students are low or declining or that our schools are not preparing students to compete in a global society. Even though some of these criticisms may not be justified (Berliner & Biddle, 1995), they add to the tensions as educators face the enormous task of creating and implementing a solid, comprehensive reading program.

Guiding the development of a comprehensive reading program is an important role of those in leadership positions. It requires a deep knowledge and understanding of reading acquisition, reading research, reading instruction, and assessment. It also requires an ability to create an atmosphere that encourages and rewards continual learning and change, and thus an understanding of the dynamics of leadership and the change process. In this chapter, we provide a framework for thinking about the essential elements of a school reading program and discuss a process model that promotes teacher empowerment and can be used to initiate and implement change in the schools.

Framework of a School Reading Program

Although individual teachers may work effectively in the classroom with students, their individual efforts do not constitute an overall reading program, nor do they provide an assurance that students will receive K–12 instruction that has been thoughtfully considered and orchestrated. An effective school reading program must be based upon a broad, comprehensive view of reading; it requires a vision of what reading is, and it demands a concerted effort that involves all professionals in the schools working toward a shared vision. These professionals include teachers, administrators, and support personnel such as reading specialists, counselors, and librarians. The development of a reading program also requires communication with parents and a knowledge of the community in which the school or district is located.

To establish an effective program, professionals must decide upon their literacy goals and establish standards that provide benchmarks for documenting the achievement of those goals. Further, activities or instructional experiences that facilitate student achievement must be agreed upon. The framework described in the following sections provides a model for thinking about goal identification. It includes three essential elements of any school reading program: curriculum (what is taught), instruction (how something is taught), and assessment (has it been learned?). Although some scholars would subsume instruction under the broad rubric of curriculum, I consider each as a separate entity for the purpose of discussion and elaboration. The framework is graphically portrayed in Figure 1.1.

Curriculum

1. Base goals and standards for reading on theory and research. The reading curriculum is the plan for guiding learning in the school; it provides the ideas for making decisions about classroom instruction. When teachers are asked to rethink the curriculum for their school, among the essential elements that they must consider is the identification of a vision with accompanying goals or outcomes for students. Often these goals reflect the current focus on standards-based curricula, which generally provide statements that indicate what students should know and be able to do at various levels. Those responsible for leading curriculum change efforts must be familiar with relevant initiatives at national and state levels and their impact on local decision making. The standards developed jointly by the National Council of Teachers of English and the International Reading Association (1996) and the primary standards developed by the New Standards Project (1999) of the National Center on Education and the Economy and the University of Pittsburgh are two examples that may be helpful. In addition, educators must, of course, refer to state standards in developing local curricula. They may also wish to compare their state standards with those of other states (Stotsky, 1997, 2000; ERIC, 2000).

Although standards aligned with appropriate assessments can be helpful in raising expectations for all students and help educators set appropriate goals, there are cautions to consider. Standards themselves may be confusing and exhaustive (Schmoker & Marzano, 1999). Further, unintended consequences of standards for students, including greater pressure and a lack of attention to what is known about student learning, need to be addressed (Gratz, 2000). These concerns must be considered in developing standards for the reading program. Schmoker and Marzano (1999) stress the importance of developing "a clear, manageable, grade-by-grade set of standards and learning benchmarks that make sense and allow a reasonable measure of autonomy" (p. 21).

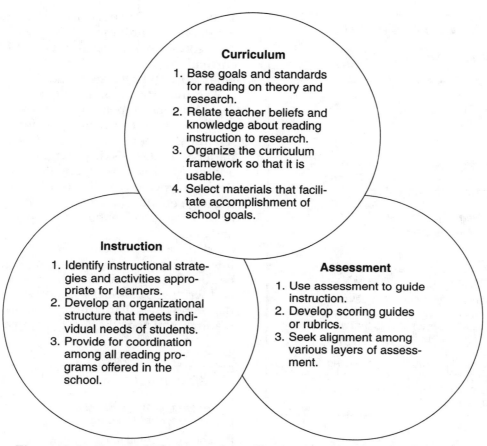

Curriculum

1. Base goals and standards for reading on theory and research.
2. Relate teacher beliefs and knowledge about reading instruction to research.
3. Organize the curriculum framework so that it is usable.
4. Select materials that facilitate accomplishment of school goals.

Instruction

1. Identify instructional strategies and activities appropriate for learners.
2. Develop an organizational structure that meets individual needs of students.
3. Provide for coordination among all reading programs offered in the school.

Assessment

1. Use assessment to guide instruction.
2. Develop scoring guides or rubrics.
3. Seek alignment among various layers of assessment.

Figure 1.1. Essential Elements of an Effective School Reading Program K–12

2. Relate teacher beliefs and knowledge about reading instruction to research. In addition to reviewing the research that is available about reading curriculum and instruction, teachers will need to think carefully about their own beliefs and values as they formulate goals and activities for students in their school. Our own life and school experiences as well as our cultural background influence our beliefs and actions. Further, beliefs are often resistant to change unless individuals are willing to think and reflect on what they believe, read new information, and be willing to relate that information to what they already know. Working with other teachers in developing an effective reading program provides much opportunity for discussion of beliefs

and knowledge and is a critical part of the curriculum development process.

3. Organize the curriculum framework so that it is usable. Another issue is how a specific school will organize its curriculum framework for reading so that essential components of reading are included. Although reading is a complex process that requires integrated use of multiple skills, there is still a need to identify the components of reading so that specific goals and instructional activities can be selected. As stated by Calfee and Drum (1986), the identified components should be simple yet coherent. The framework selected should have a sound theoretical base and at the same time be one that

---

NEW STANDARDS PROJECT

Primary Literacy Headings

Reading

1. Print-Sound Code
2. Getting the Meaning
3. Reading Habits

Writing

1. Habits and Processes
2. Writing Purposes and Resulting Genres
3. Language Use and Conventions

Example of Reading Standard 2:
Getting the Meaning (Grade 1)

Fluency

By the end of the year, we expect first grade students to be able to:

- independently read aloud from Level I books that have been previewed for them, using into-nation, pauses, and emphasis that signal the structure of the sentence and the meaning of the text; and
- use the cues of punctuation—including commas, periods, question marks, and quotation marks—to guide them in getting meaning and fluently reading aloud.

Figure 1.2

classroom teachers can use effectively. As mentioned previously, standards developed by organizations or by one's state can be used as a guide for discussion and as a basis for program development. Figure 1.2 provides the headings of the standards for primary reading and writing as identified in the New Standards (1999) document, as well as an example of a standard and its matching assessment. For comparison, similar information from the Academic Standards for Reading, Writing, Speaking, and Listening (K–12), State of Pennsylvania, is provided in Figure 1.3. In the first example, print-code or decoding is one of the major areas; in the latter example, the focus on print-sound and comprehension are subsumed under the heading Learning to Read Independently.

These frameworks may, of course, need to be modified to meet the specific characteristics of a school district. Personnel in an individual school district must think through for themselves how they conceptualize the framework for reading curriculum. In other words, they must decide what works best for them and their students.

The importance of developing a K–12 program must be emphasized. With a K–12 framework, a school can develop a broad plan that illustrates where in the curriculum various understandings, skills, and attitudes are addressed. Otherwise, students may receive little or no experience with various aspects of reading (e.g., no introduction to any study strategy), or they may receive the same experiences again and again.

Also, decisions about how to address the interrelationships among the language arts must be addressed. The relationship between reading and writing is especially important; in fact, evidence indicates that writing promotes ability in reading, and that the most effective programs

---

PENNSYLVANIA ACADEMIC STANDARDS

Reading, Writing, Speaking,
and Listening Headings

Learning to Read Independently
Reading Critically in All Content Areas
Reading, Analyzing, and Interpreting Literature
Types of Writing
Quality of Writing
Speaking and Listening
Characteristics and Function of the English
   Language
Research

Example of Standard 1
Learning to Read Independently (Grade 3)

Demonstrate fluency and comprehension in reading:

- Read familiar materials aloud with accuracy.
- Self-correct mistakes.
- Use appropriate rhythm, flow, meter, and pronunciations.
- Read a variety of genres and types of text.
- Demonstrate comprehension. (Standard 1.1.3G)

Recommend: 25 books/year

Figure 1.3

are those that enhance integration of the formal language skills of reading and writing in the school curriculum (Anderson, Hiebert, Scott, & Wilkinson, 1985; Stotsky, 1983; Spivey & Calfee, 1998). Other issues that need to be considered are:

◆ What understandings and skills are important at the emergent literacy stage that will enable students to become successful readers?
◆ In what ways can all teachers, including those responsible for teaching content subjects, assist in the development of literacy performance?

4. Select materials that facilitate accomplishment of school goals. In an effective school reading program, materials selected for the classroom should enable teachers to accomplish the standards that have been agreed upon. Too often, materials determine and drive the curriculum; they influence both activities and the content that students learn (Duffy, Roehler, & Mason, 1984). Although the basal reader is still used extensively as the predominant material and approach to reading at the elementary level, classrooms today contain a wide variety of text, print and nonprint. An extensive number of children's books are available, with many new titles published every year; there are periodicals, software, and on-line sources. Teachers have become much more knowledgeable about the availability and advantages of various types of reading materials.

In addition to experiences with narrative text, however, the program should include opportunities for students to read expository materials, including texts used in the content areas. Further, various supplemental books and nonprint materials such as films, records, maps, and charts add other dimensions and encourage students to view reading as a communication tool. The availability of technology for classroom use leads to the need for careful scrutiny of these materials.

To help schools select materials appropriate for the curriculum, various guidelines and evaluation tools have been developed. The *Guide to Selecting Basal Reading Programs* (1988) developed by the Center for the Study of Reading provides

a resource that can be used as a means of studying various materials. However, the best procedure is for those in a school district who are deciding the selection of materials to develop a checklist based upon what they perceive as important for their district.

As mentioned previously, technology is expanding our horizons relative to reading instruction. Today's technologies include a combination of the personal computer with videodisc players, CD-ROM players, modems, and television. The Internet provides endless opportunities for teachers and students to access resources once beyond their grasp. However, the selection of software can be confusing for teachers. Thus, appropriate guidelines need to be consulted (Wepner & Feeley, 1993).

In the section above, I discuss some important issues related to curriculum. However, school personnel, in addition to thinking about what it is they want students to learn at what level, must also think about how the curriculum will be delivered: that is, how instruction will take place.

Instruction

Any discussion of instruction needs to include a description of the learning activities, strategies, and organizational arrangements that help teachers meet the needs of individual learners. Although a teacher working with an individual student must have an excellent understanding of the reading process and reading methodology, this task is simple compared to the responsibility of providing instruction for 20 or more students whose range in reading performance may be wide. Thus, any reading program must provide experiences that enable each student to grow and learn in an environment that promotes risk-taking and guarantees success (Harste, 1989). This means that students who are performing at accelerated rates are challenged and encouraged to continue their learning. At the same time, students who are experiencing difficulties with grade-level curriculum need to receive specialized reading instruction that will help them to succeed and progress. One of the important tasks of the professional responsible for a total reading program is to promote communication and congruence between the special programs in schools and the classroom reading program. In this section, three major guidelines are discussed.

1. Identify instructional strategies and activities appropriate for learners.

In this general overview chapter, I identify six critical points from research and theory that school personnel need to consider as they develop their reading program.

♦ *First, instruction must be based upon what we know about the effective teaching of reading.* We hear much today about the importance of developing a reading program based upon sound scientific research that reflects effective best practice, and certainly there are seminal documents available that provide any curriculum group with a basis for discussion. The Report of the National Council on Reading (Snow, Burns, & Griffin, 1998) and the Report of the National Reading Panel (2000) provide two syntheses of research on reading instruction. The *Handbook of Reading Research* (2000) edited by M. Kamil is also an excellent source of information, as is the information provided by the Center for the Improvement of Early Reading Achievement (CIERA). Position statements from the International Reading Association can also be helpful, for example, on adolescent literacy, phonics, and assessment.

One area of contention is how to teach beginning reading. The current focus calls for a "balanced" approach to reading instruction, which is reflected in the work of the National Reading Panel (2000, p. 11): "systematic phonics instruction is only one component—albeit a necessary component—of a total reading program." In other words, phonics instruction must be embedded within a rich reading and writing curriculum and balanced with ongoing, effective comprehension instruction (Adams, 1990; Anderson et al., 1985; National Reading Panel, 2000; Snow et al., 1998).

Too often, professionals find themselves taking a side. Yet it seems as though a thoughtful discussion about the various aspects of this issue will reveal its complexities and enable teachers to make decisions in a more informed manner. Pearson and Raphael (1999) state: "teachers are not simply either whole language or skills teachers. At times, for some children, they look like the one; at other times, for other children, they look like the other. ... they make conscious, intentional decisions about individual students" (p. 31).

Freepon and Dahl (1998) have written a carefully constructed article presenting various conceptions of balanced instruction and the implications for classroom practice. They conclude that "there are differences by degrees and in the ways that people think research into practice occurs in balanced instruction" (p. 248) and recommend that teachers read the research and mediate it with contextual factors such as their own learning and needs of students.

♦ *Second, those involved in designing or selecting instructional activities need to consider the variables that contribute to success in reading, given its interactive, constructive nature.* These variables include the reader, the text, and the context. Readers approach reading with varying experiences and knowledge; they will handle some assignments better than others and will need more assistance with some than others.

Further, text material will affect students' ability to be successful. Material that is written in a clear, logical, and consistent manner should enhance understanding. On the other hand, material that is not well organized or coherent, what Anderson and Armbruster (1984) call inconsiderate text, may necessitate more teacher direction and intervention.

One current and controversial issue has to do with type of text for beginning readers, specifically, to what extent should decodable texts be used in the early stages of learning to read. Hiebert (1999) suggests that early readers need experiences with text that they can decode successfully, for example, 95% of the words. At the same time, the importance of quality literature that appeals to and interests children must not be excluded. The balance in the classroom is one that teachers need to consider.

The context for reading also influences students' performance. Context includes many factors, such as purpose for reading, classroom atmosphere, reading group composition, and interactions with the teachers.

Teachers should take these three variables—reader, text, and context—into consideration in deciding how much and what kinds of instruction are necessary, for example, the amount of prereading preparation, which vocabulary words to teach and how extensively, the degree of guided reading, the types of follow-up to text reading. In order to do this, teachers must have an excellent understanding of the reading process and how it affects instruction. They must be able to identify the what, why, and how of reading instruction (Michigan Reading Association, 1984):

— What is being read? Is it a poem, a story, a newspaper?
— Why are the students reading? For information? For enjoyment?
— How should students read? What strategies do students need to use to accomplish the task? Should they study or skim?

◆ *Third, time must be provided in the classroom for reading practice.* Research points to the importance of oral reading as a means of developing fluency (National Reading Panel, 2000). Likewise, the amount of independent reading, both in and out of school, correlates highly with reading performance (National Center for Education Statistics, 1999). Thus, in any school reading program there must be opportunities for students to read on a daily basis.

◆ *Fourth, composing should be an integral part of the reading program.* As mentioned previously, research evidence supports the connection between these two formal language skills. The notion of comprehension and composition as "two sides of the same basic process" (Squire, 1983) is an important concept for the curriculum developer. Students should participate in experiences that help them see the relationship between the reading and writing process (i.e., being an audience for someone else's writing, and writing for an audience). Both reading and writing can be used in the classroom as tools of learning (Rowe & Harste, 1985).

◆ *Fifth, students should be given opportunities to become independent and to self-monitor their literacy progress.* From kindergarten on, students need experiences that help them realize that the task

of reading relies on what readers bring to it and their purpose for reading, as well as on the type of materials or text. All lessons can be planned to help students monitor their reading and to reflect upon what they have learned.

◆ *Finally, the climate in a school must be conducive to the development of students as readers.* Not only should classrooms contain all sorts of reading material, but there should be an atmosphere in the school that promotes reading as an enjoyable and necessary part of life. There should be opportunities for teachers to read to their students, even in the upper grades, and motivational programs that encourage student reading.

2. Develop an organizational structure that meets individual needs of students. During the past 10 years, the emphasis in reading instruction has been on whole class grouping (Reutzel & Cooter, 1996). This approach has several major benefits. First, it negates the problems associated with ability grouping in which groups, once formed, tended to become permanent arrangements. Such arrangements were not beneficial for students placed in low groups (Allington, 1983; Gambrell, Wilson, & Gantt, 1981; Hiebert, 1983). Second, whole class instruction promotes the notion that becoming literate is a social endeavor and engages children in meaningful literacy activities, for example, telling stories, reading big books together, creating language experience charts, sharing student-written stories.

However, whole class teaching used extensively will not provide for the individual needs of students. There are many alternative grouping strategies that can be used by teachers. Flexible grouping, in which students may be placed into temporary groups on the basis of interest, learning styles, social needs, or instructional needs, can be used effectively by teachers (Reutzel, 1999). Another effective grouping strategy is cooperative learning, which makes use of heterogeneous groups ranging from two to five children working together (Harp, 1989; Opitz, 1992; Slavin, 1988). Guided reading, an approach in which the teacher works with a small group of children who use similar reading processes and are able to read similar levels of text with teacher support, enables students to learn how to use independent reading strategies successfully (Fountas & Pinnell, 1996). Teachers can also establish learning centers or stations in their classrooms to which children can be assigned. Cunningham, Hall, and Defee (1998) provide excellent ideas for organizing reading instruction, including Cunningham's Four Block Model.

Managing a classroom in which students are assigned or elect to do different tasks is not an easy task for teachers, especially for the novice teacher. School leaders can serve an important role in helping teachers understand the importance of providing for individual differences and, more specifically, assisting teachers in implementing grouping procedures in their classrooms.

3. Provide for coordination among all reading programs offered in the school. There has been a great deal of criticism about separate systems of education for students who experience difficulties in learning, especially those who are Title I or special education students (Allington & McGill-Franzen, 1988; Ysseldyke, Thurlow, Mecklenburg, & Graden, 1984). Much of this criticism has revolved around the pull-out arrangements that were the prevalent models for compensatory education. Although there are many concerns about pull-out models—including scheduling, loss of instructional time because of student movement, and possible stigmatizing of participants—one of the major concerns has been the nature of the instruction, specifically, that the two programs received by the students are not congruent (Johnston, Allington, & Afflerbach, 1985). Low-achieving students have had to handle the demands of two different classroom settings, approaches, and teachers. Current thinking reflects the importance of high-quality "first" teaching (Allington & Baker, 1999; International Reading Association, 2000) but at the same time recognizes that all teachers may need support in meeting the needs of struggling readers. Reading specialists can have several roles, each of which necessitates communication and collaboration with the classroom teachers. First, the reading specialist may provide direct instruction for struggling readers, but that instruction must be

intensive and personalized, taking into consideration the instruction being received in the classroom (Allington & Baker, 1999). Second, the reading specialist can assist the classroom teacher by providing advice, materials, and staff development, all focused on improving quality first teaching (Allington & Baker, 1999; Bean, Knaub, & Swan, 2000).

The climate in the school must be one that encourages communication and collaboration among all responsible for reading instruction. Teachers, whether specialists or classroom, can no longer work in isolation. All professionals need to work as members of a team to plan for the needs of students.

Assessment

Schools use assessment results for many purposes: accountability, feedback to teachers to inform instruction and to students to improve achievement, classification and certification, and reform (Asp, 2000). During the past decade, we have witnessed much change in educational assessment practices, both with large-scale, standardized tests and classroom-level practices. Much of this has been driven by the standards-based education movement, which calls for a clearer identification of what students should know and be able to do—and for evidence that students have indeed met those standards. Not only have states developed standards, but most have developed some sort of testing program based on those standards (Herman, 1997). Often, these testing programs are "high stake"; that is, decisions about resources, sanctions, and rewards may be based upon the results. In addition, local school districts often develop their own classroom assessment tools, designed for both accountability and instructional purposes. Several specific guidelines related to assessment need to be considered by those responsible for developing a schoolwide reading program.

1. Use assessment to guide instruction. A change to a constructivist perspective of learning (Sheppard, 1989) as well as a focus on higher expectations and higher-level skills (Resnick & Resnick, 1992; National Commission on Testing and Public Policy, 1991) have led to a focus on performance assessment. Such assessment "refers to a variety of tasks and situations in which students are given opportunities to demonstrate their understanding and to thoughtfully apply knowledge, skills, and habits of mind in a variety of contexts" (Marzano, Pickering, & McTighe, 1993, p. 13). As teachers develop and agree upon standards for students, they must at the same time develop and agree upon the assessment tool or tools that will be used to judge attainment of a standard. Many different assessment measures for the various elements of reading can be developed, adapted, or purchased. Assessment tools such as retellings, in which students listen to or read a story and then tell or write all that they remember, may be used as an indication that students have a sense of story and can identify relevant elements (characters, plot, setting, and resolution). Or students may be expected to read 25 books in a year and to submit a written report that indicates they have an understanding of each.

Teachers need to be involved in making decisions about which assessment tools to use if they are to use the measure in a purposeful and meaningful manner. Too often, teachers are frustrated by what they view as an overemphasis on assessment; they see little value in taking time from instruction for administering such tasks. Much of this frustration can be alleviated if teachers are involved in the decision-making process and if they have opportunities to judge for themselves the value of such measures in planning instruction.

2. Develop scoring guides and rubrics. The movement to performance assessment has had its problems, one of which is subjectivity in scoring. Rubrics, plans for assessing the quality of student work, can be helpful to teachers and can serve as a tool for involving students in their own assessment. Arter and McTighe (2000) suggest four criteria for assessing the quality of rubrics: (1) content/coverage, (2) clarity, (3) practicality, and (4) technical soundness or fairness. They also discuss the importance of teaching students how to self-assess using rubrics. The development of rubrics is a task that teachers can par-

ticipate in, using examples of student work to guide their thinking.

3. Seek alignment among various layers of assessment. The current emphasis on assessment (as related to standards) has led to overlapping and competing demands. School districts generally use their own standardized assessments, which might include large-scale testing and classroom assessment measures. At the same time, students may be required to take state-mandated tests that reflect state content standards. At times, there is little comparability among those tests; students may do well on one assessment measure and less well on another. Teachers may become frustrated and confused and ask what really matters. As Asp (2000) states, "Assessment at all levels needs to be linked together to support and reinforce a set of clearly articulated goals" (p. 151).

In sum, assessment is a critical piece of reading program development. The development of standards and curriculum, instruction, and assessment must be carefully thought through so that there is an appropriate fit of all elements. Yet these elements do not occur instantaneously, nor are they easily achieved. Sizer (1985) states it well: "A good school does not emerge like a prepackaged frozen dinner stuck for 15 seconds in a radar range; it develops from the slow simmering of carefully blended ingredients" (p. 22).

Process for Change

Reports from commissions and individuals during the past several decades have all described the need for total school restructuring and improvement efforts, and indeed many new reform movements are being initiated at state and district levels. At the same time, schools continue in their efforts to update, modify, and change their reading programs. But too many of these efforts, which start with much enthusiasm and excitement, fall short of reaching their mark. We have learned that the change process is a complex one that is more "rolling" than linear (Joyce, Wolf, & Calhoun, 1993). Specifically, changing behaviors involves collective, innovative action and constant assessment of this action (Joyce et al., 1993). The following principles are useful in thinking about and planning changes in school reading programs.

Involve All Constituents

Change is systemic; therefore, the process for change must involve all constituents. Fullan and Miles (1992) indicate that working systemically means focusing on "the development and inter-relationships of all the main components of the system simultaneously—curriculum, teaching and teacher development, community support systems, and so on," as well as on "the deeper issues of the culture of the system" (p. 751). In other words, even changing only one aspect of the school program—its reading program—involves a host of different issues and many individuals with differing perceptions of how reading should be taught. Anyone involved in a leadership position must be sensitive to the complexity of bringing about long-lasting change.

There are many different ideas about how to apply knowledge about change processes to curriculum development. The definition of curriculum development in the *Dictionary of Education* (Good, 1973) illustrates its complexity: "a task of supervision directed toward designing or redesigning the guidelines for instruction; includes development of specifications indicating what is to be taught, by whom, when, where, and in what sequence or pattern" (p. 158). An additional task, according to Oliva and Pawkas (2001), is how the curriculum will be taught, i.e., instruction. Oliva and Pawkas identify three phases in their model of curriculum development: planning, implementation, and evaluation. Ideas that may be helpful in implementing such a model in improving the reading curriculum follow.

Stage 1: Planning. As part of any process for curricular change, an initial step is reviewing the current program to determine where there is a need for change. Information should come from school sources such as test data, teacher interviews, or observations or classrooms; it can also come from published information about cur-

riculum trends or research findings. Teachers who agree to work with curriculum development can select or be given articles to read that can then be discussed and debated. School districts can also identify an expert who might make a presentation to teachers on the "state of the art" in reading instruction.

It is imperative that teachers discuss the current status of reading instruction in their school. For example, how do teachers in the elementary school teach reading? What do they emphasize? What are the reading strengths of students as a whole, and where do they appear to be having difficulties? One useful activity at this stage is to ask teachers to "map" their curriculum. According to Jacobs (1997), "curriculum mapping is a procedure for collecting data about the actual curriculum in a school district using the school calendar as an organizer" (p. 62). At least three types of data are collected: content, description of processes and skills emphasized, and the assessment produced by students. Such a procedure enables teachers to analyze the "operational curriculum," to compare what they are doing, to notice gaps as well as redundancies.

At this stage, teachers and others (consultants, parents, administrators) can investigate various ideas, materials, and approaches that may be useful for a particular school. Fullan (1999) states it succinctly: "There is no single solution. . . . The change process is too intricate and organic, organization by organization, to be captured in any single model" (p. 28). Again, outside consultants may be invited to work with teachers, and teachers should continue to search for relevant material about reading instruction. The most productive activity is for teachers to work collaboratively as they develop standards, instructional activities, and congruent assessment measures.

Stage 2: Implementation. In order that curriculum changes are truly implemented in the school, there must be staff development for all those involved. Too often, good ideas that are placed into curriculum guides or district manuals are not implemented into the daily teaching repertoires of classroom teachers. Often this is caused by inadequate staff development for teachers, who must have a solid understanding and acceptance of the proposed changes. According to Joyce et al. (1993), "a curriculum change in a major area probably requires ten to fifteen days of training rather than the one or two that are often provided now" (p. 32).

Stage 3: Evaluation. There should be formative evaluation that documents how well the change process is progressing. In addition, a process for determining the effect of the changes should be identified. This stage calls for specific attention to assessing the success of the change (Does it make a difference?) and the degree to which the changes have become institutionalized (Are teachers using the ideas?).

Encourage Professional Development

Staff development efforts must be an integral part of any change process. As stated previously, too often good ideas never become a reality in classroom practice. There are too many examples of one-shot inservice programs that provide initial enthusiasm but no more. Yet one very important finding from the Huberman and Miles (1984) studies is that commitment follows competence. Individuals are more willing to maintain and practice certain innovations if they have the competence to do them well. Thus, staff development must be ongoing and intensive in order to provide continuing support and feedback to teachers. Teachers themselves indicate that they value collaborative models of professional development, including book clubs, peer coaching, study groups, action research, and shared teaching experiences (Teberg, 1999). Alvarado (1998) concludes that in order to meet the needs of the standards movement, professional development will require a tremendous degree of collaboration and problem solving. Because teachers need feedback on what they are doing to make necessary changes, observations can also be useful as long as these observations are not used for evaluative purposes.

The principles described above illustrate the need for intimate involvement of the classroom teacher in both generating ideas for change and

implementing change in the classroom, and they acknowledge the importance of the teacher as a decision maker in creating excellent learning experiences for students. The cyclical nature of the change process is also evident. As stated by Fullan and Miles (1992), "change is a journey, not a blueprint. . . . One should not plan, then do, but do, then plan . . . and do and plan some more" (p. 749).

Conclusion

The development, implementation, and evaluation of a comprehensive K–12 reading program is an exciting and challenging task that requires the cooperation and collaboration of all concerned. In this overview chapter, we describe the three essential elements of an effective reading program—curriculum, instruction, and assessment—that can be used as a framework for conceptualizing the reading program. For each of the three elements, specific guidelines are described. We also discuss a process for change, and principles and procedures for implementing such change are suggested.

References

Adams, M. (1990). *Beginning to read.* Cambridge, MA: MIT Press.

Allington, R. L. (1983). The reading instruction provided readers of differing ability. *Elementary School Journal, 83,* 548–559.

Allington, R. L., & Baker, K. (1999). Best practices in literacy instruction for children with special needs. In L. B. Gambrell, L. M. Morrow, S. B. Neuman, & M. Pressley (Eds.), *Best practices in literacy instruction* (pp. 292–310). New York: Guilford Press.

Allington, R. L., & McGill-Franzen, A. (1988). *Coherence or chaos? Qualitative dimensions of the literacy instruction provided low-achievement children.* State University of New York at Albany. (ERIC Document Reproduction Service No. ED 292060)

Alvarado, A. (1998). Professional development is the job. *American Educator, 22*(4), 18–23.

Anderson, R. C., Hiebert, E. H., Scott, J. A., & Wilkinson, I. A. G. (1985). *Becoming a nation of readers: The report of the commission on reading.* Washington, DC: National Institute of Education.

Anderson, R. H., & Armbruster, B. B. (1984). Content area textbooks. In R. C. Anderson, J. Osborn, & R. J. Tierney (Eds.), *Learning to read in American schools* (pp. 193–224). Hillsdale, NJ: Erlbaum.

Arter, J., & McTighe, J. (2000). *Scoring rubrics in the classroom: Using performance criteria for assessing and improving student performance.* New York: Corwin Press.

Asp, E. (2000). Assessment in education: Where have we been? Where are we headed? In R. S. Brandt (Ed.), *Education in a new era* (pp. 123–157). Washington, DC: Association for Supervision and Curriculum Development.

Bean, R. M., Knaub, R., & Swan, A. (2000). *Reading specialists in leadership roles.* Paper presented at the American Educational Research Association, New Orleans, LA.

Berliner, D. C., & Biddle, B. J. (1995). *The manufactured crisis: Myths, fraud, and the attack on America's public schools.* Reading, MA: Addison-Wesley.

Calfee, R., & Drum, P. (1986). Research on teaching reading. In M. Wittrock (Ed.), *Handbook and research on teaching* (pp. 804–849). New York: Macmillan.

Cunningham, P. M., Hall, D. P., & Defee, M. (1998). Nonability-grouped, multilevel instruction: Eight years later. *The Reading Teacher, 51,* 652–666.

Duffy, G. G., Roehler, R. L., & Mason, J. (1984). *Comprehension instruction: Perspectives and suggestions.* New York: Longman.

ERIC Clearinghouse on Reading, English, and Communication (2000). *Language arts curriculum frameworks and standards.* http://www.indiana.edu/-ericrec/gninf/standards.html

Fountas, I. C., & Pinnell, G. S. (1996). *Guided reading good first teaching for all children.* Portsmouth, NH: Heinemann.

Freepon, P. A., & Dahl, K. L. (1998). Balanced instruction: Insights and considerations. *Reading Research Quarterly, 33,* 240–251.

Fullan, M. (1999). *Change forces: The sequel.* Philadelphia: Falmer Press, Taylor and Francis.

Fullan, M. G., & Miles, M. B. (1992, June). Getting reform right: What works and what doesn't. *Phi Delta Kappan, 73,* 745–752.

Gambrell, L., Wilson, R., & Gantt, W. M. (1981). Classroom observations of task-attending behaviors of good and poor readers. *Journal of Educational Research, 74,* 400–404.

Good, C. F. (1973). *Dictionary of education* (3rd ed.). New York: McGraw-Hill.

Gratz, D. B. (2000, May). High standards for whom? *Phi Delta Kappan, 81,* 681–687.

Guide to selecting basal reading programs. (1987). Champaign, IL: Center for the Study of Reading.

Harp, B. (1989). What do we know now about ability grouping? *The Reading Teacher, 42,* 430–431.

Harste, J. C. (1989). *New policy guidelines for reading.* Urbana, IL: National Council of Teachers of English.

Herman, J. (1997). *Large-scale assessment in support of school reform: Lessons in the search for alternative measures* (CSE Technical Report 446). Los Angeles: University of California, National Center for Research on Evaluation, Standards, and Student Testing.

Hiebert, E. (1999, March). Text matters in learning to read. *The Reading Teacher, 52,* 552–566.

Hiebert, E. H. (1983). An examination of ability grouping for reading instruction. *Reading Research Quarterly, 18,* 231–255.

Huberman, A. M., & Miles, M. (1984). *Innovation up close: How school improvement works.* New York: Plenum Press.

International Reading Association. (2000). *Teaching all children to read: The role of the reading specialist* (Position Statement). Newark, DE: Author.

Jacobs, H. H. (1997). *Mapping the big picture integrating curriculum and assessment K–12.* Washington, DC: Association for Supervision and Curriculum Development.

Johnston, P., Allington, R., & Afflerbach, P. (1985). The congruence of classroom and remedial reading instruction. *Elementary School Journal, 85,* 465–477.

Joyce, B., Wolf, J., & Calhoun, E. (1993). *The self-renewing school.* Alexandria, VA: Association for Supervision and Curriculum Development.

Kamil, M. L., Mosenthal, P. B., Pearson, P. D., & Barr, R. (2000). *Handbook of reading research* (Vol. 3). Hillsdale, NJ: Erlbaum.

Marzano, R. J., Pickering, D., & McTighe, J. (1993). *Assessing student outcomes performance assessment using the dimensions of learning model.* Washington, DC: Association for Supervision and Curriculum Development.

Michigan Reading Association. (1984). Reading redefined: A Michigan Reading Association position paper. *Michigan Reading Journal, 17,* 4–7.

National Center for Education Statistics. (1999). *Reading report card for the nation and the states.* Washington, DC: U.S. Department of Education.

National Commission on Testing and Public Policy. (1991). *From gatekeeper to gateway: Transforming testing in America.* Chestnut Hill, MA: National Commission on Testing and Public Policy.

National Reading Panel. (2000). *Teaching children to read: An evidence based assessment of the scientific research literature on reading and its implications for reading instruction.* Washington, DC: National Institute of Child Health and Human Development.

New Standards Project. (1999). *Reading and writing grade by grade.* National Center on Education and the Economy and the University of Pittsburgh.

Oliva, P. F., & Pawkas, G. E. (2001). *Supervision for today's schools.* New York: Wiley.

Opitz, M. F. (1992). The cooperative reading activity: An alternative to ability grouping. *The Reading Teacher, 45,* 736–738.

Pearson, P. D., & Raphael, T. E. (1999). Toward an ecologically balanced literacy curriculum. In L. B. Gambrell, L. M. Morrow, S. B. Neuman, & M. Pressley (Eds.), *Best practices in literacy instruction* (pp. 22–33). New York: Guilford Press.

Resnick, L., & Resnick, D. (1992). Assessing the thinking curriculum: New tools for educational reform. In B. Gifford & M. O'Conner (Eds.), *Changing assessment: Alternative views of aptitude, achievement, and instruction* (pp. 37–76). Boston: Kluwer.

Reutzel, D. R. (1999). Organizing literacy instruction: Effective grouping strategies and organizational plans. In L. B. Gambrell, L. M. Morrow, S. B. Neuman, & M. Pressley (Eds.), *Best practices in literacy instruction* (pp. 271–291). New York: Guilford Press.

Reutzel, D. R., & Cooter, R. B., Jr. (1996). *Teaching children to read: From basals to books.* Columbus, OH: Merrill, Prentice-Hall.

Rowe, D. W., & Harste, J. C. (1985). Reading and writing in a system of knowing. In M. R. Sampson (Ed.), *The pursuit of literacy: Early reading and writing* (pp. 126–144). Dubuque, IA: Kendall/Hunt.

Schmoker, M., & Marzano, R. J. (1999, March). Realizing the promise of standards-based education. *Educational Leadership 56*(6), 17–21.

Sheppard, L. (1989, April). Why we need better assessment. *Educational Leadership, 46*(7), 4–9.

Sizer, T. R. (1985). Common sense. *Educational Leadership, 42*(6), 21–22.

Slavin, R. E. (1988). Cooperative learning and student achievement. *Educational Leadership, 45*(2), 31–33.

Snow, C. E., Burns, M. S., & Griffin, P. (Eds.). (1998). *Preventing reading difficulties in young children.* Washington, DC: National Academy Press.

Spivey, N. N., & Calfee, R. C. (1998). The reading-writing connection, viewed historically. In N. Nelson & R. C. Calfee (Eds.), *Reading-writing connection: Ninety-seventh yearbook of the National Society for the Study of Education* (pp. 1–52). Chicago: University of Chicago Press.

Squire, J. (1983, May). Composing and comprehending: Two sides of the same basic process. *Language Arts, 60,* 627–643.

Stotsky, S. (1983, May). Research on reading/writing relationships: A synthesis and suggested direction. *Language Arts, 60,* 627–643.

Stotsky, S. (1997). State English standards: An appraisal of English language arts/reading standards in 28 states. *Fordham Report, 1*(1). (ED420879) http://www.edexcellence.net/stotsky/stottoc.html

Stotsky, S. (2000). *The state of the state standards in English language arts/reading.* Fordham Foundation. Available: http://www.edexcellence.net/library/soss2000/2000soss.html#English

Teberg, A. (1999). *Identified professional development needs of teachers in curriculum reform.* Paper presented at the American Educational Research Association, Montreal, Canada.

Wepner, S. B., & Feeley, J. T. (1993). *Moving forward with literature: Basals, books, and beyond.* Columbus, OH: Merrill/Macmillan.

Ysseldyke, J. E., Thurlow, M. L., Mecklenburg, C., & Graden, J. (1984). Opportunity to learn for regular and special education students during reading instruction. *Remedial and Special Education, 5,* 29–37.

CHAPTER TWO

Evolving Roles and Responsibilities of Reading Personnel

Shelley B. Wepner and Diana J. Quatroche

Reading specialist Anne Jackson believes that she has the best job in the entire district. She is in the district's Professional Development School (PDS) and gets to work closely with a neighboring university. A PDS liaison from the university is in her building two and a half days each week to work directly with the teachers. The PDS liaison happens to be a certified reading specialist and teaches undergraduate and graduate reading courses at the university. Every Wednesday afternoon, after students' early dismissal from school, Anne and the PDS liaison have a half-hour to conduct a mini-workshop with all K–5 teachers about an issue or idea related to literacy.

Anne is fortunate to have a principal who considers her his right-hand person for implementing the reading program for the school's 350 students. She and her principal have developed a job description that allows her to spend 49% of her time working directly with students and 51% of her time working directly with teachers.

Anne works with students with the most need, as determined by standardized test scores, informal reading assessments, and teacher recommendations. She prefers to bring students to her classroom because she has university students assisting her with instruction. In fact, every one of her remedial groups has a university student—a reading buddy—who works directly with the students.

Anne's involvement with teachers has grown steadily in the two years that she has been at the school. She works individually with teachers in the classroom. She co-teaches, conducts demonstration lessons, works with small groups and individual students, and experiments along with the teachers with new materials and techniques. Her individual work with teachers usually results from her work with groups of teachers during their preparation time. The group meetings began when the principal decided to have each teacher create a professional improvement plan related to literacy. Each three-member, grade-level team of teachers identifies an area of interest and need to pursue: for example, instructional frameworks, informal assessment techniques, test construction, technology applications, literature selections and responses, small-group instructional strategies, or strategic management of the reading series.

Anne meets with each team once a week and then uses these meetings, often in the form of a seminar, as a basis for working with the teachers individually during the remainder of the week. Recently, she was delighted with the progress of the fourth grade teachers. Unaccustomed to using critical analysis strategies with literature selections, these teachers usually resorted to assigning book reports. Anne used the seminar sessions with these teachers to have them practice different strategies that they in turn could use in their classrooms. She invited the PDS liaison to teach a few strategies and to follow up with the teachers in their classrooms.

Anne knows that she is uniquely positioned to strengthen her school's reading program because of the principal's commitment to reading, the teachers' commitment to their own professional development, and the school's access to university personnel. She is convinced that her resource role is contributing significantly to students' achievement gains in the statewide reading assessment and to their success in the school's reading program.

How is Anne's situation similar to and different from other reading personnel? What are the roles and responsibilities of persons responsible for literacy instruction? This chapter addresses these questions with the following topics:

◆ Current status of reading personnel
◆ Reading specialist's roles and responsibilities
◆ Reading supervisor's roles and responsibilities
◆ Roles of other personnel in a literacy program
◆ Reading personnel as leaders

Current Status of Reading Personnel

Anne's situation is uncommon but not unrealistic. With the advent of Professional Development Schools (PDS) and the increased recognition of reading specialists' impact on students' reading achievement (Klein, Monti, Mulcahy-Ernt, & Speck, 1997; Snow, Burns, & Griffin, 1998), school districts can position themselves to have the most qualified reading personnel for their students and teachers. This strategic use of reading personnel is especially critical for school districts challenged by a range of student diversities that detract from cohesive and manageable classroom instruction. Many schools are beginning to recognize the key role that reading specialists play as leaders of successful reading programs (Bean, Knaub, & Swan, 2000).

In 1989, when one of us wrote the first version of this chapter, we found that reading personnel had been referred to as an endangered species or, at the very least, as unnoticed and ignored (Cohen, Intili, & Robbins, 1978; Wepner, 1977; Wilson & Becker, 1984). For whatever reasons—the tightening of school budgets, the decrease in federal funding, or the establishment of new priorities— reading personnel had been suffering from a great deal of role conflict and role ambiguity

(Pierson-Hubeny & Archambault, 1985). The same concerns that existed over 20 years ago still exist today. The role of the reading specialist is at best not clearly defined and more likely endangered. Many school districts are hiring fewer reading specialists and instead hiring nonprofessional personnel to perform the duties traditionally assumed by reading specialists (Long, 1995). Paraprofessionals and classroom teachers with minimal background in reading are expected to know how to help each student develop literacy.

School districts that hire reading specialists define their roles variously, based on reading specialists' competencies and the context in which they find themselves (Bean, Cooley, Eichelberger, Lazar, & Zigmond, 1991; Bean & Hamilton, 1995; Eltink, 1990; Kletzien, 1996; Quatroche, Bean, & Hamilton, 2000; Tancock, 1995). Reading specialists continue to express frustration with the lack of clarity of their roles (Bean & Hamilton, 1995).

This role ambiguity is partially due to the varied competencies required for reading specialist certification in different states, different graduate program offerings for reading personnel, and different job descriptions by local school boards and administrators (Cotter, 2000; Weisberg, 1986). The requirements for reading specialists vary from state to state for teaching experience, type of degree, and coursework. Cotter (2000) found that only 19 states require teaching experience from one to three years, and only 21 states require a master's degree for reading specialist certification.

Anne, in our opening vignette, comes from a school district that believes her work with teachers is critical for improving literacy instruction in the classroom. Her friend in a neighboring school district, however, is directed to spend all of her time with students rather than spend time with teachers on their professional development. Research about reading specialists' roles (Barclay & Thistlewaite, 1992; Bean & Eichelberger, 1985; Cohen et al., 1978; Hesse, Smith, & Nettleton, 1973; Mangieri & Heimberger, 1980; Pikulski & Ross, 1979) indicates that Anne's friend's situation is prevalent, in that the focus is on students rather than the professional development of classroom teachers.

Meanwhile, politicians use their pulpits to declare national emergencies about the level of literacy in the United States (Levy, 2000). These same politicians and legislators need to know that the services for improving achievement in literacy are available. For example, Elaine Marker, a reading specialist in an urban-suburban school district in Pennsylvania, is able to "flex back and forth" between her role as head facilitator of professional development and her role as instructor for in-class teaching. Charlene Cox, a reading specialist in a newly formed PDS, works with the school's PDS liaison from a local university (who also is a certified reading specialist) to create for each grade-level teacher a yearlong plan of action that calls for implementation of new strategies in the classroom.

The next sections describe the various types of reading personnel who influence a reading program (reading specialists and reading supervisors), and how each works alongside other key personnel in the schools (the principal, classroom teacher, parents, local school boards) and beyond (state departments of education and state boards of education) to create the most effective literacy programs.

Reading Specialist's Roles and Responsibilities

The Commission on the Role of the Reading Specialist, convened by the International Reading Association (IRA) in 1996 was charged with developing a position paper about the roles and responsibilities of reading specialists for enhancing reading achievement. This commission reviewed existing literature, investigated how reading specialists currently function in the United States, and explored how reading specialists in exemplary programs function.

With improved learning for all students as the focus for the existence of reading specialists, the position statement *Teaching All Children to Read: The Roles of the Reading Specialist* (International Reading Association, 2000b) states that reading specialists have three major roles: instruction, assessment, and leadership. The instruction role includes planning and collaboration with teachers, supporting classroom instruction, and providing specialized support. The assessment role includes the administration and interpretation of diagnostic instruments, assisting classroom teachers in the administration and interpretation of various assessments, and the development and coordination of assessment tools. The leadership role includes literacy program development and coordination, staff development, and serving as a resource to teachers, administrators, and parents.

Recent research findings indicate a shift in the method of delivery of instructional services. The survey conducted by the Commission on the Role of the Reading Specialist (Bean, Cassidy, Grumet, Shelton, & Wallis, 1999) found that 43.9% of the respondents worked in a combination of pull-out and in-class programs, and 37% worked in a pull-out model only. This is a change from the typical pull-out model of delivering remedial instruction. For example, Tom Carter splits his time between pull-out and in-class instruction with the first, second, and third grade children. He also goes into a fifth grade social studies class where students are studying the Revolutionary War. He introduces the students to several literature books on this topic and works with the teacher to form literature groups. This approach was used in another fifth grade classroom with great success, and when the social studies teacher saw how motivated the other students were, he requested that Tom help launch it in his classroom.

Conversations with reading specialists in the elementary grades highlight approaches to working with students and teachers. A reading specialist related how she spent the first part of the school year teaching phonics to first graders by going into the first grade classrooms. The classroom teachers believed that this instruction was very beneficial to their students. Another reading specialist described how she spent the first part of the school year working with a new first grade teacher to help her assess her students and plan instruction accordingly. This reading specialist and first grade teacher team taught beginning literacy activities such as shared reading, guided writing, and language experience. A third reading specialist helped a classroom teacher adapt her reading instruction to fit the needs of several students who were having difficulty learning to read with the school's reading program.

However, many reading specialists continue to work in remedial programs that primarily follow a pull-out model (Bean et al., 1999). These specialists find it necessary to carefully work out schedules with the classroom teachers that enable them to take children out of the regular classroom at convenient times. When a pull-out model of instruction is used, it is very important for the reading specialist to keep in close contact with the classroom teachers. Tom Carter has worked out some ways to keep in contact with his classroom teachers on an ongoing basis. He visits with his teachers each morning to see how his remedial students are progressing in the regular classroom. He has found that these early morning conversations enable him to keep in constant contact with teachers as well as to help with any problems that his students may have.

Other reading specialists who work primarily with pull-out programs have found creative ways to communicate regularly with classroom teachers. Examples include providing classroom teachers with weekly written reports, conferencing informally with classroom teachers while doing hall duty, holding monthly meetings with classroom teachers to discuss students' progress, walking students to and from their classrooms, and visiting classrooms on a regular basis to discuss students' progress and to observe the classroom reading program.

Clarification of roles can occur when reading specialists, classroom teachers, and principals have an opportunity to communicate expectations for the role. The reading specialist's primary role in a school should be determined by the needs of the students. Yet the most important role for the reading teacher is to develop positive collaborative relationships with teachers (Bean, Trovato, & Hamilton, 1995).

Jaeger (1996) and Henwood (1999/2000) suggest ways that the reading specialist can create positive relationships with elementary and content-area classroom teachers respectively. Jaeger discusses how the reading specialist can be a resource to the classroom teacher with curriculum development, instructional problem solving, assessment, and parent communication. Henwood focuses on how the reading specialist can develop the role of resource to content-area teachers. She describes how to help teachers develop students' overall learning and how to become members of departmental learning teams.

Reading specialists need to know reading methodologies so they can help classroom teachers use them effectively. Anne is an example of a reading specialist who keeps classroom teachers aware of the latest literacy practices. She uses each Wednesday afternoon to help classroom teachers understand when and how to use shared reading, guided reading, independent reading, and read-alouds. During other mini-workshops, she helps teachers understand when and how to use language experience, shared writing, guided writing, interactive writing, and writing workshop. In her role as a reading specialist, Anne is providing ongoing staff development.

Reading Supervisor's Roles and Responsibilities

Some districts have reading supervisors who are responsible for coordinating and evaluating all facets of the reading program, including teacher observations and evaluation. Some districts have reading coordinators who have many of the same responsibilities as reading supervisors but without the responsibility of evaluating teachers. Reading supervisors possess the skills of reading specialists plus the supervisory skills and certification to officially observe teachers. They oversee the district's literacy curriculum and make sure that it subscribes to local, state, and national standards. They also put into place formal and informal assessment tools to measure students' learning growth.

Reading supervisors are responsible for ensuring that teachers can teach reading and that their instructional practices are aligned with the curriculum standards. Reading supervisors and their reading specialists help teachers use different instructional methods to meet diverse student needs, use different kinds of texts, and

organize classrooms for instruction (International Reading Association, 2000a). For example, reading supervisor Charles Jasper meets weekly with a committee of elementary classroom teachers to help them manage the numerous components of the district's new reading series. However, because Charles cannot give enough time to all teachers in the district, he depends on his reading specialists to work directly with the teachers in their buildings. While Charles acknowledges that he will be the one to evaluate the teachers, he knows that he can depend on his reading specialists to support teachers' work in the classroom.

Reading supervisors are couriers for trends, issues, and new research. They are responsible for preparing budgets that account for personnel and nonpersonnel expenses such as staff development, equipment, and materials and supplies. They are responsible for establishing guidelines for selecting materials and resources (core programs, trade books, textbooks, newspapers, magazines, videotapes, and CD-ROM software) and for organizing such selection (see Chapter 7). They are responsible for communicating information about the district's reading program to the community through meetings, news media, websites, or specialized school publications (see Chapter 14).

As part of the middle-level management team, reading supervisors work closely with principals and central office administrators as well as with reading specialists and classroom teachers. They use their communication skills to gain insights into the realities of the district's socioeconomic, racial/ethnic, linguistic, and achievement profile so that they can help districts succeed with students' literacy development.

Roles of Other Personnel in a Literacy Program

The Principal

Principals, as instructional leaders, are in a unique position to support the schoolwide reading program. They are responsible for ensuring that the reading program is being implemented through observations, conferencing with teachers, workshops, and professional development opportunities. As a supporter of the reading specialist, the school principal can make sure that teachers regard the reading specialist as the primary person for developing the literacy program. The principal can also help teachers understand the importance of working with the reading specialist.

If a principal has a reading background, a powerful partnership can be created. For example, the second author of this chapter is a PDS liaison to an elementary school where the principal had been a reading specialist. As the teachers in this school planned for the implementation of a Title I Schoolwide Program, this principal was especially supportive and knowledgeable about the process. She attended the planning meetings, provided time for teachers to research current practices in literacy, and encouraged teachers to consider ways to make literacy a high priority in this school. This principal is indeed involved in every facet of the program.

If the principal does not have a reading background, it is even more essential that a reading specialist be available to guide teachers with the implementation of the schoolwide reading program. The reading specialist can inform the principal about current research and best practice for reading programs, and can involve the principal in professional development along with the classroom teachers. When principals become knowledgeable about reading, they become even more supportive of the reading specialist and the total school reading program.

The Classroom Teacher

Interaction between the classroom teacher and the reading specialist is essential. Classroom teachers have consistent, long-term experience with their students in all areas of the curriculum (Jaeger, 1996) and need to make reading important. Content teachers in particular need to understand that they must teach students how to read their textbooks, and they must teach strategies that will help students make their way through their texts (Henwood, 1999/2000).

It is important for classroom teachers to realize that personnel available outside the classroom can help them teach reading. Whereas the classroom teacher has breadth of knowledge about any given student, the reading specialist has in-depth knowledge of a student's reading behaviors. The reading specialist can note the reading strategies the student uses effectively, which strategies and content areas she or he struggles with, and which ones are new and unknown in general and for different content areas. The specialist, along with the classroom teacher, can develop a plan that reinforces the student's strengths and expands her or his repertoire of strategies to help with the student's learning needs (Jaeger, 1996).

Classroom teachers need to understand the psychology of reading and reading development, the structure of the English language, best practices in reading instruction, and assessment strategies that will inform classroom teaching of reading (American Federation of Teachers, 1999). It is their responsibility to avail themselves of professional development opportunities when necessary.

Other Stakeholders

Parents. The reading specialist can build positive relationships between home and school, and can help classroom teachers do the same. They can also take on the role of advocate for students (Hamilton, 1993). Specialists can also provide workshops for parents so that children can receive positive support at home in their efforts to become or develop as readers. Parents should keep in close contact with their child's teachers and be supportive of the school reading program. They can spend time listening to their children read, take children to the library, read aloud to children, review homework assignments, limit the amount of television in the home, and provide a positive role model for their children.

Local School Boards. Local school boards should be informed of all facets of the district's reading program. It is their responsibility to endorse exemplary practice of school personnel. Local school boards should be knowledgeable about what teachers are doing to further the district's goals for the reading program. They should support the reading program by making informed decisions regarding budget, personnel, and curriculum.

State Departments of Education. The IRA's Commission on the Role of the Reading Specialist believes that state departments of education should consider six major requirements or performance standards when approving graduate teacher education programs for prospective reading specialists. Graduate programs need to ensure that graduates (1) are proficient in knowledge and beliefs about reading; (2) have a broad and deep knowledge of literacy instruction and assessment; (3) have skills to organize and enhance reading programs; (4) can communicate and collaborate with others; (5) complete a practicum where they have experience working with students experiencing reading difficulties, and experience working with adult learners; (6) have experiences that enable them to develop leadership skills (International Reading Association, 2000b).

State Boards of Education. Reading specialists can have a role in determining their state's educational policy by being active participants in statewide professional organizations and volunteering to participate in statewide committees or task forces. State boards create standards and policy that affect the curriculum and assessment that impacts local school districts. Many states have implemented high-stakes statewide assessments that affect school funding, graduation rates, and school rankings. These assessments determine curriculum and student outcomes. It is therefore important for school personnel to understand how and where these types of decisions are made, and to determine ways to help their school and district adjust accordingly.

Reading Personnel as Leaders

As part of their role as leaders, reading specialists and reading supervisors are responsible for the development and coordination of the over-all reading program. Their success in this role depends on their credibility, that is, their training and ability to do what they are charged to do. This usually means that they have taken a substantial number of graduate courses in reading education (preferably leading to a master's degree in reading or a reading specialist/supervisor certification) and that they have experience as a classroom teacher. Their teaching experience enables them to understand and assist teachers with the dilemmas that they face in addressing students' needs.

In addition to the necessary educational and professional background, reading personnel need certain leadership skills to succeed in their roles. Borrowing from a conceptual framework about the leadership of education deans (Wepner, D'Onofrio, & Willis, in press), it appears that reading personnel who are successful as leaders possess some of the same characteristics that enable them to function in four dimensions: *intellectual, emotional, social,* and *moral*. (See Figure 2.1.)

The *intellectual* dimension refers to knowledge of the various facets of a job, and the ability to juggle each responsibility within its own context. The assumption with this dimension is that reading personnel have the necessary knowledge about the field of literacy and about their own reading program. They know how their reading program addresses state and national standards and assessment mandates, and how to modify the program accordingly. They know how to administer and interpret multiple assessment instruments. They are aware of trends, research, and alternative methodologies. They know how to use specific content area reading strategies. As leaders, reading personnel know when, where, and how to use this information within their own districts to promote change. For example, reading supervisor Charles Jasper knows to work with his reading specialists to assess teachers' knowledge and use of reading strategies. He knows to offer professional development sessions that are well received by teachers and administrators. He's aware of the often conflicting demands and needs of both constituencies, and he uses this knowledge as well as his own understanding of students' needs to assist both

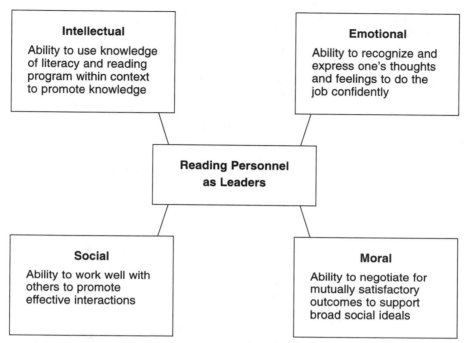

Figure 2.1. Four Dimensions of Leadership of Reading Personnel

groups. He also knows how to involve his reading specialists in follow-up work with individual teachers.

The *emotional* dimension includes an ability to acknowledge inner conflict and an ability to express feelings vividly and convincingly. Successful reading personnel are confident in overseeing their jobs, and they have a balanced perspective about their roles as leaders. They recognize their own strengths and weaknesses, and they know when they can help and when they can't. They are honest with themselves about people, policies, and practices that are bothersome, yet they know when to set aside their feelings of frustration. They also are comfortable in expressing their thoughts when people, policies, and practices inhibit learning or stifle teaching. For instance, Charles Jasper knows that many of his teachers in the high school really don't believe he can offer them anything significant. They see him as primarily serving the elementary and middle schools, and they don't want him or the high school reading specialist in their classrooms. However, Charles is so convinced

that the high school teachers need help, he continues to chip away at their resistance. He tells them what he observes with the students, and he tells them what he can do to help them be more successful with their students. He is secure enough in his role to be focused in his pursuit of best literacy practices.

The *social* dimension is about transactions with others, including societal and organizational relationships. Successful reading personnel cope with conflict rather than ignore it, are tolerant and empathetic toward others, and respect individual differences. They listen, cooperate, collaborate, and encourage others to try new things. They work effectively with teachers, administrators, students, and parents on an individual and on a group basis. Their interactions with their constituencies promote positive responses to themselves and to their ideas. Charles works particularly hard with this dimension because he saw that his predecessor used a very controlling approach with his teachers and ultimately failed to influence them. Charles spends much of his time listening to teachers express their frustration with individual students, methods that don't work, or unrealistic mandates. His reputation as an effective administrator who cares about his teachers comes from his ability to interact with them nonjudgmentally. Teachers sense this about Charles, and even if they are resistant to change, they still are willing to entertain his ideas.

The *moral* dimension has to do with a sense of conscience and accountability and the desire to negotiate energetically for mutually satisfactory solutions to problems and broad social ideals. Reading personnel who are successful know to maintain confidentiality, and they believe strongly in working together with others to get the best possible outcome for both parties. They do what they say they are going to do. They are committed as much to doing the right thing as they are to doing the thing right. In other words, short-term losses are seen as opportunities for long-term gains. Reading supervisor Charles gets particularly incensed when he sees his colleagues in neighboring school districts engage in questionable practices with the statewide assessment. Like Charles, they know that their students will have great difficulty passing the test. Unlike him, they subtly condone teaching to the test, encouraging high absenteeism on testing days, and withholding the tests of certain low-achieving students. His colleagues aren't facing reprimands from their superiors, which may seem a short-term gain to them. However, Charles will accept short-term criticism for his students' low test scores until he can plan with his reading specialists and negotiate with his teachers to achieve the long-term goal of aligning instruction, curriculum, and assessment with state standards.

Reading personnel with characteristics in the intellectual, emotional, social, and moral dimensions are able to meet the demands of their roles. Committed to the ideal of developing students' literacy, they have the intellectual and emotional stamina to work well with all constituencies to get the most from them. They know enough about their school or district to establish and communicate realistic expectations. They are able to suggest ideas and materials, conduct professional development workshops, model strategies or techniques, and conduct demonstration lessons (International Reading Association, 2000b) that fit with their teachers' needs. Their steadfast belief in the purpose of their role gives them emotional license to find ways to be heard, to be humored, and eventually to be respected.

Conclusion

As the roles and responsibilities of reading personnel continue to evolve, so do the leadership characteristics of those who assume these positions in creating a community of literacy advocates. Every success story about the impact of reading personnel on the literacy achievement of students helps others to acknowledge the need to have academically and professionally qualified reading educators in such positions. Reading personnel should be expected to have the necessary credentials and should be able to help define their roles and responsibilities. If placed in leadership positions where much of their work focuses on teachers, administrators, and the community, they should be expected to function effectively in the four dimensions (intellectual, emotional, social, and moral) described above. As more schools and districts come to accept the urgent need to use qualified reading personnel to put into place the critical elements of literacy programs (see the chapters that follow), students' potential for learning will be realized.

References

American Federation of Teachers. (1999). *Teaching reading is rocket science: What expert teachers of reading should know and be able to do.* Washington, DC: Author.

Barclay, K. D., & Thistlewaite, L. (1992). Reading specialists of the 90's: Who are they and what do they want? *Reading Research and Instruction, 32,* 87–96.

Bean, R., Cassidy, J., Grumet, J., Shelton, D., & Wallis, S. (1999). *The role of the reading specialist: A national survey.* Unpublished manuscript.

Bean, R. M., Cooley, W. W., Eichelberger, R. T., Lazar, M. K., & Zigmond, N. (1991). In-class or pull-out: Effects of setting on the remedial reading program. *Journal of Reading Behavior, 23,* 445–464.

Bean, R. M., & Eichelberger, R. T. (1985). Changing the role of reading specialist: From pull-out to in-class programs. *The Reading Teacher, 38,* 648–653.

Bean, R. M., & Hamilton, R. (1995). Focus on Chapter I reading programs: Views of reading specialists, classroom teachers, and principals. *Reading Research and Instruction, 34,* 204–221.

Bean, R. M., Knaub, R., & Swan, A. (2000, April). *Reading specialists in exemplary schools.* Paper presented at the 45th Annual International Reading Association Convention, Indianapolis, IN.

Bean, R. M., Trovato, C. A., & Hamilton, R. (1995). Focus on Chapter I reading programs: Views of reading specialists, classroom teachers, and principals. *Reading Research and Instruction, 34,* 204–221.

Cohen, E. G., Intili, J. K., & Robbins, S. H. (1978). Teachers and reading specialists: Cooperation or isolation? *The Reading Teacher, 32,* 281–287.

Cotter, M. (2000). [Requirements for reading specialist certification in the United States]. Unpublished raw data.

Eltink, M. A. (1990). Concerns of practicing reading specialists. *Journal of the Wisconsin State Reading Association, 34*(4), 7–10.

Hamilton, R. (1993). *Chapter I reading instruction: Exemplary reading specialists in an in-class model.* University of Pittsburgh, Pittsburgh, PA. Unpublished dissertation.

Henwood, G. F. (1999/2000). A new role for the reading specialist: Contributing toward a high school's collaborative educational culture. *Journal of Adolescent and Adult Literacy, 43,* 316–325.

Hesse, K., Smith, R., & Nettleton, A. (1973). Content teachers consider the role of the reading consultant. *Journal of Reading, 17,* 210–215.

International Reading Association. (2000a). *Excellent reading teachers: A position statement of the International Reading Association* [Brochure]. Newark, DE: Author.

International Reading Association. (2000b). *Teaching all children to read: The roles of the reading specialist. A position statement of the International Reading Association.* Newark, DE: Author.

Jaeger, E. L. (1996). The reading specialist as collaborative consultant. *The Reading Teacher, 49,* 622–629.

Klein, J., Monti, D., Mulcahy-Ernt, P., & Speck, A. (1997). *Reading/language arts program and personnel in Connecticut schools: Summary Report.* Connecticut Association for Reading Research Report.

Kletzien, S. B. (1996). Reading programs in nationally recognized elementary schools. *Reading Research and Instruction, 35,* 260–274.

Levy, C. J. (2000, March 29). Citing a crisis, Bush proposes literacy effort. *The New York Times,* pp. A1, A20.

Long, R. (1995). Preserving the role of the reading specialist. *Reading Today, 12*(5), 6.

Mangieri, J. N., & Heimberger, M. J. (1980). Perceptions of the reading consultant's role. *Journal of Reading, 23,* 527–530.

Pierson-Hubeny, D., & Archambault, F. X. (1985). Role stress and perceived intensity of burnout among reading specialists. *Reading World, 24,* 41–52.

Pikulski, J. J., & Ross, E. (1979). Classroom teachers' perceptions of the role of the reading specialist. *Journal of Reading, 23,* 126–135.

Quatroche, D. J., Bean, R. M., & Hamilton, R. L. (2000). *The role of the reading specialist: A review of research.* Unpublished manuscript.

Snow, C. E., Burns, M. S., & Griffin, P. (1998). *Preventing reading difficulties in young children.* Washington, DC: National Academy Press.

Tancock, S. (1995). Classroom teachers and reading specialists examine their Chapter I reading programs. *Journal of Reading Behavior, 27,* 315–335.

Weisberg, R. (1986). [Survey of state policies in reading specialist training and reading instructional practices]. Unpublished raw data.

Wepner, S. B. (1977). Are reading teachers becoming obsolete? *The Reading Teacher, 30,* 402–404.

Wepner, S. B., D'Onofrio, A., & Willis, B. (in press). From practice to theory: Personal perceptions of the education deanship. *Academy of Educational Leadership Journal.* Available: http://www.wcu.edu/cob/faculty/conf.html

Wilson, R. M., & Becker, H. L. (1984). An educational audit of a district's reading personnel. *Reading World, 24,* 69–72.

Program Development

Literacy development is both similar and different across grade levels and contexts. It is similar in that the basic principles of language and learning hold true throughout. It is different in that the application of those principles differs depending on what is developmentally appropriate at each level. Part II of this book focuses on the various settings for which administrators and supervisors must plan and carry out reading programs. It offers suggestions for responding to the differing instructional needs of students as they progress through school.

Chapter 3 emphasizes prevention and intervention during the pre-elementary school years. It stresses the pressures at the pre-elementary level brought about by state mandates for every child to achieve at predetermined levels by the fourth grade. It discusses research on young children's literacy development, including the most recent findings on brain research, and ways to develop and implement sound instructional practices for accomplishing literacy learning goals.

A set of comprehensive guidelines for developing a successful elementary reading program is the focus of Chapter 4. Included are suggestions for becoming better informed about learning to read and reading instruction, ideas for curriculum development, tips for organizing and scheduling the day, and recommendations for including skills in a meaningful context. Ideas for assessment and parent involvement are included. The guidelines are accompanied by many concrete examples for implementation.

Chapter 5 on adolescent literacy describes the needs of early adolescent and adolescent learners and offers guidelines for developing middle and high school literacy programs for these students. The International Reading Association's position statement on adolescent literacy is used to explore ways in which administrators and supervisors can create effective programs.

Chapter 6 examines reading programs offered at the collegiate level. Included here is a rationale for the existence of such reading programs and guidelines for best serving students at this level. This chapter also addresses the roles and responsibilities of reading specialists in college and university reading programs.

Broadly interpreted, the principles and guidelines presented in each chapter may be applied to all the other chapters. This is reassuring for reading specialists, supervisors, and administrators because it means that the essence of sound, effective reading instruction remains the same for students at any level.

CHAPTER THREE

Pre-elementary Reading Programs: New Expectations

Dorothy S. Strickland

The usual hectic and hurried school opening at River Falls Elementary School took on new meaning as the staff braced itself for two new classes of pre-kindergarten students. Although the state mandate to offer education to four-year-old children was greeted with enthusiasm by faculty and community, few had either the experience or training to plan and implement such a program. Last spring, Jean Porter, the District Language Arts Supervisor, began planning with the school principal. She also enlisted the help of the reading specialist to work with teachers and parents to solve what seemed to be an endless series of challenges involving space, curriculum, and staffing. Needless to say, they were ready when those pre-kindergartners and their parents arrived. But, as Jean Porter put it, "This is a work in progress."

The responsibility for pre-elementary programs has become increasingly common in the public schools. Full-day kindergarten programs are prevalent in suburban and urban settings.

Head Start and other early education programs have become more than just an adjunct to urban school district offerings; they are an important part of what the public wants and expects. One of the key motivations for pre-elementary education is the belief that it will give young people the start they need to succeed academically. Virtually everyone agrees that academic success begins with the ability to read. With this in mind, policy makers and educators have given early intervention a key role in systemic reform efforts at the state and district levels. The reforms have added a new role to the work of many administrators and supervisors of reading programs, who may have had limited experience with children at this age level.

In order to make good decisions for the very youngest children in their care, today's administrators and supervisors should be familiar with the current issues and practices in early childhood education, a term generally applied to the schooling of children from birth to age 8. While much of the information in this chapter could very well apply to the full spectrum of early childhood, the content will focus on issues most likely to affect children ages 4–6; this age group is most likely to be enrolled in pre-kindergarten and kindergarten programs within the public school. The following issues will be discussed:

◆ Linking standards, instruction, and assessment to prevent reading difficulties
◆ Language and literacy development
◆ Strategies for learning and teaching
◆ Strategies for assessing student learning and program development

Linking Standards, Instruction, and Assessment to Prevent Reading Difficulties

Increased demands to make every child a reader by the end of the primary grades have spurred early intervention efforts at the national, state, and local levels. School reform movements not only have raised expectations for what young learners should know and be able to do, but they also specify the grade levels at which these

expectations should be met. Standards have been raised for all students regardless of who they are, where they live, their linguistic backgrounds, or whether they have been classified as having a learning disability. Reform efforts have focused particular attention on literacy learning and teaching.

Early Childhood Literacy Education and Systemic Reform

Because access to pre-kindergarten education is offered by a growing number of school districts and is thus administered by the public schools, these programs are included in the reform efforts initiated at the state level. Many states and districts have established educational standards for very young children and for their teachers as well. Establishing teacher standards is in line with the thinking of most systemic reform advocates, who believe that improving teaching is one of the most direct ways to improve students' learning (Cohen, 1995).

Federal legislation has also added impetus to standards-based reform, particularly in the area of early literacy. In an effort to improve literacy instruction in Head Start programs, the federal government stipulated several educational performance standards and performance measures in the 1998 Head Start Reauthorization Act.

The *performance standards* include the development of:

◆ phonemic, print, and numeracy awareness
◆ understanding and use of oral language to communicate for different purposes
◆ understanding and use of increasingly complex and varied vocabulary
◆ an appreciation of books
◆ in the case of non-English-background children, progress toward acquisition of the English language

Performance measures that would indicate development of the standards include children's demonstration that they:

◆ know that letters of the alphabet are a special category of visual graphics that can be individually named

♦ recognize a word as a unit of print
♦ can identify at least 10 letters of the alphabet
♦ associate sounds with written words

Because Head Start is a national effort, these standards have the potential to affect large numbers of children and to have implications for the qualifications of early childhood staff in other settings as well.

The Importance of Early Intervention

Efforts to reform early childhood education were inspired largely by the desire to intervene early in children's education to prevent school failure. Special attention is given to those students who are deemed likely to experience difficulty learning to read and write. Research indicates that the cycle of failure often starts early in a child's school career. Stanovich (1986) argues, with good evidence, that children who encounter problems in the beginning stages of learning to read fall farther and farther behind their peers. Longitudinal studies (Juel, 1988) reveal that there is a near 90% chance that a child who is a poor reader at the end of Grade 1 will remain a poor reader at the end of Grade 4. As they move through the grades, these young people are apt to experience continued failure and defeat, which may account for the tendency of low-achieving students to drop out of school.

Another compelling reason to promote early intervention is the realization that supplementary remedial programs such as Title I and "replacement" programs that substitute for regular, in-class instruction have had mixed results over the years (Johnston, Allington, & Afflerbach, 1985). Some argue that such programs cause classroom teachers to over rely on special help and neglect their responsibility for less able students. Others suggest that where these programs exist, instruction within and outside the classroom is often at odds with one another. Regardless of the supplemental help offered, there is a growing recognition that more attention needs to be given to incorporating the best prevention and intervention procedures into regular classroom instructional practice (Allington & Walmsley, 1995).

Those who have turned their attention to early intervention state that it is ultimately less costly than years of remediation, less costly than retention, and less costly to students' self esteem (Barnett, 1998). This final point may be the most compelling of all because the savings in human suffering and humiliation are incalculable. Teachers in remedial programs often observe that students who feel they are failures frequently give up and stop trying to learn, despite adequate instructional opportunities. The gradual trend away from long-term remedial programs at all levels and the growing emphasis on early intervention, prevention, and good "first teaching" make the early years a key focus of reform.

What Research Says About Language and Literacy Development

Early intervention efforts were given impetus by the results of a relatively recent body of research on the literacy development of young children. Often termed emergent literacy research, the new body of information has had a profound influence on educational policy and curriculum. Teale and Sulzby (1989) list the unique dimensions of the new research: (1) the age range studied has been extended to include children 14 months and younger; (2) literacy is no longer regarded as simply a cognitive skill but as a complex activity with social, linguistic, and psychological aspects; (3) since literacy learning is multidimensional and tied to the child's natural surroundings, it is studied in both home and school environments; (4) literacy learning is studied from the child's point of view. Results of these studies provide important understandings about the nature of children's literacy learning and the kind of educational environment that best supports it. Galda, Cullinan, and Strickland (1997) list six important points to summarize these understandings:

1. *Literacy learning begins early in life and is ongoing.* It is evidenced when children begin to distinguish between their favorite books and

records and demonstrate their recognition of environmental print. As children search for patterns and make connections, they bring what they know to each new situation and apply their own logic to make sense of it.

2. *Literacy develops concurrently with oral language.* Fluency in oral language is no longer seen as a precursor to literacy but as a goal to be accomplished with and through literacy as each language process informs and supports the others. It would seem that each child stores what is learned about language and literacy in a private linguistic database and then draws on what is needed when it is needed.

3. *Learning to read and write are social and cognitive endeavors.* Children are active participants in the process. Children are not interested merely in learning about literacy; they want to actively engage in it with others.

4. *Learning to read and write is a developmental process.* Extensive observations of children reveal some general developmental patterns in the ways they acquire literacy. It is important to note, however, that these very general patterns reveal themselves in very different ways among individual children.

5. *Storybook reading, particularly family storybook reading, plays a special role in young children's literacy development.* In their accounts of parents sharing books with children, Taylor and Strickland (1986) observed that the talk surrounding the words and pictures in books inevitably turns to questions about print. Parents and teachers of young children expand, explain, and elaborate on the text as they help youngsters link the text to their personal knowledge and background experience.

6. *Literacy learning is deeply rooted in the cultural milieu and in the family communications patterns.* While it is safe to say that children growing up in our print-rich society are exposed to an abundance of print, the nature, quality, and amount of those experiences will differ from one family to another and from one community to another. The understandings children gain, largely through their everyday experiences at home, are significant and valuable.

Wolfe and Brandt (1998) outline a series of findings from brain research that help support what has already been outlined above regarding emergent literacy. For example, a child's experience and environment have a strong influence on the development of the brain. At birth, humans have limited ability in terms of speech and motor development, and their brains are not fully operational. The brain that eventually takes shape is a result of the interaction between the child's genetic inheritance and everything he or she experiences. This fits well with another important finding: that IQ is not fixed at birth. Researchers have demonstrated that early educational intervention can actually raise infants' scores on IQ tests (Ramey & Ramey, 1996). Research on the brain also suggests that some abilities are acquired more easily during certain sensitive periods, or "windows of opportunity." Because the earliest years are considered critical for learning language, the importance of stimulating environments for language development at the pre-kindergarten level is stressed.

The role of emotion in learning also has received attention from the brain researchers. Emotion appears to play a dual role in human learning. "First, it plays a positive role in that the stronger the emotion connected with an experience, the stronger the memory of that experience. In contrast, if the emotion is too strong then learning is decreased" (p. 13). This would imply that when teachers provide children with a reasonable amount of challenge, the children move forward with a feeling of success while avoiding frustration.

Establishing and Assessing a Supportive Language and Literacy Curriculum

Learning to read and write is not done in a vacuum. Nor does it begin in first grade. Long before formal schooling begins, parents and caregivers help lay the foundation for the development of essential cognitive skills and positive attitudes toward learning. Pre-elementary programs should contain (1) clear curriculum goals,

(2) evidence of intentional planning and implementation of developmentally appropriate strategies that correspond with the curriculum goals, (3) a plan for ongoing student assessment, and (4) a plan for program evaluation.

Although not all pre-elementary programs designed to prevent failure in reading will place emphasis on the same components, there is considerable agreement on the overall nature of the curriculum. The literacy curriculum components generally included in literacy programs at the pre-elementary level are outlined below. Accompanying a brief description of each topic are representative examples of the kinds of teaching strategies that supervisors and administrators should expect to see when teachers are implementing the curriculum wisely.

Literacy as a Source of Enjoyment

Early childhood educators are aware that play is an essential element in every aspect of children's learning. It follows that children who have positive attitudes and expectations about reading are more likely to be motivated to learn to read. Strategies that promote a positive view toward reading and other literacy experiences are essential to helping children learn to read and want to read.

Teaching Strategies. Teachers who are aware of children's capabilities provide activities such as singing the alphabet song, reorganizing letters to match one's name, and opportunities to write one's own name independently in the very same classroom. Each activity is approached in a way that offers a modest challenge and some degree of success for children in a nonthreatening and playful atmosphere. When selecting material to read aloud, teachers include selections that are humorous and invite participation. Throughout, they show their own enthusiasm for reading.

Language Development with a Stress on Vocabulary and Concepts

Extending children's vocabulary and discourse patterns involves both linguistic and cognitive development. Making sense of print requires the use of a combination of strategies, including the use of word meanings, sentence structure, sound and letter relationships (phonics), and background knowledge. All of these strategies help children make good predictions about print. Children who have an abundance of opportunities to expand their language and linguistic repertoires are more apt to decipher words unknown to them as readers and to make sense of what they read (Halliday, 1975; Morrow, 2000).

Teaching Strategies. Sharing and discussing books and stories may be the single most important thing teachers do to foster children's language and literacy development. Full-day programs should offer numerous opportunities throughout the day. For very young children, frequent, brief read-aloud experiences are best. Whenever possible, use volunteers to read to individuals or pairs of children. Volunteers who feel uncomfortable reading aloud may share wordless picture books. Keep in mind that it is both the reading and the talking that helps expand children's vocabularies and conceptual understandings. Figure 3.1 offers some tips for sharing literature with children.

Understandings About the Functions of Print

Knowledge of how print is used for everyday purposes helps children view literacy learning as a meaningful activity. Children who realize the functional relevance of written language are more likely to be motivated to explore its use for their own purposes (Neuman & Roskos, 1989).

Teaching Strategies. Teachers encourage the use of literacy in various interest areas in the classroom and in other purposeful ways throughout the day. Everyday purposes for writing include writing notes and letters, reading newspapers and magazines, making and using lists, and using a television guide. Real materials such as food containers, menus, cookbooks, tickets, paper and writing utensils, and sales slips should be included and used in interest centers.

**SOME TIPS FOR SHARING
LITERATURE WITH CHILDREN**

1. Vary the material: stories; poems; basic concept books, such as books about colors, numbers, the alphabet; other kinds of informational books.
2. Include some enlarged texts and big books, so that children can see the words as they hear them.
3. Put poetry, as well as recipes and songs, on charts and point to the words while reading or singing them.
4. Read and discuss a variety of material on the same theme over an extended period of time. For example, for two or three weeks you may wish to include several books and poems about families, the neighborhood, or ways to travel.
5. Link literature selections to firsthand activities tied to topics of interest, class trips, and current events.
6. Preview books before you read them. Your reading will be more expressive.
7. During a first reading, avoid interrupting the flow of a storybook with too much discussion. Revisit the story after the reading to reflect and respond.
8. When reading informational books, invite generous discussion before, during, and after the reading. They need not be completed in one sitting.
9. Do repeated readings of books, so that children become participants in the process.
10. Place the books you have read in the book center so that children have access to them for independent browsing.

Figure 3.1

Print Awareness and Concepts About Print

In order to make sense of written language, young learners need to acquire a general knowledge about reading and writing as representations of ideas, knowledge, and thoughts and an understanding of how print works. Sensitivity to print in the environment is a significant first step toward developing an understanding of what it means to be a reader and writer. Print concepts are the arbitrary conventions that gov-

ern written language, such as spaces between words, directionality, and punctuation (Galda et al., 1997).

Teaching Strategies. Opportunities for teaching concepts about print abound as part of the curriculum and in incidental ways throughout the day. When teachers read aloud from big books, children learn that it is the print that evokes the words. When teachers write aloud, children hear and see the words as they are written. In both cases, children begin to develop an awareness of the importance of top to bottom and left to right directionality and the concept of a word as it appears in print. Teachers should deliberately plan to focus on various concepts about print throughout the year, reinforcing them in a variety of ways every day.

Knowledge of Narrative Structure

Children's understanding about the nature of stories and how they are constructed greatly influences their ability to comprehend and compose. Most of the material used to teach reading to young children is written in narrative form. It follows that they are apt to understand material presented in a form with which they are familiar.

Teaching Strategies. Teachers should use prediction prompts during the reading of a story to elicit what children think might happen next. To keep their answers grounded in the story line, children should be asked: What made you think so? After the reading, children may be asked to retell the story. Teachers might use prompts that follow the elements of story structure, such as: Who were the main characters? What happened to them? What happened next? How did things turn out?

Listening Comprehension

The ability to make predictions and inferences, draw conclusions, and summarize ideas begins with opportunities to engage informally in these kinds of cognitive operations during the early years. Young children need many opportunities to listen and respond to books, stories, and various other types of texts in order to understand their content or to perform a task. Exposure to a variety of kinds of texts expands children's language and concepts and contributes to their understanding of the reading process (Robbins & Ehri, 1994; Dickinson & Smith, 1994).

Teaching Strategies. Retelling a story, which has already been described in the example above, taps into children's ability to use the structure of texts to recall information. While this is very important, it does little to help children make inferences and draw conclusions about what has been read to them. Teachers need to pose questions that require children to consider why they think a character behaved in a certain way or what they might have done under similar circumstances. Questions of this type involve the ability to use information from various sources to form an answer.

Knowledge of the Alphabet

Letter recognition is a good predictor of success in early reading. Research in this area suggests that alphabet knowledge is a by-product of extensive early literacy experiences. Thus, simply training children on the alphabet in isolation of rich literacy experiences has proven unsuccessful (Ehri, 1983).

Teaching Strategies. The alphabet should be displayed at eye level, and its use should be modeled during group writing experiences. Children's names are excellent vehicles for focusing on letters as components of words. Names should be displayed, read, and used for various purposes, such as taking attendance and identifying ownership of items. Teachers can demonstrate how names are constructed by cutting a child's name into its individual letters and then reconstructing it. Children may be given the opportunity to do the same with their own names. Children should be encouraged to learn the letters in their own names and to find them in print throughout the classroom or at home.

Phonemic Awareness

Research indicates that phonemic awareness, the understanding that speech is composed of individual sounds, is a good predictor of reading success (Stanovich, 1994). Like knowledge of the alphabet, however, there is reason to believe that phonemic awareness is best learned within a context of a variety of literacy experiences (Moustafa, 2000).

Teaching Strategies. Phonemic awareness activities should be included as part of the daily read-aloud and writing experiences. Activities should be playful and game-like. Teachers should include nursery rhymes, poems, and storybooks with patterned rhymes in their daily read-aloud offerings. They should read poetry, stories, and alphabet books that contain alliteration and word play. When reading or chanting a familiar poem or rhyme, teachers might pause before a rhyming word and let children fill in the rhyme. Children can be invited to clap the number of syllables they hear in someone's name. First the name is said, then repeated with the children as they clap along. John gets one clap. Mary gets two, Jonathan gets three, and so on.

Phonics

Learning the code involves the ability to link written symbols and sounds. Knowledge of phonics is a word identification strategy that is important to both reading and spelling (Strickland, 1998).

Teaching Strategies. Opportunities to point out patterns in the language emerge constantly throughout the day in early childhood classrooms. Attention to sound and letter relationships can be made through shared reading and writing activities. Teachers need to focus children's learning on the alphabetic principle, not simply memorizing sounds that relate to letters. In this way, children will generalize the concepts underlying phonics and be able to apply what they know to reading and writing. As teachers and children begin to informally call attention to letters, sounds, and words of interest to them, the children are helped to make the necessary connections regarding the patterns in our language. Perhaps the best evidence of children's growing awareness of phonics is the invented, phonics-based spelling they produce as they attempt to write. The child who writes "d nt t" for "do not touch" is demonstrating knowledge of at least three sound-symbol relationships. One of these, the letter "t," is used correctly in both the initial and final positions.

Opportunities to Write

Reading and writing development go hand in hand. Children learn a great deal about the purposes for writing long before they attempt to write on their own. For young children, drawing and writing blend as a way to express what they think and talk about. Children's written expression should not be mistaken as simply handwriting. It may range from scribbling to the use of letters and the beginnings of spelling. Children's attempts at spelling provide opportunities to apply what they know about written language and develop new understandings about word structure and the relationships between language and print (Sulzby, 1992).

Teaching Strategies. Teachers should demonstrate and invite children to participate in writing every day. This may be done as a group activity, before or after a read-aloud session. The Daily Journal outlined in Figure 3.2 offers a structure for shared writing activities. Various opportunities for independent writing adapt easily to children's literacy levels and past experiences with writing. A writing area where all the materials for writing are available to children should be included among the interest centers. Junk mail, clipboards, stickers, alphabet at eye level, and alphabet manipulatives may be included. Children should be encouraged to use the center during activity time and to share what they have done at the end of the day. Occasionally, teachers should offer students a prompt for drawing or writing about something relevant to the individual or to the group's activities.

THE DAILY JOURNAL

The daily journal is a group writing activity in which the teacher demonstrates and children participate in the process of writing. Chart paper or chalkboard may be used. The text may be as brief as one sentence. Simple pictures may be included. Topics may encompass current events, including personal experiences and news, responses to stories, recipes, notes, and lists of things to do or buy.

A typical daily journal entry will include the following:

1. Children participate in a hands-on activity or a read-aloud experience or simply share personal news. A discussion follows.
2. Teacher elicits comments to be written down. For example: What ideas do you want to save? What did you like best about the story?
3. Teacher writes what the children suggest and reads it aloud during the writing. Teacher may pause for children to predict the next word or letter.
4. Teacher reads and discusses finished writing with children. They discuss ideas, language patterns, words, letters. Focus is on what they know at their stage of development.
5. Group rereads with teacher.
6. Children are encouraged to draw or write their own journal entries independently during the day.
7. Children are given an opportunity to share their independent writing.
8. Extensions. Teachers may save daily journal entries and laminate them to make class big books. These are displayed and returned for rereading. Children find or match known words, letters.

Figure 3.2

Establishing an Instructional Framework

The establishment of an instructional framework within which children develop literacy and learn through literacy is critical. The Reading/Writing Workshop in Figure 3.3 is offered as an organizational guide for teachers to plan literacy experiences for children. Teachers are asked to begin each day with a literacy workshop of this type and to adjust the content to the ages and maturity levels of their students. The workshop may

A FRAMEWORK FOR READING/WRITING WORKSHOPS: PRE-ELEMENTARY PROGRAMS

1. Teacher Directed Activities

Reading/Writing Aloud involves activities in which the teacher models reading and writing process; students observe, listen, and respond.

MATERIALS: primarily trade books, chart paper, chalkboard, whiteboard

PURPOSES:

- to stretch students' experiential and literary backgrounds; expand vocabulary; concepts
- to expose students to varied forms: fiction, nonfiction, poetry
- to enlist varied forms of response: discussion; drawing/writing; drama, art, music/movement, etc.
- to expose children to various genres, literary devices, writers' and illustrators' craft
- to expose children to various purposes for reading and writing

Shared Reading/Writing involves child participation in acts of reading and writing led by the teacher.

MATERIALS: enlarged texts; may include literature trade books and content materials (books/charts) for reading; whiteboard, chart paper, chalkboard for interactive writing.

PURPOSES:

- to demonstrate/support concepts about print
- to support comprehension and interpretation
- to emphasize textual features
- to provide opportunities for children to apply what they know about reading, writing, spelling

Word Study involves activities that call children's attention to the sounds within words (phonemic awareness), letter and word recognition, and sound-letter relationships.

MATERIALS: name cards, lists, charts, enlarged texts, listening activities for phonemic awareness

PURPOSES:

- to develop sight vocabulary through environmental print
- to develop sight vocabulary through the use of students' names
- to promote phonemic awareness
- to foster understanding of the alphabetic principle; phonics

Guided Reading usually starts at the kindergarten level with children who demonstrate they are ready. Involves small-group instruction with easy materials.

MATERIALS: primarily core program materials or sets of leveled trade books

PURPOSES:

- to monitor specific strategies/skills—highly focused manner
- to provide instruction as close as possible to students' instructional levels, gradually increasing difficulty

2. Independent Reading and Writing

MATERIALS: primarily trade books (fiction and nonfiction); writing utensils, paper

PURPOSES: to provide time for child to re-enact or practice book experiences and writing experiences; self-select materials and topics; assume control, independence

3. Sharing

MATERIALS: any materials used during independent reading and writing.

PURPOSES: to provide time for children to recall and share information of common interest to the group; oral expression. At times all activities may be theme related.

Figure 3.3

last as little as 15 or 20 minutes. Materials are selected to support several areas of the curriculum simultaneously: language and literacy development, social studies and science, mathematics, and basic concept development such as sequencing, opposites, and so on.

Following are brief descriptions of the three components included in the Reading/Writing Workshop shown in Figure 3.3. (1) Teacher directed activities generally take place at circle time "on the rug" and include teacher demonstration of reading and writing with child participation and response. (2) Independent reading and writing provide time for children to re-enact and apply what they learned through direct instruction. (3) Sharing is a time for children to reconvene and report informally to others about what they did independently.

Assessing Children's Language and Literacy Development

Assessment in early childhood classrooms should reflect what is known about how young children learn to read and write. It should be based on information gathered from a variety of sources and real learning experiences. It should be an ongoing process, integral to instruction, and not take large amounts of time in preparation.

Administrators and supervisors should expect teachers to have a system in place for keeping track of children's literacy development. The system may use checklists, work samples, and anecdotal records. It should be used as an ongoing resource for making curricular decisions about the performance of individual children and about the group relative to the goals of instruction. For example, assessment during shared reading could take the form of an informal observation of the overall progress of the group. The items suggested in Figure 3.4 (Observation Checklist During Shared Reading) may be helpful in deciding upon a set of observational criteria. At times a teacher might select an individual for special monitoring. For example, a teacher might want to assess the literacy development of a child who rarely participates in the group, or

---

OBSERVATION CHECKLIST DURING SHARED READING

Book Handling and Knowledge

Students demonstrate an understanding of the following:

- Right side up of reading material
- Front and back of book
- Front to back directionality
- Title
- Author
- Illustrator

Concepts About Print

Students demonstrate an understanding of the following concepts:

- Print evokes meaning
- Pictures evoke and enhance meaning
- Left to right direction
- Sentence
- Word–Letter
- Similarities in words and letters

Comprehension and Interpretation

Students demonstrate understanding of familiar books and stories through the following:

- Discuss meanings related to characters and events
- Make and confirm reasonable predictions
- Infer words in cloze-type activities
- Remember sequence of events
- Compare/contrast events within and between books
- State main ideas
- State causes and effects
- Recall details

Interest in Books and Reading

Students demonstrate their interest in books and reading through the following:

- Show interest in listening to stories
- Participate in reading patterned and predictable language
- Engage in talk about books and stories
- Request favorite books to be read aloud
- View themselves as readers

As follow-up to shared reading, students:

- Voluntarily use classroom library
- Show pleasure in "reading" independently

Figure 3.4

take a closer look at the literacy knowledge of a particularly advanced child.

Children's growing abilities and confidence with literacy can be monitored by saving samples of their drawing and writing over time and analyzing them for content and evidence of what they know about sound-letter relationships. Evidence of oral language competence can also be gathered as teachers listen critically to children's sharing over time. Figure 3.5 contains some criteria to keep in mind regarding oral language development. Children should be praised when these criteria are evidenced. Emphasis should not be placed on specific lessons about the value of the criteria; nor should individual children be castigated when the criteria are not evidenced.

Assessing the Language and Literacy Program

Assessment of the pre-elementary program requires that administrators and teachers keep up with new developments in the field and adjust their programs accordingly. Professional cooperation among pre-kindergarten, kindergarten, and primary grade teachers must be fostered as a critical component of program continuity. All of the professionals involved should work together to design and implement a long-range plan for ongoing self-assessment and change. Teachers and administrators might engage in brainstorming activities, during which they work together to set goals for three to five years. Some possible goals for teachers and administrators are outlined below:

Possible Goals for Teachers

- Literacy will be made more visible and integral to all activities throughout the day.
  Examples: Dramatic play area will contain signs, environmental print, and materials for children to read and write; lists of children's names will be displayed and used purposefully.
- More small-group activities will be provided in which children work together on block-building, dramatic play, and literacy.

ORAL LANGUAGE CHECKLIST

1. Uses language with increasing confidence. Note that this has nothing to do with the child's home language or dialect. The focus is on self-assurance, regardless of the language in use.
2. Organizes ideas with some sense of logic.
3. Has a sense of audience: looks at audience, speaks loudly enough for all to hear.
4. Listens and responds appropriately to others.

Figure 3.5

Examples: Children will engage in supermarket play area in which counting and reading environmental print on boxes, cans, and signs are integral; group books patterned after predictable texts will be created on a regular basis.

- More opportunities will be offered children to select from a variety of literacy-related activities.
  Examples: Throughout the day, including center time, there should be "invitations" for children to engage in literacy events such as handling interesting picture books on display (with covers facing children so that they are appealing) and browsing in a writing center where writing materials are made readily accessible.
- Opportunities for children to express their imagination and creativity through a variety of literacy experiences will be emphasized.
  Examples: Response to literature make take the form of discussion, telling original stories, acting out parts of the story, moving like people, animals, or other creatures in the story, making collages, or engaging in other artistic media. There would be few, if any, times when children were asked to use commercially prepared worksheets or workbooks.
- Teachers will observe children and document their development, literacy and otherwise, in some systematic manner.
  Examples: Make use of a checklist for observing children during shared reading; collect samples of children's drawing and writing over time and make evaluative comments on their literacy development.

Possible Goals for Administrators

◆ Show continued interest in, and support of, the early childhood program.

   Examples: Meet regularly with the early childhood staff alone; support opportunities for external visits to conferences whenever feasible; stress the importance of these activities with the central administration.

◆ Place emphasis on the need for continuity of new directions and practices across grade levels.

   Examples: Help teachers find a balance between prescribed similarity of practice and a shared vision from which similar practice evolves.

◆ Work with teachers to initiate a parent involvement program and to articulate new practices to parents.

   Examples: Support development of a coordinated reporting system to parents across pre-K through second grade.

◆ Continue the dialogue in formal and informal ways.

   Examples: Continue to read and bring to the attention of teachers materials relevant to their work; conversely, read and be willing to discuss materials distributed by teachers.

◆ Help teachers rethink the current procedures for assessing and reporting children's literacy development.

   Examples: Push the district level for the elimination of standardized testing before third grade and work with teachers to help them develop informal, systematic assessment strategies and an appropriate instrument for reporting to parents.

Conclusion

One of the great dilemmas of school administrators (and supervisors, to a lesser degree), whether they are assigned to the district level or are school-based, is that they can never hope to be expert in all the disciplines, developmental levels, and areas of concern for which they are responsible. Everyone concedes that this is true. It is possible, however, for administrators and supervisors to become well enough acquainted with each area under their supervision to become effective observers and questioners of those who are expected to have the expertise.

Literacy at the pre-elementary level is a highly important, issue-laden topic. The public is increasingly interested in the topic and likely to have questions and opinions about it. Thus, administrators and supervisors should have sufficient background to serve as active, informed participants in its discussion. It is our hope that they take a true leadership role in an area in which change and controversy are likely to be present for some years to come.

References

Allington, R. L., & Walmsley, S. A. (1995). *No quick fix.* New York: Teachers College Press.

Barnett, S. W. (1998). Long-term effects on cognitive development on school success. In S. W. Barnett & W. Boocock (Eds.), *Early care and education for children in poverty* (pp. 11–44). Albany: State University of New York.

Cohen, D. K. (1995). What is the system in systemic reform? *Educational Researcher, 24,* 11–17.

Dickinson, D., & Smith, M. W. (1994). Long-term vocabulary effects of preschool teachers' book reading on low-income children's vocabulary and story comprehension. *Reading Research Quarterly, 29,* 104–122.

Ehri, L. (1983). A critique of five studies related to letter-name knowledge and learning to read. In L. M. Gentile, M. L. Kamil, & J. S. Blanchard (Eds.), *Reading research revisited* (pp. 143–153). Columbus, OH: Merrill.

Galda, L., Cullinan, B., & Strickland, D. (1997). *Language, literacy and the child.* Fort Worth, TX: Harcourt Brace.

Halliday, M. A. K. (1975). *Learning to mean: Exploration in the development of language.* Columbus, OH: Merrill.

Head Start Program Performance Standards. (1998). *Congressional Federal Record* 1304, subpart B, 1306 and 1308.

Johnston, P., Allington, R., & Afflerbach, P. (1985). The congruence of classroom and remedial reading instruction. *Elementary School Journal, 85,* 465–478.

Juel, C. (1988, April). *Learning to read and write: A longitudinal study of fifty-four children from first through fourth grade*. Paper presented at the annual meeting of the American Educational Research Association, New Orleans, LA.

Morrow, L. M. (2000). *Literacy development in the early years: Helping children read and write*. Needham Heights, MA: Allyn and Bacon.

Moustafa, M. (2000). Phonics instruction. In D. Strickland & L. Morrow (Eds.), *Beginning reading and writing* (pp. 121–133). New York: Teachers College Press.

Neuman, S., & Roskos, K. (1989). Preschoolers' conceptions of literacy as reflected in their spontaneous play. In S. McCormick & J. Zutell (Eds.), *Cognitive and social perspectives for literacy research and instruction* (pp. 87–94). Chicago: National Reading Conference.

Ramey, C. T., & Ramey, S. L. (1996, February). *At risk does not mean doomed* (National Health/Education Consortium Occasional Paper No. 4). Paper presented at the meeting of the American Association of Science.

Robbins, C., & Ehri, L. (1994). Reading storybooks to kindergartners helps them learn new vocabulary words. *Journal of Educational Psychology, 86,* 54–56.

Stanovich, K. (1986). Matthew effects in reading: Some consequences of individual differences in the acquisition of literacy. *Reading Research Quarterly, 21,* 360–407.

Stanovich, K. (1994). Romance and reality. *The Reading Teacher, 47,* 280–291.

Strickland, D. S. (1998). *Teaching phonics today.* Newark, DE: International Reading Association.

Sulzby, E. (1992). Writing and reading: Signs of oral and written language organization in the young child. In W. Teale & E. Sulzby (Eds.), *Emergent literacy: Reading and writing* (pp. 50–89). Norwood, NJ: Ablex.

Taylor, D., & Strickland, D. (1986). *Family storybook reading.* Portsmouth, NH: Heinemann.

Teale, W., & Sulzby, E. (1989). Emergent literacy: New perspectives on young children's reading and writing. In D. S. Strickland & L. M. Morrow (Eds.), *Emerging literacy: Young children learn to read and write* (pp. 1–15). Newark, DE: International Reading Association.

Wolfe, P., & Brandt, R. (1998). What do we know from brain research? *Educational Leadership, 56,* 8–13.

CHAPTER FOUR

Elementary Programs: Guiding Change in a Time of Standards

Kathryn H. Au

My purpose in this chapter is to offer guidelines an administrator, curriculum leader, or reading specialist might follow in facilitating the development of a successful elementary reading program, particularly in the context of the standards movement and pressures for accountability (cf. Schmoker & Marzano, 1999). Supporting research is noted, and practical examples are presented, drawn from my experience in working with schools to improve literacy achievement. Under most of the guidelines, I discuss issues of special significance to schools in diverse, low-income communities.

One of my key assumptions is that developing an effective reading program is not a simple matter of choosing the right commercial program or buying the right textbooks. An effective reading program can be developed only through an interactive process that is informed by current theory and research on literacy instruction and that involves teachers, students, and parents. An effective reading program cannot be selected and installed; it must evolve through a thoughtful, grassroots effort at the building and classroom levels. With this perspective in mind, I offer seven guidelines for the development of an effective elementary school reading program:

1. Become informed about current thinking.
2. Create a shared vision of the excellent reader.
3. Establish clear goals for students' learning.
4. Involve students in working toward these goals.
5. Develop an assessment system.
6. Establish conditions to support powerful instruction.
7. Summarize and evaluate student learning results.

Guideline 1: Become Informed About Current Thinking

Many educators are familiar with the heated debates about reading instruction that seem to arise every few years. The popular press tends to publicize the views of those who offer simple solutions. Yet those who work with children on a daily basis in the elementary classroom know that there cannot be a simple solution. Teachers, especially those working with students of diverse cultural and linguistic backgrounds, recognize the complexities involved in bringing all students to high levels of literacy.

The curriculum leader or facilitator who will be leading the school in improving its reading program must begin by assessing the overall situation. In a few fortunate schools, an ongoing process of professional development has supported teachers in keeping current about reading and reading instruction. More common, however, are schools with just a few teachers who have kept current because of their own professional interests. In these schools, the faculty as a whole can benefit from a process of reading and discussion that will bring them up to date with recent thinking. An understanding of the existing knowledge base in the field of reading is essential to the development of an effective reading program.

If the goal is to involve the whole faculty in the learning process, what readings might serve as a starting point? My recommendation is that the selections focus on a balanced view of reading and reading instruction (Fitzgerald, 1999), because this view invites teachers to consider the complexity of the issues and to find the middle ground. The results of a nationwide survey suggest that few teachers take a single-minded, either-or perspective on reading instruction in which phonics and skills are pitted against meaning-oriented, holistic approaches (Baumann, Hoffman, Moon, & Duffy-Hester, 1998). Of the surveyed teachers, 89% agreed with the statement, "I believe in a balanced approach to reading instruction which combines skills development with literature and language-rich activities," and 76% indicated that they had an eclectic attitude toward reading instruction and "would draw from multiple perspectives and sets of materials when teaching reading" (p. 642).

Recent thinking about balanced reading instruction suggests a definition far richer and more complex than a mere amalgamation of phonics and whole language (Reutzel, 1999). For this reason, one approach to be taken in readings and discussions might be to address questions such as the following:

◆ What are the philosophical assumptions and beliefs underlying a balanced approach to reading instruction?
◆ What are the research findings supporting this approach?
◆ What are its possible benefits to students?
◆ What are the components of a balanced reading program?

These are challenging questions, and readings that will further teachers' thinking are likely to be equally challenging. Recommended articles dealing with the philosophical assumptions underlying a balanced approach include Pearson and Raphael (1999) and Fitzgerald (1999). References to research can be found in the latest *Handbook of Reading Research* (Kamil, Mosenthal, Pearson, & Barr, 2000). Brief, teacher-friendly readings about the components of a balanced reading program are presented in the resource book developed by Au, Carroll, and Scheu (1997).

Teachers in schools serving diverse, low-income communities, including Title I schools, will find it valuable to engage in discussions of the issues that particularly affect reading instruction in their schools. Accountability pressures are likely to be felt most strongly in these schools, which often have a history of low scores on standardized tests of reading achievement. Many educators are aware of the high correlation between standardized achievement test scores and family income (Ascher, 1990), but this fact is not generally known to policy makers or to the general public. This high correlation, along with the potential for cultural bias in the test items, makes it inappropriate, especially in the case of schools in low-income communities, to rely on standardized tests as the sole or even primary means of evaluating students' achievement and the effectiveness of reading programs. Nevertheless, principals and teachers in schools in these communities frequently receive directives to "raise test scores." Such directives are often accompanied by pressure to adopt a commercial reading program, especially one with a focus on phonics and the direct instruction of skills in isolation. The claim is that such programs will raise test scores, although a close examination shows no strong evidence to support this claim (Coles, 2000; Pogrow, 1998; Taylor, Anderson, Au, & Raphael, 2000).

Teachers will want to be aware that there is no quick fix (Allington & Walmsley, 1995), and that concentrated efforts at the school level with a balanced approach to reading instruction are more likely to yield positive effects over the long run. Reasons for favoring balanced literacy instruction in schools serving diverse students are presented by Delpit (1986, 1991), Strickland (1994) and Au (1998).

Guideline 2: Create a Shared Vision of the Excellent Reader

The key to a successful elementary school reading program begins with a shared vision of what the program should accomplish for students. As implied in Guideline 1, this vision should be based upon current knowledge of the field of reading, as well as upon knowledge of the school and the students and community it serves. Each school will have a somewhat different vision, because each school presents an environment different in some respects from every other school. Schools serve different communities and different populations of students, and they each have their own unique mix of faculty members. Schools have their own histories, having used different approaches to reading instruction in the past, and they differ in their current approaches to reading instruction. In short, because of the unique nature of each school, the vision of the reading program cannot be brought in from the outside but must be developed from within. The exact process followed to develop the vision of the reading program will differ from school to school, but the process should always be a collaborative one, centering on teachers but also involving representatives of other key constituencies, such as parents.

In my work with schools, I find it helpful to start at a broad level, by first addressing issues of philosophy. I usually begin by asking the teachers to meet by grade levels to come up with two central beliefs they hold about each of the following:

- ◆ Teaching
- ◆ Learning
- ◆ Literacy

Each grade level prepares a chart with its belief statements and presents these statements to the entire faculty. Typical examples of belief statements include the notions that teaching involves accepting responsibility for every child's learning, that learning is a process of making connections between the known and the new, and that literacy cuts across all content areas. Following these presentations, I can highlight themes running across the grade levels.

Next I ask the teachers to discuss what good readers do. Each grade level compiles a list of five to 10 points, and these are shared with the whole group. Typical examples include the ideas that good readers can critically evaluate what they read, make personal connections to what they read, and decode words quickly and accurately.

Finally, I ask the teachers to come up with a vision of the excellent reader who will graduate from their school. This discussion is held within grade levels, but everyone is asked to think about the vision of the excellent fifth or sixth grade reader (depending on the highest grade in the school). The vision of the excellent reader is based on the expectations teachers hold for a representative student, neither the highest achieving nor the lowest achieving. I have the teachers imagine that this representative student has been in the school since kindergarten and has received strong instruction at every grade along the way. Grade levels write their vision statements on chart paper, and these are presented to the whole faculty. Once again, I highlight points of agreement shown in the statements. Later, the school's language arts committee, or another small group, takes the drafts and puts together a composite statement describing the whole school's vision of the excellent fifth or sixth grade reader. This statement is brought back to the entire faculty for approval.

A school's vision statement might read as follows:

> The excellent reader who graduates from Laurel Elementary School will find joy in reading and be able to read with understanding for a wide variety of purposes in school and in everyday life.

This discussion of philosophy, leading to a school's vision of the excellent reader, provides the foundation upon which a sound reading program can be built. Schools that take the time to hold such discussions have spelled out their beliefs and know what they want a reading program to accomplish. They are in a good position to move forward, because they know where they are heading. They can make decisions in a principled manner. For example, they can decide whether they should develop a reading program unique to their school, or whether a commercial program will do the job. Schools that do not take the time to hold these discussions frequently encounter difficulty because they have not made explicit the beliefs and vision that should guide

their decision making. Often these schools see their task as choosing among commercial programs. This task is difficult and sometimes leads to conflict within the faculty, because the school does not have its own, previously agreed upon criteria for assessing the merits of various programs.

Obviously, time for staff to meet for discussions is a key factor. No reading program, however wonderful in design, can be successful if staff members have not contributed to shaping it and do not feel ownership over it. The approach proposed here is based on the assumption that a school's reading program can be successful only if it is consistent with the faculty's beliefs about teaching, learning, and literacy. Furthermore, the administration, teachers, parents, students, and community must share a common vision of the excellent reader who is to graduate from the school. The reading program is the means for accomplishing this vision.

Guideline 3: Establish Clear Goals for Students' Learning

Once the discussion of philosophy has been completed and the school has a statement describing its vision of the excellent reader, the faculty is ready to begin work on the curriculum. I prefer to keep curriculum development as straightforward as possible, by thinking of the process in terms of deciding upon goals for student learning, instructional strategies, materials, and an assessment system. The first task is to set goals for student learning, which in my experience is the aspect of curriculum development that many schools find most challenging. Developing an assessment system may seem daunting, but this task becomes easier once the goals for student learning have been identified.

When I work with a school on curriculum development, I begin by referring back to its vision of the excellent reader. We review this statement and discuss its implications. Then I ask each grade level to think about the special contribution that it will make to the vision of the excellent reader. I point out that each grade level makes a contribution different from every other grade level, because of the unique characteristics of the children at that phase of reading development. For example, kindergarten teachers may teach children concepts about print, while third grade teachers may provide instruction in base words and affixes. I ask the teachers to capture their thinking in terms of grade level benchmarks, or goals they would like their students to achieve as readers by the end of the school year. I ask them to set their benchmarks to represent a high but attainable level of accomplishment for a representative or typical student.

To make the task more specific and manageable, I ask the teachers to think of benchmarks in three areas:

◆ Attitudes
◆ Comprehension
◆ Strategies and skills

I tell the teachers that they should think of at least one benchmark for each area, arriving at a total of from five to seven benchmarks all together. This is a challenging task, because teachers are accustomed to working with long lists of reading objectives, particularly in the area of strategies and skills. They quickly realize that they cannot have an objective for each skill (for example, for each initial consonant), and that skills need to be clustered under broadly stated benchmarks.

The reason for limiting the number of benchmarks is that the benchmarks form the basis for the assessment system. Eventually, forms of evidence and procedures for collecting evidence will be identified for each benchmark. Having more than five to seven benchmarks tends to make the assessment system cumbersome and overly complicated. Also, having a limited number of benchmarks makes it easier for the teachers and students to remember and work with all of the benchmarks and to keep in mind the school's overall vision of the excellent reader.

The following examples give an idea of the variety of benchmarks that teachers might develop:

◆ Children will enjoy reading every day. (Kindergarten, Attitudes)

◆ Students will have favorite authors and topics for voluntary reading. (Grade 5, Attitudes)
◆ Children will identify the problem and solution in the story. (Grade 1, Comprehension)
◆ Students will construct a theme for the story and give reasons for their idea. (Grade 4, Comprehension)
◆ Children will read a grade-level text aloud with 90% accuracy. (Grade 2, Strategies and skills)
◆ Students will monitor their comprehension and seek clarification when necessary. (Grade 6, Strategies and skills)

I am frequently asked if having teachers go through this process is not akin to "reinventing the wheel." Those who express this concern point out that the process might go faster if the teachers simply referred to one of the many existing reading scope and sequence charts, to the district's reading outcomes, or to the state's reading standards. All of these sources are valuable, and I discuss below the role they play. However, I want to highlight two important advantages to the approach of beginning with teachers' own thoughts about benchmarks, rather than with outside sources. First, this approach requires teachers to think deeply about what is important in terms of learning to read. The open-ended nature of the task of creating grade level benchmarks promotes rich, generative thinking and discussion. These professional reflections and conversations are circumvented when teachers are handed a ready-made list. Second, this approach shows respect for teachers' professional judgment and promotes their commitment to the curriculum development process. Teachers' deep knowledge of their students and their school setting can be reflected in the benchmarks. Teachers are more likely to feel ownership of benchmarks that are the result of their own best thinking and tailored to their students, not to students in general.

Each grade level prepares a first draft of its benchmarks. These benchmarks are written on chart paper and shared with the whole school. The charts are lined up so that teachers can see the progression in benchmarks, going from the lowest to the highest grade. I have the teachers do a gallery walk so they can study closely and take notes about the benchmarks proposed for each grade. Then grade levels meet again to discuss what they have observed about the benchmarks as a whole, and these observations are shared with the school. At one school, teachers observed that every grade included story elements in its benchmarks, but that it was unclear how students' knowledge of story elements was expected to differ across the grades. At another school, teachers observed that the benchmarks for the fourth through sixth grades referred to students' comprehension of informative text, but that no mention of informative text appeared in the primary grades. I welcome any and all observations, but I let the teachers know that it will take time to achieve consistency in the flow of benchmarks across the grade levels. I emphasize that at this point, when we are working with just the first draft of the benchmarks, the main goal is to have every grade level reach clarity about its own beliefs and its own benchmarks. Once this clarity is achieved, teachers can begin meeting with those at adjacent grade levels to discuss how benchmarks can be coordinated to make the flow of learning smooth and consistent for students.

After teachers have produced a first draft of their grade level benchmarks, I ask them to turn their attention to any outside sets of goals for student learning with which their benchmarks should be aligned. In most cases, one source will be the state's reading standards. Another source may be the district's reading outcomes. In some cases, the school may have a basal reading or other commercial program that includes its own outcomes. The teachers' task at this point is to align their benchmarks with the state standards and other relevant sources.

The process of alignment has not proved difficult for the teachers with whom I have worked. In general, they discover that their benchmarks address all but a few points. These omissions usually are predictable, because they involve comparatively new aspects of reading in the elementary school. For example, in schools in Hawaii, the aspects of the state's reading and literature content standards typically omitted in teachers' first drafts of grade level benchmarks are reading to perform a task (such as reading a map or bus schedule) and interacting thoughtfully with multicultural literature.

In my work with schools, I do not insist that there be a one-to-one correspondence between the grade level benchmarks and the standards. For example, although Hawaii has a separate content standard devoted to interacting with multicultural literature (Department of Education, 1999), teachers may decide that they can address this standard within a broader benchmark on responding to literature. They accomplish this by including multicultural literature as one of the categories of text to which students must respond through discussions and in writing. Thus, while there are six content standards for the state, these teachers may end up with five benchmarks. In my opinion, the purpose for alignment is not to convince the teachers to give up their own benchmarks and adopt the state standards instead. Rather, the point is to ensure (a) that the teachers develop a workable system of their own and (b) that this system enables them to teach toward and provide evidence for student learning in each of the areas specified by the state's standards. Once the process of alignment has been completed, the teachers are ready to move on to the next step.

Guideline 4: Involve Students in Working Toward These Goals

In the first round, the teachers state the grade level benchmarks in professional language. I now ask them to think about how the benchmarks might be reworded to make them understandable to students. For example, grade level benchmarks might read "Students will have the habit of daily reading" or "Students will cross-check using meaning, structural, and visual cues in order to identify words." I point out that these benchmarks have clear meanings to other educators but are much less likely to be understood by students. I ask the teachers at each grade level to put their benchmarks in the form of "I Can" statements (cf. Cleland, 1999). These I Can statements are to be shared with their classes, so that students can be aware of the expectations for achievement at each grade level and participate in assessing their own progress.

Under Guidelines 2 and 3, I mentioned the importance of teachers' participation in and ownership of the curriculum development process. Students' participation in the process of their own learning and assessment is no less important. With traditional approaches to evaluation, such as standardized tests, both teachers and students are left out of the loop (Valencia, 1998). In the context of standards, portfolios, and other innovative forms of assessment, the involvement of teachers, parents, and other interested parties becomes central to success. However, it is the involvement of students that has the potential to yield the greatest benefits of all. The aim is to put students at the center of the assessment process, so that they learn to take responsibility for setting goals for themselves as readers, for making efforts to reach these goals, and for monitoring their own progress (Valencia & Bradley, 1998).

I have the teachers imagine what it will be like to discuss the grade level benchmarks with their students. Once teachers think of themselves standing in front of their students, trying to explain the benchmarks, the need for the translation to I Can statements becomes clear. Teachers at the upper elementary grades may find that their benchmarks need little rewording, while other teachers, particularly in kindergarten and first grade, may find themselves changing nearly every word. For example, here are two kindergarten I Can statements and their accompanying grade level benchmarks. Note the difference in the wordings.

◆ I can use beginning sounds to help me read a word. (Children will use initial consonant sounds to identify words.)
◆ I can tell what will happen next in a story and why. (Children will make and justify predictions about a text.)

Creating I Can statements often leads teachers to new insights. As they put a benchmark into language their students will understand, they often find themselves gaining a better understanding of the intention behind that benchmark. After they draft the I Can statement, they revise the benchmark itself.

The next step is for the teachers to introduce the I Can statements to their classes. Usually the teachers at a grade level decide to introduce just one or two I Can statements each quarter of the school year. The reason for presenting only a few I Can statements at a time is to allow the students to become thoroughly familiar with these statements and the kinds of learning they represent. These I Can statements become the focus of assessment, although instruction related to all the I Can statements may be taking place each quarter.

Introducing the I Can statements to students for the first time often leads teachers to further discoveries. For example, they may find through discussion that another wording communicates a certain concept more clearly to the students. This experience may lead to improvements in the wording of an I Can statement and perhaps to changes in the underlying grade level benchmark as well. In any event, it does not take teachers long to learn that their grade level benchmarks and I Can statements are necessarily works in progress, especially during the first two years.

Through I Can statements, teachers have a ready means of making connections between instruction and standards explicit to students. For example, suppose that the teacher is about to teach a lesson on initial consonant sound T. The teacher can remind the children that one of their I Can statements involves learning to use beginning sounds to help them read words. She can inform them that the lesson she is about to teach is on a new beginning sound, and that learning this new sound will help them to reach the goal in this I Can statement. A fourth grade teacher once made the following comment to me about having I Can statements posted in her classroom. She said, "The I Can statements don't just help the students. They also remind me of what I'm supposed to be teaching."

Guideline 5: Develop an Assessment System

In most schools, arriving at grade level benchmarks and I Can statements seems to be the most difficult part of establishing a reading program. However, the time devoted to developing appropriate benchmarks and I Can statements is time well spent, because the benchmarks and I Can statements provide the foundation for building the assessment system.

I find that many teachers have attended workshops on content standards, performance standards, performance indicators, portfolios, rubrics, and other aspects of innovative or standards-based assessment. They have encountered so many new and different ideas about assessment, without having gained a good framework for fitting these ideas together, that they feel thoroughly confused. Given this context, my task must be to simplify the standards-based assessment process and help teachers develop an assessment system that they can implement and maintain, given the constraints on their time and energies.

Choosing a Benchmark

I start by reminding teachers that we deliberately limited the number of benchmarks so that it would eventually be possible to assess each one. The time has come to move into the assessment phase of our work. I have the teachers begin by choosing just one benchmark on which to assess their students' progress. The reason for working with only one benchmark during the first year is to allow the teachers to gain an understanding of how the standards-based assessment process works. Working with just one benchmark enables the teachers to learn the process thoroughly without feeling overwhelmed by the amount of work required.

To foster teachers' ownership of the assessment process, I prefer to let each grade level choose the benchmark they want to focus on. However, different schools take different routes in this regard. In one school, each grade level was free to choose its own benchmark, with some grade levels focusing on attitudes while others focused on comprehension or on strategies and skills. In another school, the teachers decided it would be best if they all worked on the same reading benchmark. They voted to work on a comprehension benchmark having to

do with characters, because this story element could be addressed in kindergarten through Grade 5. I find that these decisions do not make much difference in the long run, as long as the teachers all remain committed to their chosen benchmark through the year.

Gathering Evidence

Once the benchmark has been chosen, the next step for the teachers is to decide upon the kind of evidence to be collected to document students' progress. At this point many teachers have the tendency to turn to existing tests, surveys, and other measures. I assure them that these can be valuable tools. However, I encourage them to think of evidence that may be available as part of the everyday life of the classroom. For example, suppose that the benchmark selected is that students will make connections between the novel and their own lives. If the students write in literature response journals, those journals can provide evidence of progress toward this benchmark. Following this approach of gathering evidence through everyday classroom products and events makes it easier for teachers to collect evidence, because they do not have to administer separate tests. Other examples of benchmarks and classroom evidence include the following:

Benchmark	Evidence
1. Students have the habit of daily reading.	1. Logs of books read during sustained silent reading and at home.
2. Students comprehend informative text.	2. File cards with notes for research reports.
3. Students understand the characteristics of different genres.	3. Completed matrices for the genres of biography, historical fiction, and fantasy.
4. Students monitor their own comprehension.	4. Double-entry journal showing questions and reflections on the novel.

Gathering evidence in the second grade and above is made easier by the fact that students are better able to express their thoughts in writing and to maintain their own records. Teachers in kindergarten and first grade find that certain kinds of evidence can be gathered only through labor-intensive, individual assessment (e.g., running records or miscue analyses of oral reading) or observation (e.g., anecdotal records of children's behavior during time set aside for sharing and reading books). Administrators can support standards-based assessment by providing the extra help teachers need, for example, by organizing paraprofessional aides who can assist with evidence gathering at the early grades. As the assessment process becomes more comprehensive, it may become unrealistic to expect kindergarten and first grade teachers, in particular, to gather all the evidence needed while continuing to provide a rich menu of literacy instruction.

From the second grade and up, and sometimes even in kindergarten and first grade, the students themselves can and should be involved in the collecting of evidence. Students are already familiar with the I Can statements. At the end of the quarter, or at the time evidence is to be collected, the teacher can ask students what evidence they have to show that they are making progress toward the I Can statements. For example, students can be asked if they have any evidence that shows they can make connections between a novel and their own lives. Students can usually come up with ideas on their own, such as the writing in their literature response journals and in their book reports.

I suggest that the teachers at each grade level begin to assemble a simple assessment handbook. This handbook includes (1) the procedures they will follow to collect the evidence and (2) the procedures they will follow to score the evidence (rubrics). Teachers at a grade level usually discover the importance of having set procedures for collecting evidence the first time they sit down together with their samples of student work. In one school, the third grade teachers discovered that they had inadvertently assessed their students' reading comprehension under two different sets of conditions. They had agreed in advance upon the text the students would read. Three of the four teachers had simply handed students copies of the text and asked students to read and write a summary. The fourth

teacher had held a brief class discussion before students wrote their summary. As a result, her students' summaries were stronger than those from the other classes. Another discovery teachers make is that they need to be specific about their expectations. For example, a group of fourth grade teachers was disappointed to find that few of their students' summaries included discussion of the theme of the novel. Upon reflection, they realized that they had not made it clear to students that discussion of the theme was a necessary part of the summaries. The assessment handbook becomes a place for teachers to record all the decisions they have made about the exact procedures to be followed in collecting evidence. Later, the handbook becomes valuable as a means of orienting teachers new to the grade level to the assessment procedures established.

Scoring the Evidence

After teachers at a grade level have identified the evidence for their chosen benchmark, they discuss how they will score the evidence. In other words, they develop a rubric. Some teachers' previous experience has led them to believe that rubrics must involve seven-point scales with elaborate criteria. I strongly encourage teachers to think of the process of scoring evidence in a much simpler way. In standards-based assessment, a straightforward approach is to arrive at a rubric that allows student evidence to be placed in one of three categories: above grade level, at grade level, or below grade level with respect to performance on that particular benchmark. Teachers often prefer to use terms with a more developmental tone, such as exceeding, meeting, or working on the benchmark. As with the benchmarks, rubrics are geared toward end-of-year performance. The teachers work in grade levels to test their rubric on actual samples of evidence, and this reality check usually results in revisions to the rubric.

Here is an example of a rubric developed by third grade teachers for the I Can statement "I can summarize what I've read by retelling the main ideas." Students were required to read a text appropriate for the end of third grade.

◆ Above grade level
  — The response shows a clear understanding of the story and includes the elements of setting, character, problem, solution, and theme.
  — The response provides accurate and relevant information and shows sound reasoning about the story.

◆ At grade level
  — The response shows an adequate understanding of the story and includes the story elements of setting, character, problem, and solution.
  — The response provides accurate information, although not all of this information may be central to the story.

◆ Below grade level
  — The response is incomplete and shows little understanding, or an inaccurate understanding, of the story.
  — The response may include random details and unimportant information.

Several observations may be made about this rubric. First, its development and use required teachers to exercise considerable professional judgment. They had to arrive at a common understanding of exactly what they hoped to see in a summary written by their students at the end of the year. It took several meetings to arrive at this consensus. However, once the teachers had reached consensus on grade level performance, it was not difficult for them to develop the criteria for above grade level and below grade level performance.

Selecting anchor pieces often reduces the need for elaborate scoring criteria. An anchor piece is a student product used to represent a certain level of performance. For example, the third grade teachers who created the rubric presented above chose a student summary that represented the performance they wanted to see in students rated at grade level. Some teachers find it valuable as well to select anchor pieces representing performance below and above grade level. The process of selecting anchor pieces often helps teachers to clarify their thinking about scoring criteria. Having anchor pieces

helps teachers become confident in their decisions about rating students' work.

Some teachers introduce students to the teacher-developed rubric (with appropriate changes in wording). Other teachers prefer to discuss what should go into the rubric with the students themselves. If necessary, they add to the students' criteria. The rubric usually appears as a chart posted in the classroom. These charts may include anchor pieces that are not actual student products but teacher-made samples that illustrate the features of grade level, below grade level, or above grade level performance. On a regular basis, students can be guided through the process of evaluating their own work by referring to the rubric. At the end of the quarter, or whenever the period for evidence-gathering has been set, the students can select the piece of evidence that shows their best effort toward meeting the I Can statements. Students have the opportunity to assess their own performance, as well as to receive feedback from the teacher. Some teachers believe students should be aware that their reading performance is above, at, or below grade level. Many primary grade teachers, however, prefer to use terms such as "developing" or "working toward the benchmark" and do not make explicit for children the level of their performance relative to grade level standards.

Evidence of progress toward meeting benchmarks can be collected in evaluation portfolios. These portfolios usually take the form of three-ring binders containing both evidence and reflections. Valencia and her colleagues emphasize the importance of having students not only gather but reflect upon their evidence (Valencia & Bradley, 1998). Students can attach half-page reflection sheets to the evidence, indicating the I Can statement addressed, why they selected the evidence and what it shows about their progress in this area, and the goals they have for further improvement. For example, a third grade student studied by Valencia and Bradley wrote about what she liked about a journal response (the student's spelling has not been corrected):

I like it because it makes sense, it tells you whats happing in the book and its long.

In response to the question "What does it show about you as a reader?" the student wrote:

I shows that I know whats happening in the book, it shows that I read complecated books and it shows I like horse stories. (p. 186)

The authors comment that the student has gained some important understandings; she knows that reading and writing must make sense. At the same time, the student might be led to include other dimensions in her responses, such as making personal connections or questioning the author. In classrooms where students have been introduced to rubrics, the reflection sheet can include a space for self-evaluation with respect to the criteria spelled out in the rubric.

Guideline 6: Establish Conditions to Support Powerful Instruction

I believe that the standards movement has important implications for the way administrators and curriculum leaders ask teachers to conceptualize instruction. Too often in the past, teachers attended workshops on instructional strategies and came away with only a vague sense of why these strategies might be helpful. With the standards movement, instruction can be clearly defined as the means teachers use to improve students' achievement. Teachers can then make principled decisions about which instructional strategies to use, because they can weigh the potential of each strategy to improve students' learning in the areas defined by their benchmarks or standards. In the context of the standards movement, it makes more sense to begin the process of improving a school's reading program by establishing clear goals for student learning, rather than by implementing new instructional approaches. This is the reason that reading instruction appears so late in my list of guidelines. In my experience, the need for new instructional approaches becomes obvious to teachers once grade level benchmarks have been established.

When working with standards and benchmarks, teachers face the challenge not only of collecting evidence but of examining the evidence for what it can tell them about how to improve instruction and bring students closer to the goals set for their learning. In this process, teachers look for patterns within the evidence. For example, a group of third grade teachers had their students write summaries to show their comprehension of stories read. One teacher found that a good number of students in her class were retelling the entire story instead of centering their summaries on key points and events. She decided to conduct mini-lessons, including teacher think-alouds, to teach her students the difference between a summary and a lengthy retelling. Then she had students practice writing summaries, providing extensive guidance and feedback.

What are some steps that administrators can take to support teachers in the process of strengthening instruction, as this teacher did, to meet students' needs in learning to read? Research and current thinking point to several avenues. The starting point, as basic as it may seem, is to ensure that adequate time is allocated for reading instruction. Moreover, an emerging consensus about the key features of effective reading instruction suggests that elementary reading programs will generally encompass four components (cf. Flippo, 1998): access to reading materials, readers as role models, systematic instruction, and literature discussion.

Time for Reading Instruction

Estimates indicate that the average amount of time set aside for reading or language arts instruction in the early grades is about one hour and 45 minutes (Goodlad, 1983). In the primary grades, this is probably the minimum amount of time that should be allocated. Ironically, schools with a large proportion of students from low-income families usually schedule *less* time for reading instruction than other schools (Allington, 1991). The reason for this situation is not known, but certainly the students in these schools need and deserve ample time for reading instruction.

Administrators can use their leadership to make sure that the time allocated for reading instruction is not diverted for other purposes, however worthwhile or entertaining. For example, they can schedule assemblies for late in the school day, preserving the morning time for instruction. They can ask resource teachers, such as those in Title I or other remedial reading programs, to work in the classrooms instead of pulling students out for instruction. Measures such as these minimize the disruptions to classroom reading instruction and allow students of diverse backgrounds to remain a part of the classroom community of readers.

Of course, adequate time for reading instruction is only part of the solution. Close attention also must be paid to what actually happens in classrooms during reading instruction time. *Quality* of instruction must accompany *quantity* of time. Exactly what constitutes high-quality, powerful instruction may differ from school to school, just as there will be variations due to the tailoring of vision statements and grade level benchmarks to school contexts and to the students and community served.

Access to Reading Materials

Students need access to a wide variety of reading materials, especially high-quality works of children's literature. Ideally, each classroom should have its own library stocked with several hundred books. Such classroom libraries offer students a good selection during the time set aside for sustained silent reading. Materials available include works of fiction and nonfiction, as well as magazines and newspapers. A home lending program is established so that students can borrow books to read at home each evening. Students who read books independently for at least 10 minutes a day have higher reading achievement than students who do less reading (Anderson, Wilson, & Fielding, 1988). Administrators can help give students ready access to a wide range of books by setting aside funds to stock classroom libraries, as well as to increase the collection in the school library. Raising money to purchase more books is an excellent project for parent and community organizations.

Readers as Role Models

Students need the positive influence of teachers and other adults who experience joy in reading and demonstrate the real-world importance of reading. Many children come to school knowing the value of literacy in everyday life, but all are not so fortunate (Purcell-Gates, 1995). Teachers should be readers themselves, in the sense that they enjoy reading and have their own tastes and interests as readers, so that they can serve as role models for students (cf. Graves, 1990). Teachers demonstrate their enthusiasm for reading and literature by reading aloud to their classes, whether in kindergarten or Grade 6. Teachers' enthusiasm is contagious, as any school librarian can tell you. A teacher at one school was known for her love of literature and ability to win her students over to books. The librarian could always tell which author was being featured in the classroom, because the students would rush into the library at recess and borrow all of that author's books (for example, all those by Beverly Cleary).

Administrators can serve as literate role models as well, by reading aloud to students, by giving book talks, and by otherwise showing that reading has high priority in their lives. Some administrators have arranged to have the whole school, including custodial staff, engage in sustained silent reading at the same time every day. These actions send a powerful message to students about the importance of reading.

Of course, parents may be reminded that they are usually the main literacy role models in their children's lives. They can be encouraged to read books aloud to and with students, and to engage their children in discussion of these books. Administrators can help by supporting workshops that acquaint parents with books they can read aloud. Such workshops have proved to be popular events at schools, and resources such as Trelease's *The Read Aloud Handbook* (1989) offer suggestions of many suitable titles. Parents of English language learners may not be able directly to support students' learning to read in English, but they may reinforce the importance of literacy by modeling its functions and uses in other languages (Guerra, 1998).

Systematic Instruction

Students need to receive systematic instruction, including repeated demonstrations and coaching, on the strategies and skills involved in reading. Much has been written about the value of systematic instruction in word identification skills (e.g., Snow & Griffin, 1998). Clearly, knowledge of the alphabetic principle is necessary for learning to read in English, and most children benefit from explicit instruction in this regard. However, there is no evidence that any one method of teaching phonics is best, and therefore teachers are advised to make flexible use of a variety of approaches, to keep phonics instruction meaningful and interesting, and to place phonics instruction in the context of a balanced reading program (so that it occupies perhaps 10% of language arts time in the early grades) (Stahl, 2000). A significant finding from recent research is that effective and less effective teachers differ not in the amount of explicit phonics instruction they provide, but in the assistance they give to build children's independence as readers. The most effective teachers coach children in applying word identification skills when they are engaged in ongoing reading (Taylor, Pearson, Clark, & Walpole, 2000).

Literature-based instruction, combined with access to books and time for independent reading, helps students of diverse backgrounds become better readers (Morrow, 1992). Elsewhere I have discussed the continuum of instructional strategies that teachers can follow in literature-based instruction (Au, 1998). These strategies are teacher read-alouds, sustained silent reading, shared reading, guided reading, guided discussion, and literature discussion groups. Teachers may find that this or another set of instructional strategies will fit the bill in terms of improving student performance on the school's grade level benchmarks.

Administrators may wish to arrange a series of workshops to build teachers' familiarity with and ability to teach using the appropriate strategies. Most primary and upper grade teachers use literature in their classrooms (Baumann et al., 1998), but the transition to literature-based instruction requires considerable amounts of both individual and institutional learning, especially in high-poverty schools (Allington, Guice, Michelson, Baker, & Li, 1996). Administrators who are serious about lasting improvement in their school's reading program must be prepared to stay the course through the period of time required to make the transition, which may be from three to five years or even longer (Routman, 1991).

Most recent discussions of instruction in the field of reading have centered on beginning reading and phonics, rather than on the reading of older students and comprehension. This focus has been unfortunate, in the sense that some may be under the impression that the teacher's job is done once children have become fluent decoders. The ability to decode text quickly and accurately frees up attention for comprehension (Samuels, 1985). However, students who can decode every word do not automatically comprehend text (Anderson, Mason, & Shirey, 1984). Comprehension strategies (such as making inferences, identifying the main idea, summarizing, and monitoring) can and should be taught (Dole, Duffy, Roehler, & Pearson, 1991). My work in schools in low-income communities, which enroll many students of diverse backgrounds, indicates that it is far easier for teachers to bring students to grade level performance in decoding than in comprehension (Au & Asam, 1996). Comprehension instruction, especially in the context of the ongoing reading of both fiction and nonfiction texts, is a vital element in a balanced and successful reading program.

Literature Discussion

Students need to talk about their responses to reading and to share those responses with others in a variety of ways. One of the profound changes in current thinking about reading has come in the recognition that, although individual cognition certainly plays a part, literacy is ultimately social. Reading is a way of expressing our humanity and joining together with other people. Some theorists argue that the reader is never alone, even when she goes off by herself to read in a corner, because the reader remains in the company of the author (Bakhtin, 1981).

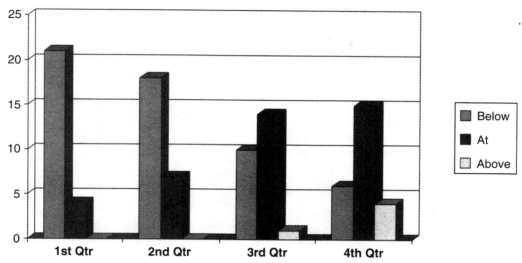

Figure 4.1. Reading Performance in the Classroom of a Teacher in Her Second Year with the Process

Part of becoming a reader is gaining membership in a community of readers who have a common background based upon their experiences with books. Literature discussions, whether with the teacher or peers, provide students with opportunities to share their responses to literature and to learn from the responses of others (Raphael, Goatley, McMahon, & Woodman, 1995). Certainly, written responses and literature discussions bring together all of the language arts: reading, writing, speaking, and listening. However, responses to literature may be expressed in other forms as well, including the visual and dramatic arts.

Guideline 7: Summarize and Evaluate Student Learning Results

I wrote earlier about having teachers focus on just one benchmark during their first year of work with standards-based assessment. By the end of the year, teachers have had the experience of gathering and scoring evidence and of obtaining results for that benchmark, usually just for the third and fourth quarters of the school year. They are now asked to display their results for student learning in the form of bar graphs. In my work with schools, I have come to appreci-

ate the importance of getting to the bottom line, which in the case of the standards movement means reaching the point where student learning results can be calculated and displayed. The use of rubrics with just three levels of performance—above, at, and below grade level—means that there generally is no difficulty in achieving reliability in scoring the evidence of student performance, with levels of agreement exceeding 90% (Au & Carroll, 1997). Once the student evidence has been scored, the results are easily presented in the form of bar graphs.

What I find valuable about these bar graphs is that they are based on evidence gathered in an ongoing way at the classroom level. They are related to standards, because classroom evidence has been organized according to grade level benchmarks aligned with these external standards. They lend credibility to teachers' work, because the results are reliable and have been quantified. Figure 4.1 shows a sample bar graph with results I have found to be typical in elementary schools with a significant number of students of diverse backgrounds from low-income families. This bar graph shows what generally happens in terms of student learning during a teacher's second year in the process I have been describing. Several observations may be made about this graph. It clearly displays improvements in students' reading performance over the course of the school year. In this case, evidence was gathered and analyzed each quarter. At the beginning of the year, almost all students were rated below grade level on this benchmark, which was to be expected, given that the benchmark was set to define end-of-year performance. Over the course of the year, a significant number of students moved from below to at grade level performance. However, a smaller number than might be expected reached levels of performance judged to be above grade level.

I believe it is important even during the first year of the change process to push forward to the point of creating these bar graphs of students' reading performance. The bar graphs serve as a reminder that the purpose of this whole process must be to improve students' learning to read. The bar graphs can address several practical needs. Obviously, they give teachers a quick picture of the overall results they have achieved with a class on a given benchmark. During the first year, most teachers find their results less than satisfactory, but they generally know exactly what they can do to improve them. If classes show different patterns of results, teachers become aware of colleagues from whom they can gain instructional ideas. Combining results for all the teachers in a grade gives an overall picture of the effectiveness of the reading program at that level. This leads to productive discussions among teachers within the grade level. Strengths and weaknesses in instruction can be identified, and steps can be taken to improve the program.

Administrators have results that they can use to evaluate the overall success of the school's reading program, and they can move forward to address issues on an objective basis: student achievement results. Administrators can use the bar graphs to meet concerns about whether students are meeting standards, whether expressed by parents, the community, the school district, or the state.

Conclusion

The approach to standards-based reform in reading described here is reflected in these words from Fullan (1993):

> When teachers work on personal vision-building and see how their commitment to making a difference in the classroom is connected to the wider purpose of education, it gives practical and moral meaning to their profession. When they pursue learning through constant inquiry they are practicing what they preach, benefiting themselves and their students by always learning. (p. 145)

One of the benefits of the present approach lies in giving teachers the opportunity to figure out for themselves how standards-based assessment works and how it can best be implemented in their own schools. When this approach is used, no pre-existing model is given for participants to copy. As they work through the process themselves, participants find that there are no shortcuts and that they must learn by doing. While many participants admit that the process is overwhelming in the beginning, they find that their confusion lifts as time goes on. This intensive, problem-solving experience, which may extend over several years, gives participants a solid working knowledge of standards-based assessment. A teacher wrote that one of the insights she gained was that the process of standards-based assessment and school improvement was ongoing and "never really finished" (Kawaguchi & Au, in press). This process can be a step toward turning a school into the kind of learning community advocated by Fullan (1993).

An important feature of the process is that it is built upon the contributions made by the teachers within each school, not by outsiders. Teachers appreciate the recognition given to them as professionals, as shown by the fact that they are being trusted to make decisions about how standards will actually be implemented in their schools. Teachers come to feel ownership over the change process, because they see that they are the ones shaping it. They can tailor their vision statement, grade level benchmarks, evidence, and rubrics to fit their own students. The constructivist nature of this process parallels the expectations for personal meaning-making and higher-level thinking that teachers expect of students in a balanced literacy program (Kawaguchi & Au, in press).

Finally, this process brings student achievement to center stage in a way that makes a practical contribution to teachers' professional development, as well as to new forms of collaboration with students and parents. When they collect and graph their own standards-based achievement data, teachers gain a greater awareness of their students' accomplishments and needs as readers. They come to understand how assessment can be a tool for improving their teaching. In many cases, because teachers help students to become aware of the standards through I Can statements and rubrics, students gain a much clearer picture of the kind of learning expected of them. When evidence is shared with parents, they can see where their children stand with respect to the rubrics. Because parents have a clear idea of what students are expected to do, they are in a better position to provide assistance at home.

Meeting high standards is currently the predominant concern in most efforts to improve reading achievement in elementary schools. In this context, a major challenge faced by administrators, supervisors, and others who seek to facilitate standards-based reform in schools is to guide the change process so that it can be perceived by teachers as supportive rather than burdensome. Meaningful change in schools requires a time-consuming and painstaking process of rethinking. Teachers are more likely to be willing to undertake this process if they can see that changes will be built on their contributions and will reflect their own best thinking about what will help their students to become better readers. This is why I believe that standards-based reform in reading must be a process of change from the inside out.

References

Allington, R., Guice, S., Michelson, N., Baker, K., & Li, S. (1996). Literature-based curricula in high-poverty schools. In M. F. Graves, P. V. D. Broek, & B. M. Taylor (Eds.), *The first R: Every child's right to read* (pp. 73–96). New York: Teachers College Press.

Allington, R. L. (1991). Children who find learning to read difficult: School responses to diversity. In E. H. Hiebert (Ed.), *Literacy for a diverse society: Perspectives, practices, and policies* (pp. 237–252). New York: Teachers College Press.

Allington, R. L., & Walmsley, S. A. (Eds.). (1995). *No quick fix: Rethinking literacy programs in America's elementary schools.* New York and Newark, DE: Teachers College Press and International Reading Association.

Anderson, R. C., Mason, J., & Shirey, L. (1984). The reading group: An experimental investigation of a labyrinth. *Reading Research Quarterly, 20,* 6–38.

Anderson, R. C., Wilson, P. T., & Fielding, L. G. (1988). Growth in reading and how children spend their time outside of school. *Reading Research Quarterly, 23,* 285–303.

Ascher, C. (1990). *Testing students in urban schools: Current problems and new directions.* New York: ERIC Clearinghouse on Urban Education, Institute for Urban and Minority Education, Teachers College, Columbia University.

Au, K. H. (1998). Constructivist approaches, phonics, and the literacy learning of students of diverse backgrounds. In T. Shanahan & F. Rodriguez-Brown (Eds.), *Forty-seventh yearbook of the National Reading Conference* (pp. 1–21). Chicago: National Reading Conference.

Au, K. H., & Asam, C. L. (1996). Improving the literacy achievement of low-income students of diverse backgrounds. In M. F. Graves, P. V. D. Broek, & B. M. Taylor (Eds.), *The first R: Every child's right to read* (pp. 199–223). New York: Teachers College Press.

Au, K. H., & Carroll, J. H. (1997). Improving literacy achievement through a constructivist approach: The KEEP Demonstration Classroom Project. *Elementary School Journal, 97,* 203–221.

Au, K. H., Carroll, J. H., & Scheu, J. A. (1997). *Balanced literacy instruction: A teacher's resource book.* Norwood, MA: Christopher-Gordon.

Bakhtin, M. M. (1981). *The dialogic imagination? Four essays by M. M. Bakhtin* (C. Emerson M. Holquist, Trans.). Austin: University of Texas Press.

Baumann, J. F., Hoffman, J. V., Moon, J., & Duffy-Hester, A. M. (1998). Where are teachers' voices in the phonics/whole language debate? Results from a survey of U.S. elementary classroom teachers. *The Reading Teacher, 51*(8), 636–650.

Cleland, J. V. (1999). We Can charts: Building blocks for student-led conferences. *The Reading Teacher, 52,* 588–595.

Coles, G. (2000). *Misreading reading: The bad science that hurts children.* Portsmouth, NH: Heinemann.

Delpit, L. D. (1986). Skills and other dilemmas of a progressive Black educator. *Harvard Educational Review, 56,* 379–385.

Delpit, L. D. (1991). A conversation with Lisa Delpit. *Language Arts, 68,* 541–547.

Department of Education, State of Hawaii. (1999). Language arts content standards. Honolulu: Author.

Dole, J. A., Duffy, G. G., Roehler, L. R., & Pearson, P. D. (1991). Moving from the old to the new: Research on reading comprehension instruction. *Review of Educational Research, 61,* 239–264.

Fitzgerald, J. (1999). What is this thing called "balance"? *The Reading Teacher, 53,* 100–107.

Flippo, R. (1998). Points of agreement: A display of professional unity in our field. *The Reading Teacher, 52,* 30–40.

Fullan, M. (1993). *Change forces: Probing the depths of educational reform.* London: Falmer.

Goodlad, J. (1983). *A place called school.* New York: Harper.

Graves, D. (1990). *Discover your own literacy.* Portsmouth, NH: Heinemann.

Guerra, J. C. (1998). *Close to home: Oral and literate practices in a transnational Mexicano community.* New York: Teachers College Press.

Kamil, M. L., Mosenthal, P. B., Pearson, P. D., & Barr, R. (Eds.). (2000). *Handbook of reading research* (Vol. 3). Mahwah, NJ: Erlbaum.

Kawaguchi, K., & Au, K. (in press). Improving reading achievement by establishing complex-wide expectations. *Educational Perspectives.*

Morrow, L. M. (1992). The impact of a literature-based program on literacy achievement, use of literature, and attitudes of children from minority backgrounds. *Reading Research Quarterly, 27,* 251–275.

Pearson, P. D., & Raphael, T. E. (1999). Toward a more complex view of balance in the literacy curriculum. In W. D. Hammond & T. E. Raphael (Eds.), *Early literacy instruction for the new millennium* (pp. 1–21). Grand Rapids: Michigan Reading Association and Center for the Improvement of Early Reading Achievement.

Pogrow, S. (1998). What is an exemplary program, and why should anyone care? A reaction to Slavin and Klein. *Educational Researcher, 27*(7), 22–29.

Purcell-Gates, V. (1995). *Other people's words: The cycle of low literacy.* Cambridge, MA: Harvard University Press.

Raphael, T. E., Goatley, V. I., McMahon, S. I., & Woodman, D. A. (1995). Promoting meaningful conversations in student book clubs. In N. L. Roser & M. L. Martinez (Eds.), *Book talk and beyond: Children and teachers respond to literature* (pp. 66–79). Newark, DE: International Reading Association.

Reutzel, D. R. (1999). On Welna's sacred cows: Where's the beef? *The Reading Teacher, 53*(2), 96–99.

Routman, R. (1991). *Invitations.* Portsmouth, NH: Heinemann.

Samuels, S. J. (1985). Automaticity and repeated reading. In J. Osborn, P. T. Wilson, & R. C. Anderson (Eds.), *Reading education: Foundations for a literate America* (pp. 215–230). Lexington, MA: Lexington Books.

Schmoker, M., & Marzano, R. J. (1999). Realizing the promise of standards-based education. *Educational Leadership, 56*(6), 17–21.

Snow, C., & Griffin, M. (1998). *Preventing reading difficulties in young children.* Washington, DC: National Academy Press.

Stahl, S. (2000). *Phonics they really use: Phonics in a balanced reading program.* Ann Arbor: Center for the Improvement of Early Reading Achievement, University of Michigan.

Strickland, D. S. (1994). Educating African American learners at risk: Finding a better way. *Language Arts, 71,* 328–336.

Taylor, B. M., Anderson, R. C., Au, K. H., & Raphael, T. E. (2000). Discretion in the translation of research to policy: A case from beginning reading. *Educational Researcher, 29*(6), 16–26.

Taylor, B. M., Pearson, P. D., Clark, K. F., & Walpole, S. (2000). *Beating the odds in teaching all children to read* (2-006). Ann Arbor: Center for the Improvement of Early Reading Achievement, University of Michigan.

Trelease, J. (1989). *The read aloud handbooks* (4th ed.). New York: Viking/Penguin.

Valencia, S. W. (1998). Why portfolios? Assessment principles and a portfolio definition. In S. W. Valencia (Ed.), *Literacy portfolios in action* (pp. 1–27). Fort Worth, TX: Harcourt Brace College Publishers.

Valencia, S. W., & Bradley, S. (1998). Engaging students in self-reflection and self-evaluation. In S. W. Valencia (Ed.), *Portfolios in action* (pp. 174–218). Fort Worth, TX: Harcourt Brace College Publishers.

CHAPTER FIVE

Adolescent Literacy Programs

Richard T. Vacca and Christine A. McKeon

On a busy road just outside Kent, Ohio, construction crews brought in huge machinery to demolish the roadbed and the narrow, curving concrete bridge over a fast-moving creek. Although rush-hour traffic was brought to a standstill by this major reconstruction project, straightening the road made a great deal of sense, and we couldn't help but wonder why the roadway had been built with such a dangerous curve in the first place. A local historian provided the answer to our question. "When the roads around here were still dirt roads," he told us, "that was a popular place to drive livestock across the creek. The current was slow there and it was relatively shallow. When roads were finally paved, they followed the original dirt roads so as not to disturb houses

and property lines." Tradition and pragmatics prevailed.

Adolescent readers today often suffer from old teaching habits and curricular decisions that no longer make sense in terms of their changing needs in the 21st century. Because of the pressure of national high-stakes assessments in the content areas, many middle school and high school teachers are driven by curricular content rather than broader issues of literacy in the lives of adolescents. Although the literacy levels of teens have attracted the attention of teachers, the media, and policy makers, as reflected in the National Assessment of Educational Progress (NAEP) reports (Bracey, 2000), little attention has been paid to *how adolescents actually view and use literacy*. Like the bridge that was designed without thinking through the implications for those who would be using it, state-mandated testing of reading achievement seems designed without thoughtful consideration of adolescents' needs or their perceptions of literacy and schooling. One Ohio teenager noted, after taking the ninth grade reading proficiency test, "I hate school; I hate those people who made up those tests" (McKeon, 1999, p. 11). His former positive perceptions of schooling during the elementary years were shattered.

An extraordinary amount of funding for the research and development of early childhood programs, though necessary, has not been balanced by research funding for adolescents (Moje, Young, Readence, & Moore, 2000; Vacca, 1998). The goals of preventing difficulties in young children (Snow, Burns, & Griffin, 1998) consumed a national agenda that focused on early reading during the 1990s. The needs of adolescent literacy learners have gone largely unnoticed, however, to the point of being marginalized (Vacca, 1998).

This chapter addresses the following:

◆ Historical overview of adolescent reading and writing programs
◆ Changing paradigms of teaching and learning
◆ Effective middle and high school literacy programs

Constructing a straight roadway for teens so they can meet the demands of the 21st century requires a substantial shift in the way adolescent literacy learning is approached and a strong commitment on the part of teachers, administrators, and policy makers to rethink traditional notions of literacy. Recognizing this need, the International Reading Association's Commission on Adolescent Literacy (Moore, Bean, Birdyshaw, & Rycik, 1999) issued a strong position statement that called for renewed commitment to adolescent reading and outlined beliefs and guidelines for instructional practices at the adolescent level. "Adolescents entering the adult world in the 21st century will read and write more than at any other time in human history.... Continual instruction beyond the early grades is needed" (Moore et al., p. 99). Before addressing the commission's recommendations and the implications for teachers and students, it is appropriate to examine the history of middle and secondary reading programs, their place in the school, and the manner in which research in psycholinguistics, sociolinguistics, cognitive psychology, composition, and literary theory has contributed to our understanding of how students learn. Understanding what it means to become literate from multiple theoretical points of view places the urgency of the International Reading Association's position statement within a contemporary paradigm based on a strong, meaning-centered pedagogical framework.

Historical Overview of Adolescent Reading and Writing Programs

The structure of the American school system and the American school day has in many ways driven the reading and writing programs for adolescents. Historically, junior high schools emerged as a result of overpopulated elementary schools during the post–World War II years. Designed as mini-high schools for Grades 7, 8, and 9, they focused primarily on a compartmentalized curriculum and had little to do with the cognitive, emotional, and social needs of adolescents. English was the subject in which reading, writing, speaking, and grammar were taught. Decades later, the middle school concept (Grades 6, 7, and 8) emerged in response to overcrowded schools and as a result of issues regarding racial integration (Simmons, 1998). Although a new notion of "language arts" is replacing the teaching of English in the middle school, language arts teachers often give little priority to the developmental literacy needs of their students (Ivey & Broaddus, 2000; Thompson, 2000).

High schools also have undergone changes over the decades. Vocational programs, collaboratives with local businesses, and career centers have allowed students to enter the job force during the school day; open enrollments and college credit courses have provided students with more options. The academic programs, however, have remained primarily subject-specific, with specialized teachers conducting lessons in the various content areas. Although some high schools have attempted innovative restructuring of the high school day such as block scheduling, and others have integrated the arts, instruction has remained primarily departmentalized by discipline. The 50-minute class period in a subject ends with the ringing of a bell, a run through the hallway, the slamming of locker doors, and quick conversations with friends on the way to the next 50-minute class period in another subject. Not much has changed from our own high school days.

In the past, most middle school and high school readers were characterized with labels similar to elementary students; they received instruction based on the notions of developmental, corrective, or remedial reading. Developmental readers were those who were near or above grade level in reading, and instruction took place in the regular classroom setting. Corrective readers fell below grade level and required additional help from the classroom teacher. Remedial readers needed some sort of specialized assistance from a reading teacher.

The concept of remedial reading and writing in middle and secondary schools was informed by a medical metaphor: Students who had a language illness, who were deficient in reading and writing, went to the laboratory for intervention and treatment; by looking at the students' symptoms (slow reading, poor comprehension, error-laden writing), the specialist could diagnose the problem, prescribe a treatment (usually worksheets or drill on isolated reading or writing skills), and effect a cure (Pemberton, 1992). The middle and secondary writing program often consisted of compositions assigned in English class without much instruction; these were often returned to the adolescents bleeding with red ink where punctuation was missing, spelling was incorrect, or words were used that didn't fit the teacher's expectations for school writing.

In the 1960s and 1970s, content-area reading— the idea that reading could not be approached separately from the content material of the subjects requiring reading—was touted as the way to reach all students who needed instructional support in using reading to learn. The phrase "every teacher a teacher of reading" was well known. It was believed that content-area teachers could best help students master vocabulary, comprehension strategies, and study skills necessary to learn that particular discipline. However, most content-area teachers misunderstood what it meant to be "a teacher of reading," believing that the skills for reading were best taught by reading teachers. Content-area teachers did not feel prepared to undertake the kinds of teaching that would enable students to be proficient readers in their disciplines. This belief prevailed through the 1980s and 1990s.

Another literacy notion that was frequently incorporated into the curriculum during the 1960s and 1970s was "writing across the curriculum." Writing to learn through all the subjects was supposed to increase students' understanding of the content areas. Yet most teachers believed it was the job of the elementary school to teach students how to read and write. High school and middle school teachers then, as now, were resistant to the notion of teaching reading strategies and assigning writing to learn. Deep-seated beliefs of content-area teachers regarding the importance of subject matter contributed to their reluctance.

Even if content-area reading and writing were part of the school's curriculum, the institutional practices worked against teachers of adolescents. The numbers of students that a teacher sees each day, the organization of subject matter specialties into departments, and the segregation of reading and writing to English classes all contribute to teachers' beliefs that their job is to teach content only. Although literacy activities may have existed in the planned curriculum, they were realized in practice in only a very few classrooms.

What were adolescents' actual experiences with the reading and writing curriculum? For the most part, teens were assigned pages in a content-area textbook, they answered questions that were narrowly focused, and they took quizzes to prove that they read the book. Often the students did not read the assignments because they found them boring and irrelevant or because the material would be addressed in a lecture the following day. School reading for many adolescents became purposeless and passive. Recently, in one of our content-area classes for pre-service teachers, when a group of 24 students was asked if they regularly read their high school textbooks, *no one* raised a hand.

Writing instruction was laborious and tended to focus on the form of the text; students were either assigned a topic or given a limited number of choices about which to write. A composition was judged as much by the number of errors the teacher found as it was by the meaning it conveyed. When asked what teachers do that inhibits writing, one teenager was critical of teachers who tell you what to write (McKeon, 2000). Although teachers mean well, the literacy experiences that adolescents undergo unfortunately seem focused more on the product than the process. It is clearly time to review literacy practices and construct a program for adolescents that makes more sense (Ivey & Broaddus, 2000; Moje et al., 2000; Moore et al., 1999; Vacca, 1998).

Changing Paradigms of Teaching and Learning

Paradigms in education are reflected in models of teaching and learning. Implicit in the assumptions of those middle school and high school teachers who resisted integrating *reading to learn* with *learning content* is a model of teaching and knowing called the *transmission model* (Pahl & Monson, 1992). In this model, teaching and learning are subject-centered, and teachers and textbooks are the primary source of knowledge. An *accommodation model,* on the other hand, is student-centered; teachers engage students in learning through hands-on, activity-oriented experiences in order to help them understand the content. Meaning, however, still resides in the text and the teacher. A third model, the *transaction model,* views learning as meaning-centered; rather than focusing on transmitting truth to students, the transaction model focuses on the *process* of how students construct meaning.

Whereas traditional teaching reflects the transmission and accommodation models of teaching and learning, responsive classrooms that mirror a transaction model more closely reflect solid principles of learning. Literacy experts agree that

the nature of adolescent literacy instruction in the 21st century must reflect a new awareness and sensitivity to responsive reading instruction. Teachers need to attend to the needs of adolescent learners, recognize their points of view regarding literacy, and address the critical thinking they will need as they embrace a complex world of visual, linear, and post-typographic print (Flood, Heath, & Lapp, 1997; Ivey & Broaddus, 2000; Moje et al., 2000; Norton & Lewis, 2000; Reinking, McKenna, Labbo, & Kieffer, 1998; Vacca & Vacca, 1999).

It is crucial that the stakeholders in middle school and high school programs have an understanding of what we know about learning. Those who teach adolescents, administer funds for middle and high school programs, and make policies need to think critically about what it takes to become literate. The fields of psycholinguistics, sociology, anthropology, cognitive psychology, child development, composition, and literary theory have contributed in multiple ways to our understanding of what it means to learn. Literacy programs based on sound pedagogical principles will be the ones that effectively pave the road for the ultimate stakeholders, the adolescents. Some essential beliefs about learning that can guide effective literacy instruction for middle school and high school students are:

1. *Connectedness is essential to learning and knowing.* Richard Prawat (1992) notes that constructivists have heightened our awareness that connection is an integral aspect of knowledge acquisition and use. Research supports cognitive structures consisting of associations (connections) among elements of knowledge. The primary difference between novice and expert practitioners, it seems, is the ability to see the big ideas in a field of study and how the elements fit together.
2. *Context is essential to learning.* There is a unique connection between knowledge and the context in which it is learned. Using knowledge contributes to understanding; the situation becomes an essential element of knowing about a skill or concept (Brown, Collins, & Duguid, 1989). Brown et al. acknowledge that

most real-world knowledge occurs naturally through a process of enculturation rather than through the learning of isolated skills.

3. *Learning is social.* Learners need to participate in a culture that provides a context for authentic activity, giving them a way of interpreting reality that is consistent with the cultural norms of the group (or the discipline).

4. *Learning is best accomplished when the environment for learning is supportive and encouraging of risk taking.* People learn when they are provided with opportunities to demonstrate knowledge and skill without fear of failure. Though proficiency is expected, environments are conducive to learning when they are supportive and allow opportunities for self-reflection. Interacting with the unknown takes both cognitive and physical energy, and a sense that mistakes will not be punished with red ink.

5. *Knowledge is transactional.* The work of Lev Vygotsky (1978) in child development, Louise Rosenblatt (1982) in reading response theory, and the research by cognitive scientists explain how human beings are part of nature and continuously transact with the environment. The individual, the learning, and the content are seen as one and cannot be separated in principle or reality. Meaning is what we construct for ourselves out of our experiences.

Effective Middle School and High School Reading Programs

Based on reading research and principles of learning, the International Reading Association's Commission on Adolescent Literacy (CAL) position statement (Moore et al., 1999) offers program directors, policy makers, teachers, community members, and parents a framework for organizing middle and secondary school reading programs. As outlined by the commission (pp. 101–106), effective programs for adolescents will provide them with the following.

1. Access to a wide variety of reading material that they can and want to read.

2. Instruction that builds the skill and desire to read increasingly complex materials.

3. Assessment that shows them their strengths as well as their needs and that guides their teachers to design instruction that will best help them grow as readers.

4. Expert teachers who model and provide explicit instruction in reading comprehension and study strategies across the curriculum.

5. Reading specialists who assist individual students having difficulty learning how to read.

6. Teachers who understand the complexities of individual adolescent readers, respect their differences, and respond to their characteristics.

7. Homes, communities, and a nation that will support their efforts to achieve advanced levels of literacy and provide the support necessary for them to succeed.

Building a highway takes incredible commitment on the part of many skilled engineers who must collaborate, plan, fine-tune, dig deep, and have a clear vision of a final roadway that will serve motorists well. Constructing effective programs for adolescent readers that will serve them well as they confront the literacy challenges of the 21st century will be much the same. Implementing the recommendations of CAL will take time, effort, and commitment on the part of many dedicated stakeholders who have a clear vision that adolescents deserve much more attention to their growth and development as readers than they previously have been given. The commission's recommendations are broad guidelines that will play out differently in different classrooms, schools, and programs. In the past, however, the *visible* organizational structure of reading instruction for adolescents was reserved for those students identified as deficient in reading and often took place in a laboratory setting. The *visible* organization ought not to be restricted to a reading lab for struggling readers. In addition to reading instruction in content-area classrooms, there may be writing centers, reading resource centers, book clubs, media centers, and even reading lounges with comfortable furniture. Not only does the commission emphasize the importance of recognizing the needs of struggling adolescent readers, but it also stresses the importance of addressing the *developmental* literacy needs of *all* adolescents in *all* areas of the curriculum in a variety of meaningful settings.

It is essential that literacy instruction, regardless of where it takes place, resonate the *invisible* principles of effective literacy learning as suggested by the commission's position statement. With the proper support, individual teachers who think critically and reflectively about their instruction and instructional alternatives will make important transformations in the way adolescents develop sophisticated literacy skills, acquire positive perceptions of themselves as readers, and use literacy as a tool for enhancing content and world knowledge.

Access to Materials

How might the commission's (Moore et al., 1999) recommendations guide effective practice? Recognizing that all adolescents need "access to a wide variety of reading material that they can and want to read" (p. 101) means that students must be given the opportunity to read text every day that taps their interests and expands their knowledge of the world in a meaningful way. They need more than textbooks; they need libraries and classrooms that are equipped with a wide variety of printed materials that cover the range of abilities and interests of adolescents (Ivey & Broaddus, 2000; McQuillan, 1998). They need access to trade books, magazines, reference materials, and technology resources from which they can choose to read and write about topics in the content areas that not only pique their interest but also stretch their abilities. Using picture books in middle school and high school classrooms, for instance, can be an effective way to enhance all content learning for adolescents (Tiedt, 2000). Using multiple texts in history can teach adolescents to be "critical consumers of the often contradictory and confusing messages about vital national issues that appear in newspapers and magazines and on television" (Hynd, 1999, p. 436). Teachers need to assist students as they search for reading material that interests them, and they need to engage in conversations

with teens about what they are reading. By tapping students' interests with a wide variety of choices, teachers will not only enhance adolescents' knowledge in the content areas but also increase the possibility that they will know a variety of ways to learn the complex subject matter that the 21st century promises to hold.

Effective Instruction and Expert Teachers

If adolescents deserve "instruction that builds both the skill and desire to read increasingly complex materials" (Moore et al., 1999, p. 102), and "expert teachers who model and provide explicit instruction in reading comprehension and study skills across the curriculum" (p. 104), what might that instruction look like? Elementary school teachers frequently model the importance of reading and instill a love of reading through read-alouds. When teachers read aloud, they have opportunities to model enthusiasm for a topic, clarify concepts by thinking aloud as they read, and broaden students' knowledge of language and the world. Middle school and high school teachers would be wise to continue the tradition of reading aloud to their students for the same reasons. By reading aloud, not only can teachers model the value of reading for pleasure, but they can also expose students to a wide range of interesting reading materials that go far beyond the content of any textbook. Social studies teachers, for example, can use read-alouds to enhance such topics as value conflict, cultural diversity, and politics. Mathematics teachers can read aloud portions of literature that lend themselves to such topics as inequality, measurement, and statistics. Physical education teachers can read aloud stories that focus on physical differences, fair play, and ethics (Richardson, 2000).

It is essential that middle and secondary school teachers provide adolescents with explicit instruction in how to question, analyze, evaluate, and synthesize—in other words, think critically—as they read. Content-area textbooks are filled with new and difficult concepts and vocabulary, and adolescents are often bewildered by the organization of texts, or see no organization at all. Teachers need to model a variety of reading strategies by demonstrating, conducting mini-lessons, and scaffolding instruction (Robb, 2000). Teachers can show students how to construct a graphic organizer, for example, to visually analyze difficult text. By explicitly modeling graphic organizers with *multiple* texts, teachers can assist students in learning how to synthesize information as they sort through complex content material. A wide variety of instructional strategies can be used to enhance learning from texts: group reading assignments, role-playing, journal writing, pre-reading strategies, reading logs, to name a few (Bintz, 1997; Harvey & Goudvis, 2000; Robb, 2000; Vacca & Vacca, 1993, 1999). Traditional assignments that insist students read to simply answer questions are not conducive to thinking, are not particularly motivating, and do not necessarily demonstrate knowledge beyond a literal level. It is important that teachers provide their students with solid, meaningful reasons for reading. Adolescents need to know why they are reading, how the information will benefit them, and strategies that help them make sense of text.

Additionally, the 21st century necessitates that adolescents leave school with rather sophisticated *technological literacy skills*. Being able to navigate the Internet to locate information, evaluate the credibility of websites, and efficiently skim and scan seamless bodies of text are only several skills that a post-typographical world of print will demand. By determining instructional goals and setting technology lessons within the context of ongoing content lessons, middle school and high school teachers will begin to prepare adolescents for the digital world of 21st-century print (Reinking et al., 1998; Rekrut, 1999).

The critical point of effective literacy instruction made by the Commission on Adolescent Literacy recognizes that teens need a wide repertoire of reading strategies if they are to become intelligent consumers of the complex world of print they will encounter when they leave the classroom. Solid strategies will lay the groundwork for adolescents who can maneuver print to meet their personal, social, cognitive, and emotional needs as adults.

Assessment

What about the commission's recommendation that adolescents "deserve assessment that shows them their strengths as well as their needs and that guides their teachers to design instruction that will best help them grow as readers" (p. 103)? Accountability, assessment, and instruction go hand in hand. Just as engineers ought to be accountable for designing a roadway that will pass the test of highway safety and maintenance standards, so too must teachers be held accountable for designing instruction that will assist adolescents in reaching literacy standards and succeeding as lifelong learners. It seems for adolescents, high-stakes testing has taken priority over more authentic forms of assessment that would provide teachers with a more balanced, useful picture of teens' strengths and instructional needs. It is important that teachers do not allow state testing to get in the way of good instruction (Thompson, 2000). Although large-scale testing is helpful in monitoring the overall achievement of standards for particular grade levels, it has little, if any, application at the classroom level.

Just as adolescents need a variety of instructional strategies that will help them develop sophisticated literacy skills, so do they need a variety of ways to demonstrate what they know and need to know. They need alternative forms of assessment in which they have a choice and voice in evaluating their progress. Content-area teachers who offer students opportunities to share what they know through the arts, for example, open doors for students whose strengths lie in their creative abilities. Other students may verbally express what they know more accurately than with paper and pencil. Keeping portfolios of students' progress, having frequent student conferences, using rubrics with small groups of learners are examples of ways teachers can document progress and assess needs.

Teachers need to set clear guidelines and expectations when alternative assessments are used; they need to be up front with students on what is acceptable and unacceptable. They need to provide students with feedback and allow students to take risks without fear that mistakes will be punished. Adolescents will benefit when assessment is viewed as a process, rather than the ultimate goal of learning subject matter for a grade. Growth in adolescent literacy is a meaning-centered entity that needs to be measured. Assessing that growth demonstrates what students know and can do, what motivates them, and what distracts them or makes it difficult for them to learn. Adolescents' literacy and content knowledge must undergo continuous maintenance, assessment, and instruction based on strengths and needs.

Reading Specialists

The Commission on Adolescent Literacy (Moore et al., 1999) strongly advocates a renewed commitment to providing middle and high school students who struggle in reading with assistance from professionals who are *reading specialists* (p. 104). Whereas reading teachers are highly visible in elementary schools, there has been much less commitment toward providing specialized help in reading to adolescents who find reading difficult (Vacca, 1998). Content teachers, many of whom have had only one course in reading, continue to feel inadequate in assisting students with reading. Their reluctance to teach reading is compounded by time constraints and the amount of content to be taught. Although their concerns are real, the literacy needs of adolescents who struggle are *just as real.* Blocked from successful learning experiences in the classroom, these teens become frustrated and disenchanted with school. Literacy specialists who have a thorough knowledge about the processes of learning to read and write are in a good position to offer these teens appropriate intervention strategies that are meaningful, challenging, and relevant. They can assist students in becoming strategic readers who will have the knowledge and literacy skills necessary for living a productive life in a complex world of print. If students who struggle in reading are not given assistance, not only are they likely to suffer lifelong feelings of inadequacy, but they will also in many cases have less of a chance to contribute to society the way literate individuals can.

How can literacy specialists productively assist teens who struggle in reading? Of primary importance is that these adolescents are not singled out as failures and sent to reading labs where they drill and practice on isolated skills. Literacy specialists need to work with small groups of students using subject matter they are expected to know, building on their interests and helping them make connections between the known and unknown. They also need to provide struggling readers with a wide variety of choices and provide *time* for the students to read materials that will entice them to want to read more (Strauss & Irvin, 2000). Reading aloud to teens, introducing them to multiple genres, allowing them to talk about what they are reading, helping them work with words, and providing them with real purposes for reading will all contribute to successful literacy experiences for struggling adolescents (Ivey, 1999; Ivey & Broaddus, 2000).

Team planning with content teachers, assisting content teachers with instructional strategies that will benefit *all* students, and modeling for students in content classes are ways that literacy specialists can foster enhanced literacy engagement, not only for *struggling* adolescent readers but for *all* adolescent readers. By providing workshops for teachers, demonstrating instructional strategies using actual content material, and suggesting alternative means of assessment and alternative ways of organizing class instructional time to meet the needs of individual students, literacy professionals can have a major impact on the nature of literacy instruction in middle schools and high schools (Henwood, 1999/2000). Fostering a *shared responsibility* for enhancing the literacy levels of adolescents will be a key ingredient in effective programs. One person cannot build a roadway; nor can one individual address the multiple reading needs, interests, strengths, and weaknesses of teen readers and non-readers.

Teachers Who Understand Adolescents

Teachers have little or no control over the diverse cultures, social and economic backgrounds, different languages, varied interests, and deep concerns that teens bring to the classroom. It is important, however, that teachers understand and respect the differences that make adolescents the complex individuals they are (Moore et al., 1999, p. 105). Adolescence is a time when teens seek self-identity, explore who they are, and define themselves through an array of social practices both in and out of school (Hynds, 1997).

How do teachers come to understand the complexities of teens? Very simply, they spend time with them. They watch how adolescents engage (or disengage) with text and how they talk (or refrain from talking) in small and large groups. Teachers observe how teens write and what they choose to write about. They notice how middle and high school students study and how they organize their work (or fail to organize it). To coin a popular phrase, one way that teachers come to understand adolescents is by "kidwatching." Teachers also come to know teens by listening to and talking with them. They listen to teens talk about movies, friends, music, clothes, school subjects, school social events, local and national events, etc., and they engage in conversations with students about those interests and concerns. When teachers carry on conversations with teens, and listen as teens talk to each other, they come to understand and appreciate their students' talents, hopes, and dreams, as well as their worries and fears, all of which contribute to the adolescents' developing self-identity.

Adolescents also begin to explore who they are as readers and writers through social interactions. In order to understand the complex nature of adolescent *readers and writers,* teachers need to spend large amounts of time with small groups of learners, as well as with individual students, talking with them and observing the strategies they use to analyze words and to make sense of text. Teachers need to notice the kinds of prior experiences adolescents bring to text and how they negotiate meaning based on those experiences. They need to observe what adolescents like to read and what they do not like to read.

It is not enough to listen, watch, observe, and notice the diversity that adolescents bring to the classroom as individuals and as readers and writers; teachers need to create literacy environ-

ments that are *responsive* to those differences. Responsive teachers realize that adolescents read much more than linear text on paper; their lives are cultural worlds in which they create "text" from the music, art, video, computer games, dance, sports, shopping malls, and television sitcoms that surround them (Alvermann, Moon, & Hagood, 1999; Hynds, 1997; McKeon, 2000; Vacca, 1998). An appreciation for the diverse pop cultures in which adolescents immerse themselves as they strive to define themselves can contribute significantly to how teachers create a responsive literacy environment. By drawing on adolescents' rich sense of pop culture, responsive teachers encourage students to relate their world outside of school to the world of classroom text (Kist, 2000; Moje et al., 2000). Allowing students to express their knowledge of an historical event, for example, through art, music, or dance creates a responsive environment that allows choice and encourages ownership in learning content. Oldfather (1993) calls this sense of responsiveness to students' individual representation of knowledge "honored voice" (p. 672).

Not only is it important that teachers provide responsive literacy environments that honor the voices and complex lives of adolescents; it is equally important that teachers provide students with meaningful curricular connections. Individuals learn best when content makes sense. Middle school reform movements have resulted in more team effort in curricular planning that goes across the curriculum (Flowers, Mertens, & Mulhall, 2000). It is rare, however, that high school teachers are given planning time to work with other subject-matter teachers and reconstruct content to reflect a more meaningful curriculum for adolescents. High school teachers need to reconsider the nature of content learning in light of how individuals learn. By connecting a literature course to a history course, for example, adolescents would get the bigger picture. Admittedly, this would take time, commitment, and a mindshift for high school teachers. If connections are not made, however, teenagers are the losers.

The paradigm we construct for organizing adolescent literacy programs cannot be simply a straight roadway across a landscape that is flat and barren. We must offer more than controlled programs that are meant to improve reading achievement. As stakeholders design a 21st-century literacy roadway for middle school and high school students, the teachers, administrators, and policy makers who engineer the landscape must be willing to let go of controlling a linear, subject-centered curriculum. They must be open to the individuality that teens bring to the classroom. Effective middle school and high school programs allow the multifaceted voices of adolescents to be heard. Programs that make a concerted effort to ensure that literacy, content learning, and schooling make sense will be the ones that work for teenagers of the 21st century.

A Supportive Community

The Commission on Adolescent Literacy (Moore et al., 1999) emphasizes that adolescents "deserve homes, communities, and a nation that will support their efforts to achieve advanced levels of literacy and provide the support necessary for them to succeed" (p. 106). Parenting involves a gradual letting go as teens explore new interests, search for self-identity, and seek independence. Parents play an important role, however, in providing support for adolescent literacy. When parents recognize the role literacy plays in teen pop culture, for example, they can support literacy growth by providing reading materials that tap these interests. Encouraging adolescents to read literature at home, whether magazines, newspapers, novels, or album covers, will assist teens in recognizing the value of literacy in everyday living. As teachers encourage self-expression of content learning through the arts, media, and visual and oral representation of content knowledge, parents can support the sense of connectedness between home and school. It is important that parents talk with adolescents about what they are reading and learning and take an interest in what they write. Parents need to be informed about the developmental nature of adolescent literacy; they need to see a more balanced picture than the one often presented in the press, namely, that reading is a score on a test.

Members of the community, boards of education, libraries, businesses, and colleges and uni-

versities need to take on active partnerships with middle school and high school efforts to support the literacy needs of adolescents. Businesses that provide support for after-school enrichment programs, book clubs, and literary circles can enhance teen literacy and provide adolescents with the strong message that literacy is important beyond the school day. Universities can be a rich resource that middle schools and high schools tap for tutoring services, technology collaboratives, and supplemental resources that enhance content learning. It is essential that libraries take an active role in the future literacy development of adolescents. Funding for libraries needs to increase dramatically; not only do libraries need to be stocked with books that recognize the interests and ability levels of teens, but they also need to offer a wide repertoire of magazines, reference materials, and technology resources that supplement the content adolescents are learning in school. School and library partnerships that support teachers' efforts to make curricular connections will have a strong impact on the effectiveness of adolescent literacy programs.

Policy makers need to recognize that the literacy needs of adolescents have been sorely neglected. The demands of the 21st century require that *all* teens need incredible support if they are going to enter the adult world with the literacy skills necessary to live productive lives and the critical thinking skills needed to make responsible decisions. Lawmakers and state departments of education need to balance their efforts toward writing documents that reflect high literacy standards with a strong commitment toward instructional and organizational support. It is crucial that government funding be allocated in support of teen literacy. Money needs to be available for the hiring of reading specialists, for ongoing staff development, and for stocking classrooms with books, visual media, and technology.

Literacy Programs for the 21st Century

The Commission on Adolescent Literacy's position statement serves as an expert blueprint for designing effective middle school and high school programs that will meet the needs of adolescents in the 21st century. We recognize that the development of such programs will take time, and that effective changes must begin with input from teachers, not with top-down administrative mandates. While school systems will vary in how changes take place regarding adolescent literacy in particular buildings, there are several common dynamics of change.

1. A new focus on adolescent literacy is needed. The organizational structure of middle schools and high schools works at cross-purposes to changing reading programs across the board. The core of an effective program will reflect a change in the mind-set of content-area teachers, administrators, policy makers, parents, the community, *and the adolescents* whose futures are at stake. Raising the awareness of the importance of adolescent literacy and giving it equal status with subject matter content is crucial and will require a shift in teachers' beliefs about the traditional subject-centered curriculum.

2. A key element in the success and substance of any new program is the support and positive attitude of a caring principal (Danehower, 1993). Administrative support is essential in encouraging participation in workshops, in-services, and professional conferences. Administrators who allocate time, resources, and materials are critical to a program's success; principals who actively support teachers and provide them with viable alternatives to solving implementation difficulties are essential.

3. Successful implementation of any curricular change takes time. The development of a responsive, meaning-centered curriculum will require a lot of time for educators to think about their educational beliefs, discuss them, and reflect on practices that mirror those beliefs (Thompson, 2000). Just as classrooms must be viewed as learning communities, so must schools become learning communities for teachers. The groundwork for responsive literacy programs will be laid when educators are given time to actively share insights, reflections, suggestions, failures, and successes.

A team of teachers at the North Canton Middle School in North Canton, Ohio, serves as an exemplary case of how one group of educators addressed in a meaningful way the literacy and curricular needs of adolescents at the seventh grade level. This example illustrates how the underlying principles of the IRA's position statement on adolescent literacy unfolded with real teachers in a real classroom. One of our teens, Jimmy, typically unmotivated by school, enthusiastically recalled this experience several years later.

Administrative decisions regarding the structure of the school day allow Mr. Donnelly, the math teacher, Ms. Greek, the language arts teacher, and Ms. Wyckoff, the social studies teacher, 45 minutes of daily planning time together. When the team realized that a local cultural center was hosting a Norman Rockwell exhibit, the administration supported the teachers' efforts to collaborate. In social studies, the seventh graders read about and critiqued social issues of the 1940s and 1950s as they analyzed postcards and magazine covers that captured the essence of Norman Rockwell's art. In language arts, the students read and explored connections between biographical snippets of the artist and his art. With the assistance of Ms. Donnelly, the art instructor, the math teacher designed lessons that incorporated measurement through scale drawing. The class reproduced a Norman Rockwell illustration by measuring fiberboard tiles and creating an oversize mosaic rendition of the artist's work that was displayed in the gymnasium. Recognizing the significance of the team's efforts, the administration funded an extra field-trip to the cultural center, where the students were able to view the works of Norman Rockwell firsthand.

These teachers were given time to develop goals as a team through thoughtful curricular planning that enhanced student learning; they provided Jimmy with literacy and learning connections that made sense. The curricular experiences were motivating, providing Jimmy with memorable learning in the middle school that he vividly recalled as a high school student. He was clearly engaged in learning, clearly engaged in meaningful reading, and clearly saw curricular connections. Jimmy's often disenchanted attitude toward school was replaced with requests to revisit the cultural center that year, and the year after, and the year after that.

Conclusion

The literacy needs of adolescents have been overlooked as a result of multiple complex and conflicting educational and political issues. Education agendas at national, state, and local levels during the 1990s reflected a strong commitment to preventing reading difficulties in young children. Energy, funding, and support for early childhood literacy highlighted the importance of effective reading instruction for beginning readers during the 1990s. It is clearly time for educators, policy makers, and program directors to recognize that literacy development does not end in the elementary years. It is crucial that educational agendas of the 21st century be strongly committed to the developmental literacy growth of adolescents at the middle and high school levels.

The position statement by the International Reading Association's Commission on Adolescent Literacy (Moore et al., 1999) will help educators, policy makers, and program directors attend to teenage literacy. We must construct new roadways for adolescents if we are truly to become a nation of readers. For too long, teens have been trying to maneuver a literacy agenda that resembles an outdated bridge crossing shallow water. Adolescents deserve more, and construction ought to begin now.

References

Alvermann, D. E., Moon, J. S., & Hagood, M. C. (1999). *Popular culture in the classroom: Teaching and researching critical media literacy.* Newark, DE: International Reading Association.

Bintz, W. P. (1997). Exploring the reading nightmares of middle and secondary school teachers. *Journal of Adolescent and Adult Literacy, 41,* 12–24.

Bracey, G. W. (2000). Literacy in the information age. *Phi Delta Kappan, 82*(1), 91–92.

Brown, J., Collins, A., & Duguid, P. (1989). Situated cognition and the culture of learning. *Educational Researcher, 18*(1), 32–42.

Danehower, V. (1993). Understanding the change process. *Schools in the Middle, 2*(4), 45–46.

Flood, J., Heath, S. B., & Lapp, D. (1997). *Handbook of research on teaching literacy through the communicative and visual arts.* New York: Macmillan Reference Library.

Flowers, N., Mertens, S. B., & Mulhall, P. F. (2000). What makes interdisciplinary teams effective? *Middle School Journal, 31*(4), 53–56.

Harvey, S., & Goudvis, A. (2000). *Strategies that work: Teaching comprehension to enhance understanding.* York, ME: Stenhouse.

Henwood, G. F. (1999/2000). A new role for the reading specialist: Contributing toward a high school's collaborative culture. *Journal of Adolescent and Adult Literacy, 43,* 316–325.

Hynd, C. R. (1999). Teaching students to think critically using multiple texts in history. *Journal of Adolescent and Adult Literacy, 42,* 428–436.

Hynds, S. (1997). *On the brink: Negotiating literature and life with adolescents.* Newark, DE: International Reading Association.

Ivey, G. (1999). Reflections on teaching struggling middle school readers. *Journal of Adolescent and Adult Literacy, 42,* 372–381.

Ivey, G., & Broaddus, K. (2000). Tailoring the fit: Reading instruction and middle school readers. *The Reading Teacher, 54,* 68–78.

Kist, W. (2000). Beginning to create the new literacy classroom: What does the new literacy look like? *Journal of Adolescent and Adult Literacy, 43,* 710–718.

McKeon, C. A. (1999). The Ohio proficiency test from the eyes of a child. *Ohio Reading Teacher, 32*(2), 10–11.

McKeon, C. A. (2000). Lessons from a teenage writer. *Ohio Journal of English Language Arts, 40*(2), 66–70.

McQuillan, J. (1998). *The literacy crisis: False claims, real solutions.* Portsmouth, NH: Heinemann.

Moje, E. B., Young, J. P., Readence, J. E., & Moore, D. W. (2000). Reinventing adolescent literacy for new times: Perennial and millennial issues. *Journal of Adolescent and Adult Literacy, 43,* 400–410.

Moore, D. W., Bean, T. W., Birdyshaw, D., & Rycik, J. A. (1999). Adolescent literacy: A position statement. *Journal of Adolescent and Adult Literacy, 43,* 97–112.

Norton, J., & Lewis, A. C. (2000). Middle-grades reform: Kappan special report. *Phi Delta Kappan, 81*(10), K1–K20.

Oldfather, P. (1993). What students say about motivating experiences in a whole language classroom. *The Reading Teacher, 46,* 672–681.

Pahl, M., & Monson, R. (1992). In search of whole language: Transforming curriculum and instruction. *Journal of Reading, 35,* 518–534.

Pemberton, M. (1992). The prison, the hospital, the madhouse: Redefining metaphors for the writing center. *Writing Lab Newsletter, 17*(1), 11–16.

Prawat, R. (1992). Teachers' beliefs about teaching and learning: A constructivist perspective. *American Journal of Education, 100*(3), 354–395.

Reinking, D., McKenna, M. C., Labbo, L. D., & Kiefer, R. D. (Eds.). (1998). *Handbook of literacy and technology: Transformations in a post-typographic world.* Mahwah, NJ: Erlbaum.

Rekrut, M. D. (1999). Using the Internet in classroom instruction: A primer for teachers. *Journal of Adolescent and Adult Literacy, 42,* 546–557.

Richardson, J. S. (2000). *Read it aloud: Using literature in the secondary content classroom.* Newark, DE: International Reading Association.

Robb, L. (2000). *Teaching reading in the middle school.* New York: Scholastic.

Rosenblatt, L. (1982). The literacy transaction: Evocation and response. *Theory Into Practice, 21,* 268–277.

Simmons, J. S. (1998). The study of language for adolescents: A U.S. historical perspective. In J. S. Simmons & L. Baines (Eds.), *Language study in middle school, high school, and beyond* (pp. 6–18). Newark, DE: International Reading Association.

Snow, C. E., Burns, M. S., & Griffin, P. (Eds.). (1998). *Preventing reading difficulties in young children.* Washington, DC: National Academy Press.

Strauss, S. E., & Irvin, J. L. (2000). Exemplary literacy learning programs. *Middle School Journal, 32*(1), 56–59.

Thompson, S. C. (2000). Overcoming obstacles to creating responsive curriculum. *Middle School Journal, 32*(1), 47–55.

Tiedt, I. M. (2000). *Teaching with picture books in the middle school.* Newark, DE: International Reading Association.

Vacca, R. T. (1998). Let's not marginalize adolescent literacy. *Journal of Adolescent and Adult Literacy, 41,* 604–609.

Vacca, R. T., & Vacca, J. L. (1993). *Content area reading* (4th ed.). New York: HarperCollins.

Vacca, R. T., & Vacca, J. L. (1999). *Content area reading: Literacy and learning across the curriculum* (6th ed.). New York: Addison Wesley Longman.

Vygotsky, L. (1978). *Mind in society.* Cambridge: Harvard University Press.

CHAPTER SIX

College and University Literacy Programs

Arlene D. Wartenberg

"I got all A's at my high school but don't feel prepared to do college work," said Kelly.

"I was quarterback on my high school football team, so it was easy to get good grades. How am I going to get through my classes here?" asked Tom.

"I have been out of school for 15 years and am terrified about taking exams and writing papers," said Marie.

"I graduated from high school by the skin of my teeth," said Mark. "In fact, I don't know how I got into college. This is really scary."

"I don't know what I'm doing in this course. After all, I got into this college. Who needs help with studying anyway," muttered Amy.

What do all of these students have in common? They are all enrolled in a college or university reading program. This chapter will do the following:

- ◆ Provide an historical overview
- ◆ Describe the typical components of college and university reading programs
- ◆ Give examples of college reading programs
- ◆ Suggest the role of reading personnel in such programs
- ◆ Explore characteristics of a successful program

Purpose of College and University Literacy Programs

The comments by Kelly, Tom, Marie, and Mark are typical of college and university students who feel unprepared for the literacy demands of coursework. The comment by Amy is typical of students who are informed they must enroll in a reading course because of low scores on placement tests. Many post-secondary institutions test all entering freshmen in reading, writing, and math (National Center for Education Statistics, 1996). Students who perform poorly on such tests must enroll in a course to help them learn the skills necessary to succeed. Boylan (1995) reported that in 1991, 74% of colleges and universities offered at least one course in remedial reading and writing; by 1995 that number had risen to 78%.

While the literacy courses and programs might differ among colleges and universities, they have the same purpose: to provide students with the assistance they need to succeed in post-secondary study. "It is a truism to say that the 21st century is bringing more to read, more ways to read it, and more reasons to be an effective reader than ever before" (Pugh, Pawan, & Antommarchi, 2000, p. 25). The rapid acceleration of knowledge and the diversity of ways to access knowledge, therefore, increase the demands on all students, especially those who lack literacy strategies.

Historical Overview of College and University Literacy Programs

An issue of the *Yale Report* calls for an end to the admission of students with "defective preparation" (Roberts, 1986, p. 6). The president of the University of Michigan, in his inaugural address, states that colleges in America are too involved in instruction that is more suitable for students of secondary school (Lissner, 1990). Despite the fact that these two sentiments were expressed in 1828 and 1852 respectively, they might have been said today. The acceptance of underprepared students has been documented since the first colleges were established in America, well before the more contemporary open admission policies and equal opportunity legislation (Roberts, 1986). In 1776 there were nine colleges in the new nation. Unlike the European model of higher education, the idea early on was that education was for all (Wyatt, 1992).

To help underprepared students, colleges established preparatory departments. Students could be admitted to the university and study in these preparatory departments until they acquired the necessary basic skills and were deemed ready to begin regular coursework (Roberts, 1986). Although these programs were not welcomed enthusiastically, they flourished throughout the middle to late 1800s. Wyatt (1992) suggests that one reason for their continued existence was the admission requirements of just basic skills in grammar, reading, and spelling. Another reason offered by Wyatt was that during this period there were no formal secondary schools. The result of this was that students went to college from grammar school with or without the help of a tutor and often as young as age 12.

While some prestigious schools tried to maintain high admission standards, even they had underprepared students. Brier (1984) noted the presence, in 1828, of students at Yale who needed help with academic subjects. Harvard University, early on, provided college assistance in Latin, the tongue of instruction (Wyatt, 1992). By the middle of the 19th century, preparatory departments were springing up in many colleges and universities. These programs consistently increased, despite complaints that students in need of such help should not attend institutions of higher learning. By the conclusion of the 19th century, approximately 84% of American universities had preparatory programs (Wyatt, 1992).

The 20th century saw many changes that influenced college literacy programs. One change was the advent of secondary schools; these schools provided the type of education previously offered by preparatory programs, which as a result gradually declined. However, underprepared students continued to attend post-secondary institutions. The Morrill Acts of 1862 and 1890 opened numerous new colleges. Because these colleges competed to fill classes, underprepared students continued to be accepted (Boylan & White, 1987). Leedy (1958) suggested that the demise of the classical instruction model with its focus on repetition and recitation to an elective system which was a more reading-oriented approach ultimately led to the need for college remedial reading courses (p. 53).

While some schools in 1915 still maintained preparatory programs (Maxwell, 1979), others followed the lead of Wellesley College, which had initiated the first documented remedial reading program in 1883 (Mason, 1993). The early 1900s saw growth in the number of these remedial reading courses, the major focus of which was study skills instruction (Wyatt, 1992). By the mid 1900s, the focus of remediation shifted to some of the more mechanical aspects of reading such as eye movements and span that improved the rate of reading, as well as isolated skills such as skimming and vocabulary development (Charters, 1941).

The Great Depression and World War II brought changes in the number of available students; colleges competed for students who could pay tuition and often accepted students who needed academic assistance (Bonner, 1986). Following the war, the Serviceman's Readjustment Act of 1944, the GI Bill of Rights, encouraged applicants and greatly impacted the need for college remedial reading and study skills programs (Wyatt, 1992). Federal funds were provided to colleges and universities to establish programs to help these veterans succeed in college. Although this population gradually declined, remedial reading and study skills programs were institutionalized and available to all students (Maxwell, 1979). Institutions of higher learning had now adjusted to a new population: adults, both male and female.

The 1960s brought about the establishment of open admission policies and federal aid to higher education (Bonner, 1986). The presence of nontraditional students and minorities increased on campuses nationwide, as did the expansion of "How to Study" courses and individualized instruction, including programmed instruction,

mastery learning, and peer tutoring (Lissner, 1990). While the number of literacy courses continued to grow, the 1970s saw the growth of the learning center, which by the 1980s was the most frequently used system to aid students (Lissner, 1990). Writing was included in many reading programs in the 1990s as educators focused on the connectedness of reading and writing.

This historical survey shows that developmental reading programs, as these programs have come to be called, have always been part of the educational programs of institutions of higher education. While the components of programs might have changed, they tend to incorporate the current educational beliefs and aim to facilitate the learning of students with literacy needs.

Components of College and University Reading Programs

Learning Assistance Programs is the name given by Johnson and Carpenter (2000) to today's literacy programs. They suggest that these programs include "any remedial or developmental program intended to help students succeed academically in college" (p. 321). They believe that although programs might have other names such as Reading Laboratories or Academic Skills Centers, the name Learning Assistance Program is preferred to Developmental Reading to avoid the "remedial" connotation. Regardless of the name, the structure of the programs ranges from a single course in reading or study skills, with or without a reading laboratory, to a comprehensive program that might include courses, a computer laboratory, and peer or professional tutoring.

Reading and study skills courses of today focus on the important aspects of successful learning: text reading, test taking, and lecture note taking. To facilitate the understanding of texts, students are presented with a variety of organizational strategies whose purpose is to activate and develop schema, focus attention, and help set purposes for reading (Nist & Holschub, 2000). These organizing strategies might include graphic organizers, concept maps, and text previews.

Grant (1993) recommends that students have explicit training in strategy use if they are to become independent text readers. She designed SCROL, a framework to help students use headings to improve text comprehension. The SCROL framework includes the following five steps.

- *Survey* headings and subheadings, questioning and thinking about what you already know.
- *Connect* headings and subheadings, writing key words that show relationships.
- *Read* headings, one at a time, for information relevant to each. Underlining or marking key ideas is recommended at this time. Rereading is suggested if a section is unclear.
- *Outline* twice main ideas and important details, first using the text as a guide and second from memory.
- *Look back*, verifying accuracy and correcting outline inaccuracies.

An important component of SCROL, according to Grant (1993), is teacher modeling. First the teacher models and discusses the strategy. Then students practice using SCROL in small groups, with students taking turns thinking aloud as they go through the steps. Finally, students practice independently. Grant recommends that even in this phase of learning, the teacher should identify the headings to be used and help those students who need assistance.

Nist and Holschub (2000) concur that strategy training should be direct and include instructor modeling as well as numerous opportunities for student practice and evaluation of usefulness. They also stress that students need instruction in how to underline and annotate texts, self-question, and self-test.

Reynolds and Werner (1994) believe that no one strategy works for all learners. They recommend that students need to understand their learning style, analyze the strategies they currently utilize, and learn ways to improve their strategies as well as learning effective alternative ones.

Reading courses frequently include practice taking and studying from lecture notes. After reviewing research, Armbruster (2000) concludes that student achievement is positively related to both the quantity and quality of the lecture notes they take. To help students improve, she suggests they should be provided with outlines, other advance organizers, and videotaped lectures for practice. Spires and Stone (1989) recommend the Directed Notetaking Activity (DNA), a strategy for taking lecture notes, which incorporates metacognition as a way to make the students actively involved. DNA uses a split-page design in which the listener puts main ideas in the left column and supporting details in the right. Self-questioning is an important component of DNA. Students are taught to raise questions before the lecture (to motivate and set purposes), during (to determine main ideas, details, and progress), and after (to process information and satisfy purposes).

Studying for and taking tests is another area often included in college reading courses. Flippo, Becker, and Wark (2000) believe that students profit from coaching on how to take tests. They suggest that programs should include learning how to schedule study time, review materials, anticipate test questions, and use memory strategies.

In addition to reading and study skills courses, some programs also include tutoring. Johnson and Carpenter (2000), in their review of college reading programs, found a variety of tutoring formats that include individual or small-group tutoring, peer tutoring, or on-line tutoring. They also mention paired or adjunct classes that are reading strategy courses paired with content courses. Some programs include workshops that are designated for all students. Topics of sessions include studying for and taking exams, and time and stress management.

Examples of College Literacy Programs

Following are descriptions of four reading and study skills programs. The purpose of these descriptions is to show how each program is designed to adapt to its population and setting.

Program One:
Supplemental Instruction Model

Dr. Dianna C. Martin developed Supplemental Instruction in the 1970s at the University of Missouri–Kansas City in response to a rising attrition rate. The model was designated an exemplary program by the United States Department of Education in 1981. Since then, over 100 institutions have offered or continued to offer Supplemental Instruction. The program, as described in a handbook printed by the University of Missouri (*An Integrative Model,* 1985), is a nonremedial support program that should be available to all students. A competent content leader is trained to lead out-of-class study sessions starting in the beginning of the semester. The primary task of the leader is to help students develop thinking and reasoning skills through the provision of information on note taking, anticipating test questions, vocabulary development, and memory aids.

Commander and Smith (1995) describe Supplemental Instruction courses taught by trained graduate students who act as learning leaders in classes paired with designated content courses, such as history, psychology, or biology. Student attendance is voluntary. In each session, students learn strategies that develop metacognitive awareness and an appreciation of the structure of the discipline. Leaders provide frequent quizzes to help prepare participants for examinations in the regular class, and they model how to function in that course.

Commander and Smith (1995) recommend that, in order to be successful, instructors of Supplemental Instruction courses need to be familiar with the course content of paired courses. In their program, instructors visit a section of the course the semester prior to pairing, take notes, and observe students and teacher. They also recommend offering a variety of Supplemental Instruction courses, encouraging students to take the hardest courses after having success with a more comfortable paired course.

The advantage of Supplemental Instruction is that participants immediately see the applicability of strategy use in a content course.

Program Two:
Reading and Skills Course and Center

This literacy program in a mid-sized, four-year university located minutes from a large city consists of a reading and study skills course and a reading and academic skills center. Freshmen take The Nelson-Denny Reading Test (Brown, Bennett, & Hanna, 1981) prior to their first semester. The test, according to the program's director, was selected because it measures comprehension separately from vocabulary and is easy to administer and score. She has used the Nelson-Denny for many years and believes it helps differentiate students with needs from those who can succeed unassisted. Students are advised to take the reading and skills course if they score at or below the 11th reader level as well as below 450 on the verbal portion of the SAT.

Students receive two credits for the course, which meets four hours each week: three hours of class and one hour in a study group. Rather than using a traditional college reading and study skills text, the director has worked with a publisher to put together a text that includes two types of material: (1) information and exercises that develop vocabulary, comprehension, critical reading, and the student's role as a learner (metacognition, learning styles, and scheduling time); (2) chapters and exercises from the very texts used in freshmen courses at that university. Utilization of these chapters, according to the director, has enhanced students' transfer of skills.

Reading literature is an important component of the course. The program director believes that many students lack skills because they are not readers. She has also seen a lack of interest in the selections provided in anthologies; therefore, all instructors of reading and study skills classes require students to read popular novels and nonfiction that are then discussed in class and summarized. Instructors report that at the beginning of the semester, it is difficult to get students to write a paragraph; by the end of the semester, they write pages.

The director, a certified reading specialist, teaches sections of the course. The other instructors are certified in either reading or English. The fourth hour of the course, the study group, is led by either the reading course instructor, a graduate student, a peer, or a combination. In each study group, a content course is selected that tends to be difficult for the group. Students explore difficult course vocabulary, compare lecture notes, and discuss course-specific test-taking strategies.

Because of the time involved in having an instructor attend all classes of a content course, study groups have taken the place of the Supplemental Instruction model. Study groups have also taken the place of assigning students to attend the reading skills center a certain number of hours during the semester; the study groups have been viewed as more beneficial by both students and group leaders. The course is effective because it encourages students to enjoy reading, provides opportunities for them to transfer skills to their coursework, and has trained staff.

The Reading and Academic Skills Center is available to all students of the university. Open during the day and evening, it is staffed by course instructors, graduate students, and peer tutors who have all participated in a tutor training program. The director reports that tutors who are majors in specific disciplines, such as chemistry or psychology, are very effective as tutors. Some students come to the Skills Center for one-on-one clinical instruction with a reading specialist. Others come to participate in a small-group tutorial for assistance with specific courses.

Program Three:
Learning and Advising Center

This program is located in a major university in a large city. The director of the program is a trained reading specialist. The program includes a reading and study skills course as well as tutoring in reading and study skills, mathematics, and writing. The staff includes faculty with doctorates or master's degrees in different disciplines, including reading or English. The director trains all staff who work with students in the Learning and Advising Center.

Originally, the reading course was paired with a content course. The director suggests this was effective but too labor intensive. Currently, the course includes three components: (1) a reading and study skills text, (2) focus on time management, and (3) use of duplicated chapters of texts currently in use at the university. The strengths of this course, according to its director, include using the Internet for the location and reading of primary documents, visuals and videos to help students draw conclusions, and case studies to help students go from the specific to the general.

The Learning and Advising Center is widely used; the director reports that half of the university's student body visits the center each year. They attend for individual assistance with coursework, math review sessions, or help with written assignments. The advantages of having all assistance in one location are the centralization of files for staff and ease of access for students.

The literacy course is successful because it encourages students to use the Internet to read primary documents and develop skills for reading content texts.

Program Four:
Learning Center

The Learning Center, located in a small liberal arts college in a suburban area, was originally a language laboratory, but its director, a certified reading specialist with wide experience working with adults, has begun to transform it into a reading and study skills center. There is no reading course as yet; instead, students who are conditionally accepted because of low SAT scores or borderline high school grade point averages are required to come to the Learning Center for eight visits their first semester.

The program's director administers learning style inventories and designs sessions that meet the specific needs and styles of each learner. Students who come to the center utilize computer assistance programs, watch videos on how to study, listen to language tapes, and work individually and in small groups with a peer tutor or the director on literacy skills or content needs. The director, the only full-time employee and reading specialist, is assisted by part-time teachers and peer tutors. She wrote a tutor manual and trains tutors one-on-one.

The strength of this program is the background of its director, who is training those who work with students, regardless of their lack of reading background, to appreciate ways to help students understand their learning styles, learn to improve their memory, and learn how to use specific study strategies.

Role of Reading Personnel

While there are differences in the programs described, each focuses on applying learning directly to coursework, whether through a literacy course or a learning center. Each program has a training component for those who work with students.

Although no certification is required for individuals to teach reading and study skills at the post-secondary level, it is beneficial for those who direct literacy programs to have expertise in the field. Interviews with those who hire directors of programs in community colleges and colleges and universities suggest that applicants with degrees or certification in reading are preferred.

Characteristics of Successful Programs

Each of the programs described in this chapter depends on the available resources of its institution. Despite its size and resources, however, each program focuses on helping students learn strategies they can immediately use in coursework, and each includes a staff training component.

Just because students have graduated from high school, we cannot assume they have developed efficient and effective learning strategies. College reading programs, therefore, should provide opportunities for students to learn how to approach diverse texts, take notes in class, and study for and take tests. Those who teach read-

ing courses and work in learning laboratories need to help students appreciate the benefits of these strategies, model how to use each, and provide sufficient opportunities for guided practice that leads to independent use.

Research has shown the importance of background knowledge and metacognition to new learning. Strategies such as SCROL for reading texts and a systematic note taking format incorporate the use of background information and stress metacognition. Helping students with pre-reading and scaffolding strategies will enhance this development. These strategies are more effective if teachers utilize material from students' courses, because the students will see immediate impact on their learning.

Successful programs require trained staff. Two essential factors for reading course instructors and tutors are a background in reading and knowledge of learning strategies that can be used regardless of the discipline. Therefore, program directors need to stay current and provide training sessions for staff.

Literacy program leaders need to have knowledge of tests that screen students with learning needs. Johnson and Carpenter (2000) suggest that 75% of institutions have reading placement tests and require courses for students who do not do well on such tests. The most commonly used test, they say, is The Nelson-Denny Reading Test.

Reading personnel at the post-secondary level need to work with faculty of all disciplines to help them gain an appreciation of the needs of the underprepared student. They should work with administrators to design programs that fit the needs of their institution as well as encourage them to appreciate that most college students could profit from programs that help develop stronger learning strategies.

Conclusion

The historical overview has shown a progression from seeing reading courses taking the place of secondary education, to laboratories that focus on speed reading and specific skill training, to today's focus on the development of a learner-centered paradigm. Education today is viewed as a lifelong experience. The purpose of today's post-secondary literacy programs, therefore, is to help students learn the strategies they need to enhance their learning. People who work with students in reading courses and learning centers have to have the expertise to help students develop strategies that encourage improvement of note taking, reading texts, test taking, and time management.

With the increased role of technology in all facets of society, college literacy educators need to keep abreast of technological changes and develop students' ability to succeed in a workplace that functions through the exchange of technical text. As in the past, the components and characteristics of post-secondary literacy programs will be linked to the ongoing learning needs of students accepted to colleges and universities.

References

An integrative model of student academic support. (1985). Kansas City: University of Missouri.

Armbruster, B. B. (2000). Taking notes from lectures. In R. F. Flippo & D. C. Caverly (Eds.), *Handbook of college reading and study strategy research* (pp. 175–199). Mahwah, NJ: Erlbaum.

Bonner, T. N. (1986). The unintended revolution in America's colleges since 1940. *Change, 18,* 44–51.

Boylan, H. R. (1995). The scope of developmental education: Some basic information on the field. *Research in Developmental Education, 12,* 1–6.

Boylan, H. R., & White, W. G. (1987). Educating all the nation's people: The historical roots of developmental education (Part 1). *Research in Developmental Education, 4,* 1–4.

Brier, E. (1984). Bridging the academic preparation gap: An historical view. *Journal of Developmental Education, 8,* 2–5.

Brown, J. I., Bennett, J. M., & Hanna, G. (1981). *Nelson-Denny Reading Test.* Chicago: Riverside.

Charters, W. W. (1941). Remedial reading in college. *Journal of Higher Education, 12,* 117–121.

Commander, N. E., & Smith, B. (1995). Developing adjunct reading and learning courses that work. *Journal of Reading, 38,* 352–360.

Flippo, R. F., Becker, M. J., & Wark, D. M. (2000). Preparing for and taking tests. In R. F. Flippo &

D. C. Caverly (Eds.), *Handbook of college reading and study strategy research* (pp. 221–260). Mahwah, NJ: Erlbaum.

Grant, R. (1993). Strategic training for using text headings to improve students' processing of content. *Journal of Reading, 36,* 482–488.

Johnson, L. L., & Carpenter, K. (2000). College reading programs. In R. F. Flippo & D. C. Caverly (Eds.), *Handbook of college reading and study strategy research* (pp. 321–363). Mahwah, NJ: Erlbaum.

Leedy, P. D. (1958). *A history of the origin and development of instruction in reading improvement at the college level.* Doctoral dissertation, New York University. (University Microfilms No. 59-01016)

Lissner, L. S. (1990). The learning center from 1829 to the year 2000 and beyond. In R. M. Hashway (Ed.), *Handbook of developmental education* (pp. 127–154). New York: Praeger.

Mason, R. B. (1993). *Selected college reading improvement programs: A descriptive history.* (ERIC Document Reproduction Service No. ED 366-907)

Maxwell, M. J. (1979). *Improving student learning skills.* San Francisco: Jossey-Bass.

National Center for Education Statistics. (1996). *Remedial education at higher education institutions in fall 1995.* Washington, DC: U.S. Department of Education, Office of Education at Research and Improvement [On-line]. Available: http://nces.ed.gov/pubs/97584.html

Nist, S. L., & Holschub, J. L. (2000). Comprehension strategies at the college level. In R. F. Flippo & D. C. Caverly (Eds.), *Handbook of college reading and study strategy research* (pp. 75–104). Mahwah, NJ: Erlbaum.

Pugh, S. L., Pawan, F., & Antommarchi, C. (2000). In R. F. Flippo & D. C. Caverly (Eds.), *Handbook of college reading and study strategy research* (pp. 25–42). Mahwah, NJ: Erlbaum.

Reynolds, J., & Werner, S. C. (1994). An alternative paradigm for college reading and study skills courses. *Journal of Reading, 37,* 272–278.

Roberts, G. H. (1986). *Developmental education: An historical study.* (ERIC Document Reproduction Service No. ED 276-395)

Spires, H. A., & Stone, P. D. (1989). The directed note-taking activity: A self-questioning approach. *Journal of Reading, 32,* 36–39.

Wyatt, M. (1992). The past, present, and future need for college reading courses in the United States. *Journal of Reading, 36,* 10–20.

PART III

Program Implementation and Evaluation

T his section includes four chapters about program implementation and evaluation. Many factors contribute to effective reading program development. The collaborative efforts of administrators and teachers to select and use appropriate materials, evaluate teacher's instructional practices, participate in professional development, and assess students' progress with instruction are examined.

Chapter 7 presents ideas for selecting materials and resources for the elementary and secondary levels. The administrator's role is examined. Issues surrounding material selection are addressed as different types of instructional and assessment materials and resources are described. Guidelines for organizing the selection of materials such as textbooks, magazines, videotapes, and other supplemental tools are also included in this chapter.

Chapter 8 offers ideas and guidelines for teacher observation at the elementary and secondary levels. Choice, activity, and authenticity are explained as essential elements to observe when focusing on the interactions between the teacher and students. A Reading Lesson Observation Framework is used as a guidepost for evaluating teachers' growth as instructional leaders.

Chapter 9 addresses professional development and its impact on the practices of those involved in literacy instruction. Information about the National Board for Professional Teaching Standards, portfolios, and action research as forms of professional development are included. Examples of school-university partnerships as another form of professional development also are included.

Chapter 10 looks at the impact of standards on assessment patterns and trends. It addresses both large-scale assessment trends and classroom assessment practices, and it suggests ideas for educators to use to put these two assessments together into a coherent program.

This part of the book helps leaders of literacy to provide the best possible instructional reading programs by focusing on four critical areas of implementation and evaluation: selection of materials, teacher observation, professional development, and assessment.

CHAPTER SEVEN

Selecting Materials for the Literacy Program

Diane Lapp, Douglas Fisher, James Flood,
Kelly Goss-Moore, and Juel Moore

While there is evidence that children are performing better in the area of literacy than ever before (Berliner & Biddle, 1995; McQuillan, 1998), debate continues about the most appropriate ways to further enhance children's growth in literacy. Since educational administrators and teachers are critical to the success of classroom reading instruction, they must share a viable plan that ensures literacy success for every child.

This chapter identifies key factors that need to be addressed as literacy materials are selected.

First, we examine the role of the administrator in selecting materials. We then offer guidelines for the selection of materials for literacy programs. Finally, we describe how one principal's team selected materials for an elementary school.

The Administrator's Role in Selecting Materials

We begin this discussion by sharing the findings from a survey that we administered to 65 elementary, middle, and high school principals from nine states. We asked them: "What do you believe are your primary responsibilities?" and "What role do you believe you should play in selecting instructional materials at your school site?" After the surveys were completed, we interviewed 35 of the principals.

The first question on the survey asked principals to rank order their responsibilities. Their answers were compiled into these overall rankings:

1. Overseeing student learning as the instructional leader
2. Providing teachers with professional development
3. Evaluating teacher performance
4. Administering student discipline
5. Developing public relations with parents and community leaders
6. Improving test scores
7. Conferencing with teachers
8. Selecting curriculum materials
9. Working with budget
10. Implementing state standards

While the ordered list created enough conversation among literacy leaders to fill a chapter, if not a book, we will be concentrating on number 8, selecting curriculum materials.

It is interesting to note that selecting curriculum materials was listed as number 8 in terms of importance out of the top 10 perceived responsibilities of administrators. The only items that scored lower were working with budgets and implementing state standards. One administrator stated, "While this is low on my list of current responsibilities, it is critical. When we are selecting reading materials, I have to support my teachers to make sure they select the best materials. Once the materials are selected, my job really begins—making sure that the materials are used effectively."

Since we had designed the survey to collect information about the principal's role in materials selection, we asked a specific question about the responsibility the principal felt he or she played in material selection. Their answers overwhelmingly indicated that their role was to provide informational support to teachers who would then make the selections. One principal voiced the sentiment of many when she said: "We're going to have the materials we select for several years, and I want to know that they are the best for our students. I'm not sure that I have enough current knowledge about each curriculum area to make the decision alone, but my teachers know a lot and are very clear about what materials they need to be effective."

What Procedures Are Used to Select Materials?

We asked the principals what they believed were the best ways to identify effective literacy materials. Their most common responses were: (1) they checked with other instructional leaders about the effectiveness of the materials they used, (2) they asked their teachers and literacy specialists for suggestions, and (3) they invited publishers to present their materials to the teachers at the school site. Of those interviewed, 94% stated that they also got insights about materials when they attended professional conferences.

Based on survey and interview responses, we believe that principals rely heavily on their teachers and curriculum specialists to select the materials. We wondered if this philosophy might be altered by the amount of funding that was available for the task, so we asked in the survey who would have the primary decision-making authority for selecting materials if the school were given $10,000, $20,000, and $100,000. Regardless of the increase in amount of funding, their answers remained consistent, that the teachers and curriculum specialists should make the decisions on the materials for the literacy program.

What Factors Aid Selection?

In addition to the procedures and responsibilities questions, we were also interested in identifying the types of materials that would be purchased. In response to the question "What type of materials would you like to purchase?" the principals identified, in rank order, the following:

1. Quality literature selections
2. A wide array of information articles, books, and magazines

3. Those containing a strong emphasis on decoding at the early grades
4. Those containing explicit directions for teachers on how to use the materials
5. Those having a strong assessment component
6. Those with useful suggestions for teachers about grouping and management
7. Effective workbooks to accompany the texts

All principals were interested in the support that the selected materials would provide to the teachers who used them. As one administrator noted, "If I'm going to spend money, I want a package. I want to know that everything a teacher needs to use with the materials is included. I don't want to have to secure additional money for staff development and then more money for assessments and then more money for supplemental readings."

What Materials Should Be Purchased?

When asked what would be purchased if they were given money other than the dollars specified for basal materials, the number one priority noted by all principals was quality fiction and nonfiction literature that is written at students' instructional reading level. One administrator wrote, "We would spend all our money on books. We get textbook adoption money from the state but hardly any extra money to create really good classroom libraries. Every teacher needs hundreds of leveled books in his or her classroom to be effective with read-alouds and SSR. They need fiction and nonfiction."

The principals' second priority was to purchase class sets of supplemental phonics, spelling, and vocabulary materials. The elementary principals noted the need for the phonics materials, while all survey participants identified the need for the spelling and vocabulary resources.

Survey Findings

The results from this study highlight several issues pertaining to materials selection. First, information matters. The administrator needs to be informed about the materials and their use. Further, the administrator needs to arrange for this information to be secured and shared with teachers and community members as decisions are made.

Second, participation matters. The results of this survey are very clear: Administrators believe that teachers, specialists, and community members must be involved in the selection process. As one administrator stated, "I have the authority to make the decision. However, I don't have to use the materials. If I really want the materials used well, I need to make sure that those closest to the result of the decision are involved in the decision-making process."

Third, extended resources should matter. While these leaders identified many extended instructional materials they would purchase with additional dollars, very few of them identified the need for children's magazines or for computer software or other media as part of their materials selection. This is interesting, given the number of teachers who use technology and media in their classrooms (e.g., Fisher, Lapp, & Flood, 2000), and we wonder if these extended resources were not considered because they are not traditionally purchased with "textbook" money. We plan to repeat this survey yearly to determine when and if these additional resources become a part of the purchase plan.

Additional Considerations

We believe that many principals, like the ones surveyed, will ask the literacy specialist or lead teacher to assist with materials selection. It is important to note that the selection of materials is highly dependent on the local literacy guidelines. For example, if teachers are expected to read aloud every day to their students, they must have quality, interesting materials to do so. Similarly, if teachers are expected to provide guided reading instruction, they require a number of leveled texts and appropriate assessment materials. The remainder of this chapter focuses on selecting various materials for the classroom, including basals and textbooks, children's literature, children's magazines, and media.

Selecting Basals and Textbooks

Although there have been criticisms about basals, anthologies, and textbooks (e.g., Hudak-Huelbig, Keyes, McClure, & Stellingwerf, 1991), they are still the most significant component of the literacy curriculum (Fawson & Reutzel, 2000; Hoffman et al., 1998) because of the range of possible lessons that they provide and their comparatively low cost.

At the secondary school level, the administrator often has a limited role in the review or selection of the primary textbooks that are used in the classroom. A district committee of content-area specialists and teachers often adopts textbooks used in high school. However, more and more often, administrators and their faculties ask for and are given the opportunity to choose between a number of adopted textbooks in a subject area. Additionally, secondary school administrators and supervisors can review and select books to supplement the primary textbook.

What Counts as a Basal or Textbook?

Most basals or textbook series are programs that consist of several components, including student and teacher editions. They are designed for students in Grades 1 through 6 or through 8. Traditionally, they include a collection of emergent literacy materials, several "little books" for beginning reading instruction, and at least one student textbook per grade level. Current basals focus on age-appropriate, quality literature with pictures and illustrations. Supplementary or companion materials to a core basal program often include sets of library books, which relate to thematic units under study. Often these will include books by authors or full versions of text excerpted in the student editions. Other materials include classroom assessments, such as informal inventories, rubrics for writing, and checklists of a variety of types. A variety of technology components are also included in modern basals. Interactive software for independent practice in comprehension or writing is common.

Current basals attempt to embrace the entire spectrum of language arts: listening, speaking, reading, and writing. They also attempt to provide activities that integrate the language arts with the content-area curriculum. Activities span a wide range of language and literacy skills, including vocabulary, text structures, comprehension, and fluency. Lessons are generated from narratives, expository texts, poetry, and other texts that students may encounter in real life.

Student Texts. The most important part of any basal is the content of the books the students read. The contents of the student texts have changed considerably over the past several decades; current editions reflect a wide range of cultures and genres. Children's texts include a variety of genres, and many selections are complete or excerpted works of major authors. Levels are designated in an attempt to ensure a grade level match with the reading competency of the students. Companion libraries or lists of supplementary books are offered to help teachers provide materials that match students' levels.

Teacher Editions. Teacher editions of the past ranged from a low of 672 pages to a whopping 1,035 pages. Current teacher editions are more compact, helpful guides designed to present systematic, explicit instructional examples and suggestions. Additionally, teacher editions often provide a range of alternative grouping, extension, and assessment activities, home involvement connections, and ideas for working with gifted and talented education (GATE) students, special need students, and those who are learning English as a second language. More innovative teacher editions also include curriculum connections to assist teachers in planning thematic lessons, as well as technology connections and websites.

How Can Basals Be Selected?

Figure 7.1 contains a checklist with questions that literacy leaders should ask before purchasing a basal series. This checklist can serve as a basis for evaluating differences among texts. The basal with the best score may not necessarily be the best choice for a school, but the checklist will provide the selection committee with information to discuss during their deliberations.

CRITERIA FOR BASAL OR TEXTBOOK SELECTION

Name of Basal _____ Publisher _____

Philosophy   Scale (1 = weak; 5 = excellent)

1. Is the program based on accessible, current research?   1   2   3   4   5
2. Does it have a philosophy that is compatible with yours?   1   2   3   4   5
3. Does it address the literacy needs of your population?   1   2   3   4   5
4. Does it encourage reading for enjoyment?   1   2   3   4   5

Content of the Student Text

5. Are there a variety of types of selections?   1   2   3   4   5
6. Are selections grouped by themes?   1   2   3   4   5
7. Are texts leveled?   1   2   3   4   5
8. Are questions that involve an array of thinking strategies included?   1   2   3   4   5
9. Are many cultures represented?   1   2   3   4   5
10. Are selections systematically sequenced?   1   2   3   4   5
11. Is vocabulary presented, discussed, and practiced in a way that promotes
    reading independence?   1   2   3   4   5
12. Do comprehension skill and strategy lessons promote independence?   1   2   3   4   5

Practice Books

13. Are activities related to text selections?   1   2   3   4   5
14. Are instructions and examples clear enough to foster student independence?   1   2   3   4   5
15. Are skills presented in a spiral format (e.g., grammar, comprehension,
    phonics)?   1   2   3   4   5

Teacher Manual

16. Are before, during, and after reading strategies included?   1   2   3   4   5
17. Is instruction thoroughly explained and modeled?   1   2   3   4   5
18. Are skills initially contextualized?   1   2   3   4   5
19. Is there a systematically presented phonics sequence?   1   2   3   4   5
20. Do comprehension skills build from concrete to abstract?   1   2   3   4   5
21. Are consistent routines suggested that aid classroom management and
    instruction?   1   2   3   4   5
22. Is a week-by-week and a five-day planner included that provides a week-
    at-a glance overview of what is to be taught?   1   2   3   4   5
23. Are teacher and student editions numbered exactly the same?   1   2   3   4   5
24. Is a copy of the student's page included on the teacher's page?   1   2   3   4   5

Supplementary Materials

25. Are there big book and matching little books?   1   2   3   4   5
26. Are there sets of leveled little books?   1   2   3   4   5
27. Are there tapes of songs and poems?   1   2   3   4   5
28. Are there alphabet, word, and sentence strips?   1   2   3   4   5
29. Is there useful software?   1   2   3   4   5
30. Is a CD-ROM teacher planner system included?   1   2   3   4   5

Assessment

31. Are pre/post assessments in various formats (oral/written) included for
    each unit?   1   2   3   4   5
32. Are the end-of-lesson assessments included?   1   2   3   4   5
33. Do assessment selections (fiction and exposition) match those of
    standardized tests?   1   2   3   4   5
34. Do assessments incorporate response formats similar to those appearing
    on standardized tests?   1   2   3   4   5
35. Is instructional information provided that enables regrouping based on
    assessment?   1   2   3   4   5

                                                        TOTAL:

Figure 7.1

Selecting Children's Literature

Once basal funding has been spent, many principals believe that the next task is to select children's literature books and anthologies. Literature encourages students to learn about people they may never meet and to visit places they may never see in their lifetimes. As Cullinan (1989) notes, literature is both a window and a mirror to the world. Teachers use literature as a significant part of the reading or language arts program for at least three reasons: modeling of language structures, connecting lessons to students' prior knowledge, and motivating readers (e.g., Fisher, Flood, & Lapp, 1999; Roser & Martinez, 1995).

It is important to note that books selected for classroom use should support the goals and themes of the curriculum and should reflect the languages spoken in the classroom and the reading fluency of students. In classrooms throughout the United States, Strickland, Walmsley, Bronk, and Weiss (1994) found that basal reading anthologies containing the very best children's literature are used jointly with the classroom libraries. One's concept of what counts as a text continues to expand (Diamondstone, 2000; Wade & Moje, 2000).

What Counts as Children's Literature?

Each year, thousands of books for children are published; tens of thousands more are in print. The field of children's literature is expanding rapidly, with children having significantly greater access to quality books. A number of sources may help teachers identify appropriate materials. For example, book reviews in journals such as *The Journal of Children's Literature, The Horn Book, The School Library Journal,* and *The New Advocate* provide educators with information about new books as well as previously published titles.

In addition, several awards are given each year that highlight quality new books. The Newbery Award is based on literary quality, while the Caldecott is given for quality illustrations. Committees that read all of the children's books published during the year select the medal and honor winners. The Coretta Scott King Award is presented annually to both an African American author and an African American illustrator for outstanding contributions to children's literature.

Organizations such as the International Reading Association (IRA) and the National Council of Teachers of English (NCTE) have established committees that annually develop lists of notable books. The IRA's Teacher's Choices is a national project involving teachers in the selection of books for use across the curriculum. The Teacher's Choices lists are published annually in *The Reading Teacher.*

How Can Children's Literature Be Selected?

The following criteria may help with the selection of children's literature:

◆ Books chosen for classrooms should cover a wide variety of genres, including folk tales, tall tales, fables, myths, legends, poems, fantasy, realistic and historical fiction, nonfiction, and science fiction. Books should depict a variety of family structures and perspectives on the world. Good writing and engaging illustrations in a wide array of genres will elicit thoughtful responses from children and also offer opportunities to venture to unique discoveries and places.

◆ Selections should provide examples of well-developed characters, interesting language, and engaging plots. Literacy leaders must also be aware of gender, racial, and ability stereotypes that might exist within the text. Literary quality of the selection should have been demonstrated by reviews, awards, and trusted word-of-mouth recommendations.

◆ A wide range of difficulty levels should be a part of every classroom library. This will ensure that readers can grasp concepts and ideas with and without guidance.

Selecting Children's Magazines

Children need to become proficient at reading a wide range of genres if they are to be literate as adults. To this end, opportunities must be provided for them to read periodicals written for

CRITERIA FOR MAGAZINE SELECTION

Magazine Title _____

	Scale (1 = weak; 5 = excellent)
1. Is current information provided?	1 2 3 4 5
2. Is a wide range of interest areas covered?	1 2 3 4 5
3. Is there a range of difficulty within a periodical?	1 2 3 4 5
4. Do the graphics support the text?	1 2 3 4 5
5. Are various types of graphics included (e.g., photographs, drawings, illustrations, cartoons)?	1 2 3 4 5
6. Is there a range of genres (e.g., stories, poems, essays, cartoons, experiments, puzzles)?	1 2 3 4 5
7. Are students invited to submit their writing, poetry, art?	1 2 3 4 5
8. Does the content support the curriculum goals?	1 2 3 4 5
9. Are instructional suggestions offered to the teacher?	1 2 3 4 5
10. Will the content motivate students to read?	1 2 3 4 5
	TOTAL:

Figure 7.2

their grade and interest levels. Children's magazines have been developed to address this need.

What Counts as Children's Magazines?

Children's magazines come in many forms and styles. There are some very popular magazines for elementary age students, such as *Highlights* and *Weekly Reader*. In addition, there are children's magazines targeted toward specific markets, such as *Music Express, Sports Illustrated for Kids, American Girl,* and *Kids Discover*. Further, there are magazines for older students, such as *Teen Life, Music Alive,* and *Teen People*. The appendix to this chapter provides a list of children's magazines by age level. To identify new titles in children's magazines or to find current subscription prices, simply search the World Wide Web for "children's magazines."

How Can Children's Magazines Be Selected?

When selecting periodicals for a particular grade level, you may want to consider the criteria outlined in Figure 7.2 in order to ensure that you have addressed the range of literacy among the students.

Selecting Media

Standards documents for English and language arts now frequently note the importance of visual literacy as a component of a comprehensive and balanced literacy curriculum. Over the past decade, research on the effects on achievement when using multiple forms of media has grown significantly (e.g., Flood, Heath, & Lapp, 1997; Lapp, Flood, & Fisher, 1999).

Visual representations of complex ideas help students organize information (Dillner, 1993/1994; Flood, Lapp, & Bayles-Martin, 2000; Mayer, 1990; Pailliotet, Semali, Rodenberg, Giles, & Macaul, 2000). Developing concept or semantic maps is one strategy used by teachers because it provides insights about students' knowledge of the topic (Armbruster, 1996; Irvin, 1998; Valerio & Readence, 2000). In addition to concept maps and character webs, teachers use art, illustrated vocabulary, videos, and computer websites to assist students in creating visual representations and in understanding text (Flood, Heath, & Lapp, 1997). Media literacy, especially through the use of videos and films, has become a mainstay for many teachers. There is evidence that even a single, short, powerful film can alter perceptions and behaviors (e.g., Eisenman, Girdner, Burroughs, & Routman, 1993).

CRITERIA FOR VIDEO SELECTION

Title _____

Scale (1 = weak; 5 = excellent)

	1	2	3	4	5
1. Does the video support curricular goals?	1	2	3	4	5
2. Are there corresponding text materials?	1	2	3	4	5
3. Is there an instructor's manual?	1	2	3	4	5
4. Are the graphics appropriate for the target grade level?	1	2	3	4	5
5. Is the language grade level appropriate?	1	2	3	4	5
6. Does the publisher provide a viewer's guide?	1	2	3	4	5
7. Is the information in the video historically accurate?	1	2	3	4	5
8. Does the video display people in respectful ways?	1	2	3	4	5
9. Does the video encourage students to read more about the topic?	1	2	3	4	5
10. Is the video reasonably priced?	1	2	3	4	5

TOTAL:

Figure 7.3

Dahl and Farnan (1998) note in their book *Children's Writing* that computers and technology have significantly impacted literacy instruction. However, the selection and use of technology was not given high priority by the principals in the survey or interviews we conducted. Here we will highlight the importance of computer software as a primary component of the literacy program. Chapter 12 of this volume extends the conversation about literacy and technology.

Researchers have attempted to document positive outcomes when students use computers as part of a comprehensive literacy curriculum. For example, Russell (1991), in her meta-analysis, found that the relationship between technology and writing was significantly influenced by the social interactions that students had in the computer lab, and the writing was higher-quality when students used word processing software and computers. Similarly, Owston, Murphy, and Wideman (1992) found that students wrote higher-quality essays using word processing software than they did when they wrote their essays in cursive. Odenthal (1992) found similar results among English-language learners. Haas (1989) documented similar results; she found that easy-to-use software programs facilitated the revision process. The results of these studies indicate that technology:

1. helps children to focus on content rather than mechanics
2. encourages the production of more and better-developed essays
3. reduces the drudgery of editing

What Counts as Media?

The term *media* comprises a variety of traditional and nontraditional print and nonprint sources, including videos, films, computer software, Internet sites, graphics, and songs. We consider these sources together because in classrooms they are used to supplement textbooks and basals.

How Can Media Be Selected?

While there are many forms of media, the two most common are videos and software programs.

Videos. Realizing the value of videos as instructional media is sometimes difficult for administrators who are not sure of the educational significance. The criteria outlined in Figure 7.3 may assist in the selection of videos that will form a component of the literacy program.

Software. As the studies on technology suggest, educational software is another type of material

CRITERIA FOR SOFTWARE SELECTION

Title _____

	Scale (1 = weak; 5 = excellent)
1. Does the topic match curriculum goals?	1 2 3 4 5
2. Do the instructional strategies and content complement our philosophy?	1 2 3 4 5
3. Is the material interactive?	1 2 3 4 5
4. Is instructional feedback provided?	1 2 3 4 5
5. Is the material easy to navigate?	1 2 3 4 5
6. Are the directions language and user friendly?	1 2 3 4 5
7. Can the material be used independently by the student?	1 2 3 4 5
8. Can the program be re-entered without starting over?	1 2 3 4 5
9. Are the skills levels appropriate for the student population?	1 2 3 4 5
10. Is learning enhanced by the graphics?	1 2 3 4 5
11. Is there an evaluation component?	1 2 3 4 5
12. Is a class spreadsheet available?	1 2 3 4 5
13. Is there a way to ensure student privacy?	1 2 3 4 5
14. Are additional extension lesson plans or materials included?	1 2 3 4 5
15. Can technical support be easily secured?	1 2 3 4 5
TOTAL:	

Figure 7.4

that can aid students in acquiring and expanding literacy. You may wish to use the criteria in Figure 7.4 to select and match software with your instructional goals.

How One Principal's Team Selected Materials

We had the opportunity to be involved with and to observe the process of materials selection at Oak Park Elementary School in San Diego, California. The Materials Focus Group (named by the principal in collaboration with her staff) assumed the task of selecting a basal so that they could get other teachers involved in staff development and a search for a basal that would best fit with their philosophy about literacy development. Under the leadership of the principal, and one of the authors, the 15–20 members of the committee met regularly to orchestrate the staff development and adoption process. Over the course of a year and a half, monthly workshops on language, literature, and learning given to the entire staff by focus group members and outside experts were interspersed with presentations by

publishers' representatives who were invited to display materials at the district level.

Basals

Everyone was gaining a broader view and, consequently, was able to look at basal materials with an informed view of how literacy develops. The choice was narrowed to two balanced literacy basals; the committee had to look closely to determine which one best met the adoption criteria that evolved through the staff development and screening process.

The chain of events that led to the selection of the basal at Oak Park included:

1. The principal asked for teacher volunteers to pilot the basals that had been approved at a district level.
2. Volunteer teachers were randomly assigned by the district to pilot a program.
3. Pilot teachers attended publisher-supported meetings about the materials.
4. Using a checklist similar to the one included in Figure 7.1, pilot teachers evaluated the selections.

5. Pilot teachers reported to other grade level faculty what was being learned about the materials from meetings and use.

6. Faculty from all grade levels met to discuss how effectively the program was meeting the needs of students at various grade levels.

7. Each faculty member voted, and the selection was made.

Other Materials

At Oak Park, supplementary materials are also selected by grade level teams who bring their selections to share with a focus group. The sharing of information about materials is important in order to ensure that the entire school knows what is available for different classrooms at various levels of literacy. A grade level team may invite publishers to display materials at the school or present at a focus group meeting. The presentations may be done at any time other than adoption years, to protect the integrity of the district's selection process. The principal then allocates funding to each grade level and allows them to purchase the supplemental materials that they wish to use at their grade level.

Conclusion

While the majority of teachers use many different types of materials, the mainstay is a large library of trade books (single and multiple copies) and components of a major basal system. The target material must be assessed to determine its alignment with school goals, curriculum, and student need. This chapter has attempted to offer insights about the process of selecting materials for the schoolwide literacy effort, including the administrator's role.

As we have noted throughout this chapter, the role of the principal, the instructional leader, is very complex; it encompasses working with teachers, parents, and other policy makers, building support personnel, and most importantly of all, creating a safe, supportive school learning environment for the students. To this end, it is important to reemphasize that students of all ages learn in classrooms where they are engaged. Guthrie (1996) identifies many factors that promote engagement. Selecting appropriate, motivating materials is one of the most significant of these. We have therefore offered research-based insights as well as criteria related to effective materials selection. Additionally, we have described how a principal cooperatively engages teachers in the selection of literacy materials.

Appendix: Children's Magazines

Young Children, Grades K–2

Spider
An on-line magazine
http://spider.tm/may2001/checkem.shtml

Scienceland
P.O. Box 1177, Scarsdale, NY 10583
212-490-2180
A science magazine for young people

Jack & Jill
Magazines.com, 180 Freedom Avenue, Murfreesboro, TN 37129
http://hallmags.com/title/jack_and_jill.shtml
Famous biographies, new games & sports, comic adventures, kids' health questions, poems and stories

Sesame Street Magazine
Sesame Street, P.O. Box 52000, Boulder, CO 80321-2000
http://www.sesameworkshop.org
A pre-school reading publication

Elementary Age, Grades 3–5

Cricket
Cricket, Box 593, Mt. Morris, IL 61054-0593
http://www.cobblestonepub.com
Quality literature and illustrations for children

Ranger Rick's Nature
Ranger Rick, The National Wildlife Federation, 8925 Leesburg Pike, Vienna, VA 22184-0001
http://www.nwf.org/rangerrick
Well-illustrated and reliable nature magazine

Sports Illustrated for Kids
   Time Inc., P.O. Box 830609, Birmingham, AL 35283-0609
   http://www.sikids.com
   Sports-oriented subjects
National Geographic World
   National Geographic World, Box 2330, Washington, DC 20013-2330
   http://www.nationalgeographic.com/media/world
   Outstanding illustrations and content in this nature and science magazine
Weekly Reader
   Weekly Reader Corporation, 200 First Stamford Place, P.O. Box 120023, Stamford, CT 06912-0023
   http://www.weeklyreader.com
   A current events magazine for youth
Highlights
   Highlights for Children, P.O. Box 269, Columbus, OH 43272-0002
   http://www.highlightsforchildren.com
   "Fun with a purpose" recreational yet educational features; an all-purpose magazine for children
Music Express
   Cherry Lane Magazines, P.O. Box 53063, Boulder, CO 80322
   http://www.cherrylane.com
   Music interests for younger students
Odyssey
   Cobblestone Publishing, 7 School Street, Peterborough, NH 03458
   http://www.odysseymagazine.com
   For children with an interest in astronomy and space science; quality photography and illustrations

Teens, Grades 6+

Teen Newsweek
   Weekly Reader Corporation, 2000 First Stamford Place, P.O. Box 120023, Stamford, CT 06912-0023
   http://www.weeklyreader.com/teennewsweek
   A current events magazine for teens
Time for Kids
   1271 6th Avenue, 25th Floor, New York, NY 10020
   http://www.timeforkids.com
   A current events magazine
Music Alive
   Cherry Lane Magazines, P.O. Box 53063, Boulder, CO 80322
   http://www.cherrylane.com
   Music interests for adolescent students
Teen People
   3000 University Center Blvd., Tampa, FL 33612
   http://www.teenpeople.com
   Uses the "People magazine" format
Black Beat
   Sterling/Macfadden, Dept. 2000, 66 West Merrick Road, Valley Stream, NY 11580
   http://www.blackbeat.com
   A current magazine for the African American teen
Latingirl
   70 Hudson Street, 5th Floor, Hoboken, NJ 07030
   http://www.latingirlmag.com
   A current magazine for the Latina teen
Footsteps
   Cobblestone Publishing, 30 Grove Street, Suite C, Peterborough, NH 03458
   http://www.footstepsmagazine.com
   Exciting magazine that celebrates the heritage of African Americans and explores their contributions to our culture
Twist
   270 Sylvan Avenue, Englewood Cliffs, NJ 07632
   http://www.twistmagazine.com
   Advice and information for teens

References

Armbruster, B. B. (1996). Considerate texts. In D. Lapp, J. Flood, & N. Farnan (Eds.), *Content area reading and learning: Instructional strategies* (pp. 47–57). Needham Heights, MA: Allyn and Bacon.

Berliner, D. C., & Biddle, B. J. (1995). *The manufactured crisis: Myths, fraud, and the attack on America's public schools.* Reading, MA: Addison-Wesley.

Cullinan, B. E. (1989). *Literature and the child* (2nd ed.). San Diego, CA: Harcourt Brace Jovanovich.

Diamondstone, J. V. (2000). A view of what a text can be: Encouraging novel perspectives. *Journal of Adolescent and Adult Literacy, 44,* 108–120.

Dillner, M. (1993/1994). Using hypermedia to enhance content-area instruction. *Journal of Reading, 37,* 260–270.

Dahl, K. L., & Farnan, N. (1998). *Children's writing: Perspectives from research.* Newark, DE: International Reading Association and National Reading Conference.

Eisenman, R., Girdner, E., Burroughs, R., & Routman, M. (1993). Attitudes of Mississippi college students toward David Duke before and after seeing the film "Who Is David Duke?" *Adolescence, 28,* 527–532.

Fawson, P. C., & Reutzel, D. R. (2000). But I only have a basal: Implementing guided reading in the early grades. *The Reading Teacher, 54,* 84–97.

Fisher, D., Flood, J., & Lapp, D. (1999). Literature in the literacy process. In L. Gambrell, L. Morrow, S. Neuman, & M. Pressley (Eds.), *Best practices in literacy instruction* (pp. 119–135). New York: Guilford.

Fisher, D., Lapp, D., & Flood, J. (2000). How is technology really used for literacy instruction in elementary and middle school classrooms. *NRC Yearbook, 49,* 464–476.

Flood, J., Heath, S. B., & Lapp, D. (Eds.). (1997). *Handbook of research on teaching literacy through the communicative and visual arts.* New York: Macmillan.

Flood, J., Lapp, D., & Bayles-Martin, D. (2000). Vision possible: The role of visual media in literacy education. In M. A. Gallego & S. Hollingsworth (Eds.), *What counts as literacy: Challenging the school standard* (pp. 62–84). New York: Teachers College Press.

Guthrie, J. T. (1996). Educational contexts for engagement in literacy. *The Reading Teacher, 49,* 432–445.

Haas, C. (1989). Does the medium make a difference: Two studies of writing with computers. *Human Computer Interaction, 4,* 149–169.

Hoffman, J. V., McCarthy, S. J., Elliott, B., Bayles, D. L., Price, D. P., Ferree, A., & Abbott, J. A. (1998). The literature-based basals in first grade classrooms: Savior, Satan, or same-old, same-old? *Reading Research Quarterly, 33,* 168–197.

Hudak-Huelbig, E., Keyes, M. L., McClure, A., & Stellingwerf, E. (1991). *You can't judge a basal by its cover: A comparison of seven basal reader series.* Unpublished report, William Paterson College, Wayne, NJ.

Irvin, J. L. (1998). *Reading and the middle school student* (2nd ed.). Boston: Allyn and Bacon.

Lapp, D., Flood, J., & Fisher, D. (1999). Intermediality: How the use of multiple media enhances learning. *The Reading Teacher, 52,* 776–780.

Mayer, R. (1990). When is an illustration worth ten thousand words? *Journal of Educational Psychology, 82,* 715–726.

McQuillan, J. (1998). *The literacy crisis: False claims, real solutions.* Portsmouth, NH: Heinemann.

Odenthal, J. M. (1992). *The effect of a computer-based writing program on the attitudes and performance of students acquiring English as a second language.* Unpublished doctoral dissertation, San Diego State University and Claremont Graduate University, San Diego, CA.

Owston, P. D., Murphy, S., & Wideman, H. H. (1991). On and off computer writing of eighth grade students experienced in word processing. *Computers in the Schools, 8,* 67–87.

Pailliotet, A. W., Semali, L., Rodenberg, R. K., Giles, J. K., & Macaul, S. L. (2000). Intermediality: Bridge to critical media literacy. *The Reading Teacher, 54,* 208–219.

Roser, N., & Martinez, M. (Eds.). (1995). *Book talk and beyond: Children and teachers respond to literature.* Newark, DE: International Reading Association.

Russell, R. G. (1991, April). *A meta-analysis of word processing and attitudes and the impact on the quality of writing.* Paper presented at the Annual Meeting of the American Educational Research Association, Chicago, IL.

Strickland, D., Walmsley, S., Bronk, G., & Weiss, K. (1994). *School book clubs and literacy development: A descriptive study* (Report No. 2.22). Albany: State University of New York, National Research Center on Literacy Teaching and Learning.

Valerio, P. C., & Readence, J. E. (2000). Promoting independent study strategies in classrooms of the twenty-first century. In K. D. Wood & T. S. Dickinson (Eds.), *Promoting literacy in grades 4–9* (pp. 331–343). Boston: Allyn and Bacon.

Wade, S. E., & Moje, E. B. (2000). The role of text in classroom learning. In M. L. Kamil, P. Mosenthal, P. D. Pearson, & R. Barr (Eds.), *Handbook of reading research* (Vol. 3, pp. 609–627). Mahwah, NJ: Erlbaum.

CHAPTER EIGHT

Observing the Reading Teacher: Teacher Evaluation and Growth

Bill Harp

In the time that has passed since the publication of the previous edition of this book, unprecedented changes have taken place in the field of reading education. Never in my career have I seen such scrutiny of literacy practices, such criticism of teachers, and such politicization of education. The national media have given thorough coverage to limited improvement in performance on the National Assessment of Educational Progress, lowered reading test scores in California, and the cries of politicians of all stripes to improve teaching and learn-ing. We have witnessed the legislation of cur-riculum, a national movement toward standards-based education, and calls for changes in teacher education. On the topic of how children learn to read, some have even tried to narrowly define what we consider acceptably "scientific" research (Taylor, 1998). There are many who paint a dark picture of the work we do in bringing children to literacy.

All of this means that literacy leaders must do an ever better job of making sure that learn-ers are becoming readers in the best learning environments we can possibly create. One important way to achieve this goal is for reading specialists, principals, and language arts supervisors to be present in classrooms, helping reading teachers improve their work from kindergarten through Grade 12. Our observations of teachers, the feedback we give them, and the collaboration we offer in improving instruction are keys to the growth of reading teachers.

This chapter addresses the following:

- Key assumptions that inform supervision
- Trends in supervisory practice
- Guidelines for thinking about teacher observation
- A suggested sequence of evaluation activities

Let's begin with an examination of some of the key assumptions and understandings that inform our practice as reading supervisors.

Assumptions That Inform Supervision

My work with reading teachers in hundreds of classrooms has led me to a set of assumptions and understandings about reading teachers that should inform supervision of these professionals. These understandings are:

1. Teachers make clear decisions about what drives the curriculum. In some schools, the curriculum is driven by state-mandated, high-stakes tests. In some schools, the instructional materials drive the curriculum. In some schools, instructional decisions are based on the needs of the learners. I have come to believe that the most effective reading teachers base instructional decisions on the needs of learners, with an eye toward mandated tests, materials, and standards.
2. Teachers of reading are also teachers of writing. Reading and writing are inverse processes that are best taught together.
3. The reading teacher is a knowledgeable teacher whose instruction is informed by a solid knowledge base. This knowledge base is ever growing and changing, because the reading teacher is a continual researcher and learner.

4. A well-defined philosophical base guides the reading teacher's instruction. The teacher's philosophy is the filter through which all instructional decisions are made.

Trends in Supervisory Practice

In addition to the personal understandings described above, there are clearly some trends in supervisory practice that can further inform our observation of reading teachers. Three trends examined here are portfolios, observation as ethnography, and peer observation and reflection.

Portfolios

One trend in supervisory practice is the use of teaching portfolios to document the work of reading teachers in school settings from elementary school through high school. Portfolios have been proven to be an effective method to encourage teachers to evaluate their abilities and enhance their skills (Campbell, Cignetti, Melenyzer, Nettles, & Wyman, 1997). Portfolios contain written documentation of planning, curriculum, organization and presentation methods, interactions with students and parents, assessment methods and data, classroom management approaches, and professional development activities (Perkins & Galfer, 1998). The collection of work samples, often a part of building a portfolio, has proven to be an effective evaluation tool (McConney, Schalock, & Schalock, 1998). Conversations about portfolio entries have proven to offer opportunities for enhancing teaching expertise as teachers develop from beginners to experts (Bartell, Kaye, & Morin, 1998).

Observation as Ethnography

Our observation of reading teachers may also be informed by the work of those who are attempting to take a more ethnographic stance toward supervision. The supervisor or observer views the literacy classroom as a complex culture in which the participant-observer is focused on the actions of learners. Steve Flores (1999), a principal in California, says his understandings of ethnography have caused him to rethink his observational style when he visits classrooms. He has shifted his focus from the teacher to the actions of the students in the classroom. He particularly focuses on looking and listening for evidence of previously learned skills, emerging skills, and where the community of learners is headed.

Brian Cambourne (2000) has been observing literacy classrooms as an ethnographer for nine years. He offers the following thoughts:

> These classrooms were very complex settings. I don't think I'll ever fully understand this complexity, nor will I understand how teachers manage to orchestrate it in ways that promote productive literacy learning. The best I can do is provide some preliminary insights to the nature of this complexity. (p. 512)

Cambourne asserts that the best way to understand the complexity of the literacy classroom is to make sense of the following aspects of classrooms he has observed.

1. The inanimate physical paraphernalia present in the setting.
2. The human behaviors that take place in the midst of these paraphernalia.
3. The programs (i.e., routines and events) that typically occur within settings.

The central message in Cambourne's work is that while teachers skillfully manipulate the paraphernalia of teaching reading, the most powerful element that the teacher manipulates is the discourse that pervades the classroom. Of this discourse Cambourne (2000) says:

> The discourse features I identified could be grouped under a general heading that I described as strong 'pro-reading/pro-writing' ethos. By *ethos* I mean something that is akin to climate, atmosphere, tone, and other such terms. Each one describes a rather ubiquitous, ethereal 'thing' that pervades all that takes place in the setting but is not immediately obvious to observers and is difficult to capture in language, except in broad terms. One only becomes aware of it after prolonged immersion in the settings where it occurs. (p. 513)

We need to be certain that our observations of the reading teacher assess this climate.

Peer Observation and Reflection

Among the trends in staff development are peer observation and reflection. In a study of peer observation techniques in both elementary and secondary settings, Munson (1998) reported that teachers liked the feedback and felt more comfortable with peer rather than administrator observation. Perhaps peer observation could be coupled with supervisor observation in order to involve more persons in faculty development efforts.

Written and oral reflections on portfolio contents coupled with peer and supervisor conferences have been effective in helping teachers assess progress they have made toward stated goals (Andrejko, 1998). One school's faculty members so fully believed in the value of reflection and collaboration that they divided faculty into three groups. Each group undergoes an evaluation year, a learning development year (with reduced teaching load), and a consolidation and practice year (Zederayko & Ward, 1999).

Guidelines for Thinking About Teacher Observation

In observing the work of reading teachers, we need to focus more on the learners than on the teacher. We need to examine the paraphernalia, the human behavior, and the routines and events that take place in the classroom, with particular attention to the nature of the discourse—discourse that establishes an atmosphere, a climate, and a tone that is pro-reading and pro-writing. We need to engage teachers in a supervisory, faculty development process in a variety of ways, including peer observations, portfolios, and reflection. In order to have teachers involved in the process, we need to give them choices, focus on activities, and strive for authenticity.

Choice

Reading teachers must be permitted to exercise choice in the evaluation process. Ownership of one's own growth as a teacher invites (if not requires) reflective practice. Reflective practice leads to the teacher identifying his or her next learning step—the next step of personal growth to take. The evaluation process for reading teachers must offer them opportunities for choice in the direction and scope of changes in practice.

Choice is critical to the evaluation process in another dimension as well. We have recognized that if learners are to take ownership of their learning, they must be empowered to evaluate their own learning, based on work samples they help choose, and against criteria they help establish (Harp & Brewer, 1996). The evaluation process for reading teachers must offer them opportunities to evaluate their own work, to offer samples of their work, and to help identify the criteria against which their work will be evaluated.

Yet another aspect of choice comes into play in the evaluation of the reading teacher. Reading teachers are becoming more and more skillful at looking at their learners as readers and writers. In the process, reading teachers are beginning to ask their own research questions. The teacher as researcher is becoming accepted practice. As researchers, reading teachers behave reflectively: asking questions, seeking answers, and contributing to educational theory and practice. Their classrooms become teaching and learning laboratories. The questions the reading teacher identifies for research reflect another aspect of choice in the professional life of the teacher. The evaluation process for the reading teacher should examine the choices a teacher makes as a researcher. Such choices include the types of research questions asked and the ways in which the reading teacher uses the research data.

Activities

The role of the reading teacher is to create, in collaboration with the learner, the environment that encourages active reading, researching, experimenting, writing, thinking, speaking, and investigating. In evaluating the work of the reading teacher, attention must be focused on the nature of the activities he or she creates for learners. Two issues seem critical here: the pro-reading and pro-writing atmosphere the teacher creates, and the degree to which the lessons the teacher designs reflect current understandings about best practice. You will be able to evaluate the atmosphere in the room by carefully observing and listening, engaging learners in dialogue, and being present in that culture for extended periods of time. Of particular importance is your attention to the discourse between teacher and learners.

Classroom Discourse. Cambourne (2000) identified six basic expectation messages being constantly communicated in the classrooms he observed. You may wish to consider these (paraphrased here) in examining the discourse in classrooms you observe. As you gain experience in examining the culture and discourse within a classroom, you will no doubt develop your own criteria. The six themes identified here are offered as a starting point for you.

1. Becoming an effective user of literacy is extremely worthwhile and will further the purposes of your life.
2. All members of this learning community are capable of becoming readers and writers. No one can fail.
3. The best way to learn is to share and discuss your learning problems with others, take risks, make approximations, and reflect on the feedback you get.
4. All statements, comments, and judgments must be justified using plausible and sensible arguments and examples.
5. It is safe to try things out in this setting.
6. You must take responsibility for your own learning. Take the lessons and demonstrations of others and make them your own.

Let's now turn our attention to identifying best practices and observing the lessons taught by the reading teacher.

An Observation Framework. The Central Dauphin School District in Harrisburg, Pennsylvania, has developed a Reading Lesson Observation Framework (RLOF) that can serve as a model for you in helping your district develop such a framework (Henk, Moore, Marinak, & Tomasetti, 2000). Development of the framework began with the staff agreeing upon goals for the literacy program and then developing shared understandings of effective literacy practices. This was accomplished by careful study of the research literature, reflection, and dialogue among all of the stakeholders. Once effective practices had been agreed upon, teams of teachers were engaged in creating the classroom observation framework consistent with these practices. Of the Central Dauphin framework, the authors reporting on the process said:

> Knowing that effective change requires years of ongoing staff development and support, the RLOF remains a working document within the district. Teachers use it as a basic guidepost for their reading instruction. They recognize that the framework represents an organized set of recommended principles and practices that can lead to better reading instruction for their children. They also realize that it serves as a blueprint for their continued professional development since they can decide which components and aspects will be addressed in the future. (p. 363)

The Reading Lesson Observation Framework is included in Figure 8.1 in the hope that you will use it as a springboard for discussion and development of an observation framework designed or adapted by the teachers with whom you work. Two things are critical here. The framework must represent agreed upon "best practices in reading," and there must be opportunity for teacher choice in what is included and how it is used. Please note that within the Classroom Climate component of the RLOF, consideration is given to the pro-reading/pro-writing element. Also, within each component, space is created for teachers to add elements.

Authenticity

I frequently tell reading teachers in my classes that I want them to orchestrate *authentic* learning activities for children. By this I mean that I want them to have children read and write for real, communicative reasons. For example, I would want to evaluate children's spelling ability by their spelling performance in creating connected text, not just with a spelling-list test on Friday. In other words, I urge the evaluation of children's literacy learning by observing them as they engage in real reading and writing activities.

I believe this notion of authenticity may be applied to evaluating the work of the reading teacher.

An authentic evaluation of the reading teacher would not look only at the test scores of his or her students. Instead, we would observe this teacher in the learning environment to see how skillfully the environment is created and managed to support the literacy learning of students. We would examine the interactions with students to see how effective the teacher is in coaching developing readers and writers. We would observe planned and impromptu lessons as well as examine the products and test scores produced by the students. Our observations would consist of a sequence of activities designed to learn as much as possible about the teacher's work and the children's learning.

Suggested Sequence of Evaluation Activities

The following is a set of activities in which the teacher and supervisor might engage in the evaluation process. The list is presented here only as one possibility, not as a definitive prescription. The activities should be agreed upon in advance and designed to best meet the needs of the teacher. The five-step process outlined here includes creating a professional portfolio, conducting an environmental scan, writing a self-assessment and goals, conducting a reading lesson observation, and engaging in an evaluation conference.

Step One: Professional Portfolio

The reading/writing teacher assembles a portfolio to document strengths and draw conclusions about his or her next learning goal. The teacher working with emergent readers might include running records, developmental reading checklists, developmental writing checklists, samples of children's writing, copies of the Reading Lesson Observation Framework collected over time, and summaries of anecdotal records.

Teachers working with developing and fluent readers in Grades 3–5 might include many of the

THE READING LESSON OBSERVATION FORMAT

Teacher _____ Observer _____

School Year _____ Date of Observation _____ Observation # _____

Observation occurred: Before reading _____ During reading _____ After reading _____

Component I. Classroom Climate   O   C   R   N

A. Many different types of authentic reading materials such as magazines, newspapers, novels, and nonfiction works are displayed and are available for children to read independently. ☐ ☐ ☐ ☐

B. The classroom has a reading area such as a corner or classroom library where children are encouraged to go to read for enjoyment. ☐ ☐ ☐ ☐

C. An area is available for small-group reading instruction. ☐ ☐ ☐ ☐

D. Active participation and social interaction are integral parts of reading instruction in this classroom. ☐ ☐ ☐ ☐

E. The classroom environment indicates that reading and writing are valued and actively promoted (e.g., purposeful writing is displayed, journals are maintained, Word Walls are used, book talks and read-alouds by teacher occur regularly). ☐ ☐ ☐ ☐

F. ☐ ☐ ☐ ☐

G. ☐ ☐ ☐ ☐

Component II. Pre-reading Phase   O   C   R   N

A. During the pre-reading discussion, the teacher asked the children to preview the text by having them read the title of the selection, look at the illustrations, and then discuss the possible contents of the text. ☐ ☐ ☐ ☐

B. Children were encouraged to activate their background knowledge through the use of K-W-L charts, webs, anticipation guides, etc. ☐ ☐ ☐ ☐

C. By generating a discussion about the topic before reading the selection, the teacher created an interest in the reading. ☐ ☐ ☐ ☐

D. The teacher introduced and discussed the new vocabulary words in a meaningful context, focusing on those new words that were central to the understanding of the story. ☐ ☐ ☐ ☐

E. The children were encouraged to state or write predictions related to the topic of the reading selection. ☐ ☐ ☐ ☐

F. Before reading occurred, the teacher helped the children identify the type of material that was to be read to determine what their purpose should be for reading it. ☐ ☐ ☐ ☐

G. The objective for the reading lesson was clearly identified for the children, along with how the objective related to previous lessons. ☐ ☐ ☐ ☐

H. The teacher continually assessed children's prereading discussion and made appropriate adjustments. ☐ ☐ ☐ ☐

I. ☐ ☐ ☐ ☐

J. ☐ ☐ ☐ ☐

(continued)

Figure 8.1

THE READING LESSON OBSERVATION FORMAT *(continued)*

Component III. Guided Reading Phase

	O	C	R	N
A. At appropriate points during the reading of the selection, the children were asked to evaluate their initial predictions.	☐	☐	☐	☐
B. The children were asked to identify or read aloud portions of text that confirmed or disproved predictions they had made about the selection.	☐	☐	☐	☐
C. The comprehension discussion focused on the purposes that were established for reading the selection.	☐	☐	☐	☐
D. An appropriate mix of factual and higher-level thinking questions were incorporated into the comprehension discussion.	☐	☐	☐	☐
E. During the reading lesson, the teacher modeled fluent reading and then encouraged the children to read fluently and with expression.	☐	☐	☐	☐
F. The teacher encouraged the children to adjust their reading rate to fit the material.	☐	☐	☐	☐
G. The teacher monitored the children and gave proper assistance and feedback while they read or completed practice activities.	☐	☐	☐	☐
H. The teacher modeled and encouraged the use of new vocabulary during the discussion.	☐	☐	☐	☐
I. The children were encouraged to use a variety of word study strategies (e.g., words within words, context, syllabication) to decipher the meaning of unknown words as appropriate.	☐	☐	☐	☐
J. The children were encouraged to use appropriate comprehension monitoring and fix-up strategies during reading (e.g., paraphrasing, rereading, using context, asking for help).	☐	☐	☐	☐
K. The teacher reminded the children to make use of their knowledge of text structure (e.g., fictional story grammar, nonfiction text structures).	☐	☐	☐	☐
L. The teacher periodically assessed the children's ability to monitor meaning.	☐	☐	☐	☐
M.	☐	☐	☐	☐
N.	☐	☐	☐	☐

Component IV. Post-reading Phase

	O	C	R	N
A. During the post-reading discussion, the children were asked to read aloud sections of the text that substantiated answers to questions and confirmed or disproved predictions they had made about the selection.	☐	☐	☐	☐
B. The teacher asked the children to retell the material they had read, concentrating on major events or concepts.	☐	☐	☐	☐
C. The children were asked to explain their opinion and critical judgments.	☐	☐	☐	☐
D. The teacher had the children provide a written response to the reading (e.g., written retelling, written summarization, written evaluation).	☐	☐	☐	☐
E. Children were encouraged to use new vocabulary in written responses. Examples and modeling were provided by the teacher.	☐	☐	☐	☐
F. Writing was used as a natural extension of reading tasks.	☐	☐	☐	☐
G. The teacher continually monitored children's comprehension and provided appropriate feedback.	☐	☐	☐	☐
H.	☐	☐	☐	☐
I.	☐	☐	☐	☐

(continued)

Figure 8.1 *(continued)*

THE READING LESSON OBSERVATION FORMAT *(continued)*

	O	C	R	N
Component V. Skill and Strategy Instruction				
A. The teacher provided a clear explanation about the structure of the skill or strategy to be learned and described when and how it could be used.	☐	☐	☐	☐
B. The teacher modeled the use of the skill or strategy so children were able to see how it would be used in an appropriate situation.	☐	☐	☐	☐
C. Any direct teaching of a phonemic element was immediately followed by children using the skill in a meaningful context.	☐	☐	☐	☐
D. Explicit skill and strategy instruction was provided and applied in the context of the reading selection.	☐	☐	☐	☐
E. The children were encouraged to use before, during, and after reading strategies as appropriate.	☐	☐	☐	☐
F. Reading skill and strategy instruction moved children toward independent use through scaffolding.	☐	☐	☐	☐
G.	☐	☐	☐	☐
H.	☐	☐	☐	☐

	O	C	R	N
Component VI. Materials and Tasks of the Lesson				
A. The selections used for the reading lesson were appropriate for children of this ability and grade level.	☐	☐	☐	☐
B. The reading materials represented authentic types of texts.	☐	☐	☐	☐
C. Reading materials and tasks reflected a sensitivity to the diverse learning needs of the children.	☐	☐	☐	☐
D. The amount and type of independent work was appropriate for the level of the children and instructional goals it was designed to achieve.	☐	☐	☐	☐
E. Independent work often contained open-ended questions that encouraged children to enhance and extend their understanding of the selection.	☐	☐	☐	☐
F. The literacy tasks the children were asked to perform during the lesson were meaningful and relevant.	☐	☐	☐	☐
G. The children engaged in various modes of reading during the lesson (e.g., silent, oral, guided, shared).	☐	☐	☐	☐
H. The teacher provided opportunities for the children to read for enjoyment.	☐	☐	☐	☐
I. Children were encouraged to respond personally or creatively to the reading material.	☐	☐	☐	☐
J. A balance existed in the reading lesson between teacher-initiated and student-initiated activities.	☐	☐	☐	☐
K. Reading materials and tasks were organized around themes when appropriate.	☐	☐	☐	☐
L.	☐	☐	☐	☐
M.	☐	☐	☐	☐

(continued)

Figure 8.1 *(continued)*

THE READING LESSON OBSERVATION FORMAT *(continued)*

Component VII. Teacher Practices	O	C	R	N
A. The teacher focused on reading as a meaningful process.	☐	☐	☐	☐
B. The instructional techniques used by the teacher and the ways they were executed reflected an awareness of recommended practices.	☐	☐	☐	☐
C. Children were grouped appropriately and flexibly.	☐	☐	☐	☐
D. The teacher's management of the reading lesson provided for active student engagement.	☐	☐	☐	☐
E. The pace and flow of the various phases of the reading lesson represented an effective use of time.	☐	☐	☐	☐
F. The teacher's instruction was sensitive to the diversity of children's experiences and their social, cultural, ethnic, and linguistic needs.	☐	☐	☐	☐
G. The teacher actively promoted the integration of the language arts in this lesson.	☐	☐	☐	☐
H. The teacher encouraged the children to take informed risks and promoted safe failure.	☐	☐	☐	☐
I. The teacher's conferences with children were timely, focused, and positive in nature.	☐	☐	☐	☐
J. Authentic assessment practices were used in this lesson.	☐	☐	☐	☐
K. The teacher's planned goals, actual instruction, and assessment practices were aligned.	☐	☐	☐	☐
L.	☐	☐	☐	☐
M.	☐	☐	☐	☐

Key to Checklist

O = Observed	This component was observed and was judged to be of *satisfactory* quality.
C = Commendation	This component was observed and was judged to be of *very high* quality.
R = Recommendation	This component either was not observed or was judged to be of *unsatisfactory* quality.
N = Not applicable	This component was *not observed* because it was not appropriate for the lesson.

Figure 8.1 *(continued)*

items listed above. Additional items might be samples of work produced by children as part of themes or integrated units, records of genres children have read and written, and documentation of children's progress in meeting the challenges of content-area reading, including research using print and electronic media.

At the middle school level, teachers might include many of the items listed for upper elementary teachers. Teachers working in remedial reading settings would probably include only an adapted version of the Reading Lesson Observation Framework.

Teachers working with students beyond the middle school level might include many of the items listed above and a variety of critical and analytic pieces from across a wide range of genres, well-researched term papers, and pieces documenting highly advanced use of computer and electronic media. An adaptation of the Reading Lesson Observation Framework would be used only in remedial settings. Beyond the emergent reader stage, running records would be a good way to document work with struggling readers.

Step Two: Environmental Scan

The teacher joins the supervisor in doing an environmental scan of the classroom, documenting evidence of conditions that promote literacy. These conditions should be determined in advance at the district or school level consistent with philosophy and curriculum goals. The examples included here are drawn from the work of Cambourne (1988), who identified conditions conducive to literacy learning. His work here is fast becoming considered classic. Cambourne helped us understand that the conditions that foster learning oral language and the conditions that facilitate coming to fluency in reading and writing are the same. The conditions that exist to facilitate oral language learning must exist to promote fluency in literacy. I suggest that we draw from these conditions in conducting an environmental scan.

At the elementary school level, all seven of Cambourne's conditions (described below) should be included in the scan, as in the form shown in Figure 8.2.

1. Immersion. As learners of oral language, we were constantly immersed in language. Many parents talk to children who are in the womb. We assign intentionality to the gurgles of newborns. Just as these very young children are immersed in oral language, so must emergent and developing readers be immersed in texts of all kinds. Evidence of the existence of this condition would be a classroom in which print is used for a variety of purposes: informing, persuading, directing, controlling. The classroom library is well stocked, including the publications of class members.

2. Demonstration. Each time the oral language learner was immersed in language, the use of language was demonstrated. Literacy learners need many demonstrations of how texts are constructed and used. Children need to be read to many times during the day, not just for 15 minutes after lunch, and it seems easy for teachers

to demonstrate reading. However, teachers seem to have difficulty demonstrating writing. This is probably because we have received so few demonstrations of writing ourselves. By demonstrating writing, I mean actually showing children how you think through and execute the process of writing a piece.

Cambourne makes the critical point that unless children are engaged with immersion and demonstration, little learning will occur. Engagement implies that the learner is convinced that he or she is a potential doer or performer of the demonstrations, that learning these things will be beneficial, and that this new learning can be tried out without fear of harm if the performance is not "correct."

3. Expectation. Parents of young children fully expect that their toddlers will make tremendous leaps toward oral language fluency, and that they will accomplish the task within a few years. Rarely do parents (barring unfortunate circumstances) worry about their children coming to fluency in oral language. Why, then, do some parents respond so negatively when young children spell a word the best they can at the time or make a mistake when reading orally? Teachers of reading must have high expectations that children will learn to read and write, and at the same time they must help parents (and others) value the importance of successive approximations.

4. Responsibility. Parents are often grateful that they do not have to teach their children to speak. In fact, in coming to fluency in oral language, children take responsibility for their own learning. They appreciate the need for clear, useful communication and modify their language to maximize its use. Children can also be responsible for learning to read and write. We need to help children decide what their next learning steps are to be and how they will take them.

5. Use. As oral language users, we practiced our control over language in very real ways—to get things done and to get our needs met. In the reading/writing classroom, children need many daily opportunities to practice reading and writing in ways that are real, communicative, and

ENVIRONMENTAL SCAN FOR ELEMENTARY LEVEL	
Condition	Classroom Evidence
Immersion	—Classroom library includes books from a variety of genres, including student publications. —Teacher uses print to inform, for example, in bulletin boards, classroom displays, and student work.
Demonstration	—Teacher conducts read aloud for 20 minutes each day. —Teacher models the process used to write a narrative story about a personal experience.
Expectation	—Teacher has students reading and writing daily, and communicates specific expectations for parents to model.
Responsibility	—Teacher uses self-assessment forms to help students determine their next steps for reading and responding to their literature books.
Use	—Students read their literature books 10–20 minutes each day.
Approximation	—Teacher communicates to students ways to use their mistakes as opportunities for learning.
Response	—Teacher gives feedback regularly that is relevant, appropriate, timely, and non-threatening.
Pro-reading/pro-writing	—Numerous children's writings are prominently displayed in the classroom. —Browsing boxes for independent reading and an author's chair are part of the classroom.

Figure 8.2

authentic. Probably no one reading this text has, as an adult, drawn three rectangles on a piece of paper and then practiced addressing envelopes in the rectangles. Why? This is a truly inauthentic exercise. We address envelopes for the purpose of mailing something. Children need non-artificial ways to use reading and writing.

6. Approximation. In most families, certain words or phrases that a youngster approximated were deemed so charming, they have become part of that family's vocabulary. When the 2½-year-old approached with a plate at a 45-degree angle and said, "Mommy, cookies all gonded, all

gonded," Mommy didn't reply with, "Now, honey, that isn't the way we would say that." Mommy responded to the communication and probably enjoyed the child's approximation of standard speech. Why is it that parents who were so charmed by approximation in oral language are so disturbed by their children's approximation in reading and writing? Mistakes are a natural, developmental part of all learning. Knowledgeable teachers of reading see the mistakes as road signs that lead to better understanding of the developing reader and writer. Such teachers are very careful about how they respond to approximations.

7. Response. Cambourne asserts that learners must receive feedback on their attempts at reading and writing that is relevant, appropriate, timely, readily available, nonthreatening, and with no strings attached. We must help children understand that mistakes are a natural part of learning, that mistakes help them define what they need to learn next. The responses parents and teachers make to the child's efforts in literacy are critical factors in success.

The elements in the environmental scan illustrated in Figure 8.2 are appropriate for the early elementary years. From third grade on, the nature of the evidence of approximation changes as children are approximating less with increased fluency in both reading and writing. There probably are fewer teacher demonstrations of reading and writing, and possibly more demonstrations by children. Arguably, the nature of responses from the teacher changes.

At the middle school and high school levels, the environmental scan should include expectation, responsibility, and use as defined above. At all grade levels, we should be looking for evidence in the classroom of a pro-reading/pro-writing climate by the nature of the discourse. We should also seek evidence that the six expectation themes we described in the section on classroom discourse are present.

Step Three: A Written Self-Assessment

The reading/writing teacher is asked to write a self-assessment of strengths as a teacher and to identify desired next learning goals as a professional. This self-assessment and goals statement should be included in the portfolio the teacher assembles in Step One.

Step Four: The Reading Lesson Observation Framework

The final aspect of observing the work of the reading teacher is the use of the Reading Lesson Observation Framework. Ideally, the framework designed in your school or district would be used. Teachers would have the choice of getting this feedback from a grade level colleague, a peer mentor, the principal, or another supervisor. If the framework is being used several times throughout the school year, the teacher could select one from the beginning, middle, and end of the year to include in the portfolio, rather than having the framework used as a separate step in the evaluation process.

Step Five: The Observation Conference

Here the teacher and supervisor meet to explore the contents of the portfolio, to review the data from the environmental scan and lesson observation, and to agree on the teacher's strengths, next learning goals, and a plan for meeting those goals.

Conclusion

Throughout this discussion, I have stressed the importance of viewing supervision as a process of growth and evaluation. This process must be informed by a set of solid assumptions and consistent with recent trends in supervisory practice. I encourage you to take an ethnographic stance to supervision, paying close attention to the classroom environment and the interactions of reading teacher and students. My hope is that this shift in supervisory practices will result in creating the best learning environments for learners to become readers.

References

Andrejko, L. (1998). The case for the teacher portfolio. *Journal of Staff Development, 19*(1), 45–48.

Bartell, C. A., Kaye, C., & Morin, J. A. (1998). Portfolio conversation: A mentored journey. *Teacher Education Quarterly, 25*(2), 129–139.

Cambourne, B. (1988). *The whole story: Natural learning and the acquisition of literacy in the classroom.* Auckland, New Zealand: Ashton Scholastic Limited.

Cambourne, B. (2000). Conditions for literacy learning: Observing literacy learning in elementary classrooms: Nine years of classroom anthropology. *The Reading Teacher, 53,* 512–515.

Campbell, D. M., Cignetti, P. B., Melenyzer, B. J., Nettles, D. H., & Wyman, R. M. (1997). *How to develop a professional portfolio: A manual for teachers.* Boston: Allyn & Bacon.

Flores, S. (1999). Classrooms as cultures from a principal's perspective. *Primary Voices K–6, 7*(3), 54–55.

Harp, B., & Brewer, J. A. (1996). *Reading and writing: Teaching for the connections.* Fort Worth, TX: Harcourt Brace.

Henk, W. A., Moore, J. C., Marinak, B. A., & Tomasetti, B. W. (2000). A reading lesson observation framework for elementary teachers, principals, and literacy supervisors. *The Reading Teacher, 53,* 358–369.

McConney, A. A., Schalock, M. D., & Schalock, H. D. (1998). Focusing improvement and quality assurance: Work samples as authentic performance measures of prospective teachers' effectiveness. *Journal of Personnel Evaluation in Education, 11,* 343–363.

Munson, B. R. (1998). Peers observing peers: The better way to observe teachers. *Contemporary Education, 69*(2), 108–110.

Perkins, P. G., & Galfer, J. L. (1998). Producing teacher/staff portfolios: A method for effective evaluation. *Catalyst for Change, 28*(1), 17–20.

Taylor, D. (1998). *Beginning to read and the spin doctors of science: The political campaign to change America's mind about how children learn to read.* Urbana, IL: National Council of Teachers of English.

Zederayko, G. E., & Ward, K. (1999). Schools as learning organizations: How can the work of teachers be both learning and teaching? *NASSP Bulletin, 83*(1), 35–45.

CHAPTER NINE

Professional Development

JoAnne L. Vacca and Maryann Mraz

Professional development is undergoing transition as teachers engage in practice-centered research and collaborate with administrators. Those responsible for overseeing reading programs exert considerable influence on professional development even as changes occur in their own roles. This chapter discusses:

◆ The shifting role of administrators
◆ Strategies to support change (with portfolios and collaboration)
◆ Guidelines for professional development programs

The Shifting Role of the Administrator

The primary role of administrators (principals, reading supervisors, staff developers) is one of enabling teachers to talk about teaching and to create and use knowledge about their own teaching. Instead of handpicking a speaker for inservice sessions, "it is important that teachers, administrators, and policy makers become aware of new and broader conceptions of professional development" (Lieberman, 1995, p. 591). This, in turn, should lead to greater, more meaningful, involvement of administrators and teachers in the entire professional development program initiative.

The administrator must be an active and informed participant in the professional development team. Administrators should be able to meaningfully discuss educational research and theory with other team members and to model teaching practice based on this research and theory (George, Moley, & Ogle, 1992). The administrator should be committed to the program and eager to collect data, do observations, experiment with new strategies, and reflect with the rest of the staff on what is happening in the classroom. The administrator must sustain change through his or her continuing presence in workshops, immediate response to teachers' concerns, and spirit of celebration over successes (Courtland, 1992).

Administrators can be supportive of professional development in many ways. One resource that is in short supply for teachers is time. Teachers need time during the school day to meet and talk about their students, their schools, and their visions of education (Murphy, 1993). Careful arrangement of planning times may facilitate the formation of study groups or planning groups among the faculty. Part of weekly staff meetings can be set aside for sharing questions, observations, and concerns about a staff project (Clyde, Condon, Daniel, & Sommer, 1993). Articles relevant to classroom practice, such as the action research projects described in *Teachers Are Researchers* (Patterson, Santa, Short, & Smith, 1993), can be read by all faculty members and discussed.

A systemwide commitment to change could be demonstrated by support for release time, reimbursement for conferences, and establishment of local workshops. Teaching materials to support literacy, access to technology resources, a video library of model lessons, and a print library for teacher study on literacy issues also illustrate the administration's commitment to change. Growth-oriented evaluations, where teachers can choose to set personal or team goals for the year and work on these goals without fear of punishment if goals are not met, provide a new level of understanding for teachers' professional development (Duke, 1993).

Just as students must be partners in the construction of their own knowledge, so must teachers have a voice in both the process and the content of professional development (Pahl & Monson, 1992). Teacher input must be "sought, valued, and considered" (Henk & Moore, 1992, p. 48) during the process of implementing curriculum initiatives. When participation in programs is voluntary, teachers are empowered to make choices about their own professional development (Courtland, 1993).

In a recent study by Mraz (2000), school district administrators were asked for their perspectives on professional development and the literacy program. These curriculum directors and assistant superintendents cited teachers' own fear of risk taking as an obstacle to curriculum innovation. They emphasized the need to include building administrators in professional development initiatives related to language arts education. One explained, "The building administrator is the prime mover in that process. If you have a building principal who's dynamic, who doesn't spend a lot of time in the office, who is willing to learn more and get resources, that whole building structure can change."

In one district, building principals participated not only in the materials selection process, but also in the professional development programs that followed. The goal was to help administrators understand how the components of an effective literacy program operated and how the implementation of such a program could be monitored. As a result, when teachers had questions about how to use the materials, principals were able to assist.

What, then, constitutes high-quality professional development? Among the findings of a two-year study by the National Foundation for the Improvement of Education (NFIE), Renyi (1998) reported "the greatest gains in teacher learning were in places where whole schools studied their student results and agreed on what they needed to learn collectively and to do differently to improve those results." In the final analysis, "high quality professional development is not a program or an activity, but an ethos—a way of being where learning is suffused throughout the teachers' working lives" (Renyi, 1998, pp. 73–74).

Strategies to Support Change

Change can be uncomfortable and demanding. Moving toward the goal of effective literacy education "requires teachers who are empowered, careful thinkers about their day-to-day interactions with students—teachers who are able to reflect on their practice" (Vacca, Vacca, & Bruneau, 1997, p. 445). To support teachers as they continue to develop professionally, a number of strategies are useful (Courtland, 1992; George, Moley, & Ogle, 1992; Henk & Moore, 1992; Vacca, Vacca, & Bruneau, 1997):

- Small-group seminars for reflective dialogue
- Journal writing with response or feedback
- Regularly scheduled meetings with a predictable pattern
- Discussion of research theory and literature with other teachers
- Strategy modeling with peers
- Microteaching lessons in follow-up sessions (lesson demonstrations)
- Peer coaching (co-workers give feedback to one another as they use strategies with their classes)
- Guided practice (facilitator leads participants in trying out strategies)
- Structured feedback sessions (facilitator elicits participant response after strategy is tried)
- Peer support teams (co-workers share the ups and downs that accompany change)
- Mentor and lead teacher models
- On-site and off-site consultants
- Telephone hotlines
- Visits to functional sites either in one's own or another building

Portfolios

An especially powerful tool for professional development is the portfolio, used for assessment, for evaluating the progress of learners in the classroom, and for selecting prospective teachers. Teachers can use this tool to assess their own progress in implementing a program or in documenting accomplishments.

Administrators of reading programs encourage educators to view their students as active readers and writers. What better way to understand the process of writing and of portfolio development than for educators to be involved in the development of their own portfolios? Graves (1992) states, "We need more policy-makers, administrators, and teachers who know portfolios *from the inside.* Their decisions about portfolio use must include the reality of living and growing with the process of keeping one" (p. 5).

The person responsible for professional development may choose to gather the teachers together to discuss the expectations for personal portfolio development. The group would meet periodically to share the material from their portfolios and the experiences they have had in selecting this material. This dialogue gives educators firsthand experience with a strategy they may be using with their students and also encourages teachers to look at their own continuing development.

National Board for Professional Teaching Standards. An independent, nonprofit organization for the voluntary certification of highly accomplished teachers, the National Board for Professional Teaching Standards (NBPTS) requires the preparation of a portfolio that provides evidence of a candidate's good teaching practice. The portfolio contains videotapes of classroom teaching, lesson plans, samples of student work, and written commentaries in which the teacher reflects on what she or he is doing and why. Teacher candidates have about five months to compile portfolios. Most teachers report spending about 120 hours on their portfolios, the equivalent of about one day a week over a semester.

Portfolio entries and assessment exercises focus on challenging teacher issues such as communicating with parents and meeting diverse learner needs, and include interviews and exams in the teacher's field. Scoring is done by teachers who have attended an intensive training workshop and have qualified for scoring by demonstrating an understanding of the National Board standards, the directions to candidates, and the scoring guides. Scoring is based on the collection of a candidate's responses: videotapes, student work samples, and the candidate's analysis of written responses to assessment exercises. Each of these pieces of evidence helps scorers evaluate a candidate's work in light of the conscious, deliberate, analytical, and reflective criteria the National Board standards endorse. The following section tells one teacher's story of the certification process and how it contributed to her professional growth.

The NBPTS Certification Process. Karen is a 30-year veteran teacher who completed the NBPTS certification process in 1998. She has taught every grade and is currently teaching a variety of subjects in a middle childhood program, in South Euclid–Lyndhurst city schools in northeast Ohio.

Karen describes the process as being more involved than she anticipated. A substantial amount of writing was required, including six 10–15-page papers on various aspects of the curriculum. She received her box of portfolio materials in the summer of 1997, and completed the portfolio process in April 1998. The portfolio was sent to a central location, and from there, sections of it were sent to six reviewers. She took the qualifying exam in June 1998; 1½ hours were allowed for each of four questions. She described the questions as fair and pointed out that, "if you've taught for a number of years, you've lived them." For example, one question required her to develop a unit on pioneers for a fifth grade social studies class.

Feedback on her portfolio was very detailed and came in the form of an "answer key"—pamphlets that outlined the responses that evaluators were seeking. Although questions and requirements were very specific, the board seemed not to look for teachers who were "perfect," but rather to look for teachers who could evaluate what they were doing and why, who could recognize when an aspect of a lesson needed to be altered in order to meet the needs of the students.

Throughout this process, Karen participated in a support group through Cleveland State University, one of several northeast Ohio universities offering such groups. At the time, only she and one other teacher from her district were embarking on the certification process. She found the

support group and the mentoring from teachers who had completed the process to be invaluable and questioned how a person could complete the process without such support. Her group met once a month in the beginning, twice a month toward the end, and additional times to prepare for the exam.

Monetary rewards for going through this process vary from state to state. While such rewards can provide an initial incentive, Karen sees additional benefits as she reflects on the NBPTS process. She believes the process forced her to keep on top of pertinent issues and to articulate a philosophy of education. It also opened the door to opportunities such as the Governor's Advisory Board. Was it worth it? "Yes, if you are really into the profession. I learned a lot about myself as a teacher."

University-School Collaboration

A major support system results from the link between ivory tower and real world when professors and pre-K–12 educators work together. Following are several examples with components of their respective effective collaborations.

Teacher Apprenticeship Programs. At John Carroll University in University Heights, Ohio, the one-year intensive school-based program for students with an undergraduate degree in a field other than education leads to a master's degree and teacher certification. The gap between theory and practice is bridged as students spend one year in a participating school as they complete coursework. The program is currently affiliated with several public and private schools in the greater Cleveland area.

School-based, cooperating teachers who are involved in the program benefit from "implicit" learning, for example, from dialoguing about students, being involved in teacher education by collaborating on ways to develop and advance the novice teacher. Teachers also benefit from "explicit" learning by attending sessions that target professional areas of interest.

In the Ursuline College and University School Teacher Apprenticeship Program (TAP), school faculty are involved in three roles: (1) mentor, (2) lead instructor for graduate classes, and (3) guest presenters for graduate courses. (Approximately 50% of the teachers on staff do this.) TAP pays for teachers to attend workshops and classes to qualify to teach the graduate courses. Teachers must be thoroughly familiar with state licensure standards in order to coach and mentor novice teachers. Like the students in the John Carroll program, students in the Ursuline College program hold an undergraduate degree in a field other than education. They earn an advanced degree and a teaching certificate through the program.

Partnership Network. Through the KENT (Kent Education Network for Tomorrow) Partnership, eight school districts in a three-county area formally partner with Kent State University to "create better lives for children and futures for our communities." The ongoing professional development component includes a lowered tuition rate (approximately $100 less per credit hour) for district partners. Professional development workshops and courses are often brought to the schools. In the Akron and Canton school districts, an entire master's degree program is taken to convenient local sites; interested teachers may obtain an M.A. in Curriculum and Instruction with an emphasis on urban education. These districts, in turn, provide practice sites for student teachers from Kent. Each year, a free, one-day conference for anyone in partnership districts is held; this facilitates sharing and collaboration among the schools.

The response from teacher participants to the partnership initiatives has been very positive, although overall participation in the programs is not yet as high as desired. KENT Partnership hopes that, in the future, school administrators will engage in more strategic planning with regard to the professional development of their faculty, particularly in light of the new Ohio licensure standards of 2001, mandating teachers to take 30 graduate hours for every 10 years of teaching. Ideally, school administrators will play a more active role in informing teachers about professional opportunities that coincide with the individual goals of the faculty member and with

the strategic goals of the school. Currently, communication about the partnership offerings does not always seem to get from the main office to the classroom level.

Teacher as Researcher: Action Research

Often tied to the university-school collaboration model is *action research,* the practice of teachers in the classroom investigating questions that they have generated about teaching and learning. This type of practice-centered inquiry begins with the questions "What do I think?" and "How will I know?" Teacher-researchers gather evidence in their classrooms to test their hypotheses and then evaluate their results (Gove & Kennedy-Calloway, 1992).

What better person to raise questions about practice, test assumptions, and evaluate results on student learning than the classroom teacher? For example, Colleen, a fifth grade teacher, is frustrated that her students, despite the Harry Potter publicity, do not do more independent reading. She wonders if they will be motivated to read more books if they are asked to share their book thoughts in letters to friends. She decides to investigate this question through her own classroom inquiry. The steps she takes—the steps in an action research sequence—are shown in Figure 9.1.

Colleen initiates a program of dialogue journal writing in which her students write letters to a partner in the class, describing their thoughts about the books they read. She introduces this new method through mini-lessons and modeling, and she allocates time for writing letters during writing workshop. She decides what evidence she will need to determine what effect the journal writing has on student reading. Colleen sees herself as a professional, a researcher, and a learner. She has come to "see all events, behaviors, institutions, and intentions as open to teacher research and, therefore, changeable" (Patterson & Shannon, 1993, p. 9).

At the end of the quarter, Colleen evaluates what has happened. She reads her students' dialogue journals, reviews the charts where they have recorded the books they have read, reflects on her own professional journal, and asks the

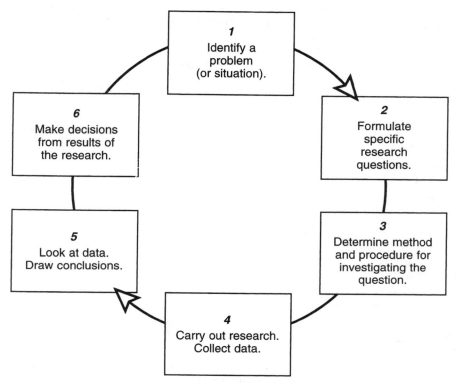

Figure 9.1. Action Research Sequence

students how they felt about dialogue journals and independent reading. Colleen concludes that most of her students enjoyed the dialogue journals and that the number of books read increased significantly. She will probably make letter-writing part of her writing workshop from now on.

Action research closes the gap between theory and practice, creates a problem-solving mind-set in teachers, improves instructional practice, improves the professional status of teachers, empowers teachers, and provides the potential for an improved educational process for children (Olson, 1990).

Teachers should be encouraged to share the results of their work with other professionals through publication, newsletters, staff meetings, or simply professional conversation. In addition, teachers will find that *the investigation into one research question will raise more questions.* Research is an ongoing process. "Teacher researchers know that when it comes to research, the joy is

in the doing, not in the done" (Hubbard & Power, 1993, p. 24).

Three trends seem to have merged, according to teachers who have participated in practice-centered inquiry: (1) there is greater involvement in teaching; (2) collegiality among members of the research team is enhanced; (3) focused, data-based feedback is generated.

Guidelines for Professional Development Programs

The successful planning and implementation of a professional development program is a collaborative effort. It requires reflection, on the part of both teachers and administrators, about the current needs and strengths of the school's program. Together, the members of the school team can then coproduce a systematic plan for meeting those mutually agreed upon needs. The

SURVEY OF COMPETENCY NEEDS FOR INTERMEDIATE GRADE TEACHERS

Directions: Indicate whether or not you would like assistance in each area of competency related to reading comprehension in the intermediate grades:

	Needs		
Competency	I feel confident in this area	I would like a little more help here	I would like lots of help here
1. Building background activities to develop a frame of reference			
2. Showing students how to generate their own questions			
3. Involving students in process of predicting and verifying			
4. Getting students involved in group discussions			
5. Sensitizing readers to sources of information where answers to questions can be found			
6. Using literature in response groups and in journal writing			

Figure 9.2

following section offers guidelines for generating and implementing such a plan.

Before making any consequential decisions, all administrators involved need data-based information. Next, they need to work with participants in goal setting. Studies have confirmed the importance of including teachers (Rycik, 1986) and administrators (Mraz, 2000) in all phases of the professional development program. When both groups have a say in targeting goals for improvement, a balance across individual, instructional, school, and school district priorities is more achievable.

Probably the most efficient and effective way to engage in planning is to follow a model that is both systematic and participatory. It should be orderly and flexible and depend on input from those most directly involved. Above all, the cyclical design is conducive to collaboration among teachers, administrators, coordinators, and committees. A plan such as this virtually guarantees that professional development will

be well designed and tailored to meet participants' needs.

Another way to assist a committee in planning is to focus on three major types of questions in designing the professional development program: What? Why? How? What is the current situation? What needs to be improved? What is the baseline? What exists right now? Why do we want improvement in a particular area? Why are teachers and administrators doing what they are doing in the classroom, in the building? How can we begin to make some changes in the status quo? How should we initiate the professional development, and how do we proceed?

As a rule, planning proceeds in phases, beginning with a proposal to initiate change in the school's reading program. This phase of planning should rely on information and ideas from several sources, especially the group for whom professional development is intended. Needs assessment enables the reading supervisor and planning committee to identify needs, attitudes,

---

SURVEY OF NEEDS AND CONCERNS FOR PRIMARY GRADE TEACHERS

Directions: Please number in order of importance (1 = most important; 5 = least important) the areas in which you feel you need additional help in order to teach reading in the primary grades. Then, answer each question as completely as possible.

_____ Using shared reading with beginners (for example, big books, songs, charts, poems)

_____ Using conversation to encourage individual or group language experience stories

_____ Linking singing, dancing, and other rhythmic activities to reading and writing instruction

_____ Creating a dress-up area for dramatic activities

_____ Using evaluation procedures that are developmentally appropriate for the children

_____ Using the language children bring to school as a base for language activities

1. What is your area of greatest concern about teaching reading?

2. What is your area of least concern?

Figure 9.3

interests, and potential resources. Two types of assessment surveys to collect information from the teaching staff are shown: one for intermediate grade teachers in Figure 9.2, and one for primary grade teachers in Figure 9.3. At this juncture in the planning process, basic goals and objectives can be set by the committee. The next phase—actual implementation of content and process—is soon underway.

The implementation of professional development centers on delivery of the program. It should occur over a series of planned activities, lasting anywhere from a month to a year or two. To work effectively with teachers, the reading supervisor or staff developer needs to be open to new ideas and demonstrate identified strategies and techniques for improving instruction. Interpersonal skills, as well as one's basic delivery and knowledge base, are important whether conducting a workshop or assisting in an action research project. Following are some personal characteristics that are associated with effective presenters at professional development sessions (Vacca & Vacca, 1996, 1999).

♦ Demonstrates enthusiasm and interest in the topic.
♦ Stimulates excitement.
♦ Relates in an open, honest, and friendly manner.
♦ Answers questions patiently.
♦ Doesn't talk down to participants.
♦ Displays a sense of humor.

As reading supervisors take on the role of staff developer, they need to be confident and collaborate with teachers on ways to work with each other. They need a tolerance for ambiguity and a realization that participants are involved in a learning effort, with no one having the "right" answer.

One of the most practical ways to implement a professional development project is to incorporate the process of change with the best principles of adult learning. Essentially, adults go

116

JoAnne L. Vacca and Maryann Mraz

through a change process beginning with un-freezing or readiness, next moving forward and gaining experience, then refreezing, and finally, incorporating changes into the environment. Implementing professional development with this process allows reading specialists and supervisors to introduce a range of action-oriented instructional options to participating teachers. The key to effective delivery is involvement through hands-on activities such as role-playing, demonstration teaching, observations, interviewing, and problem-solving groups. As the teachers sense the process of reading by playing the role of reader and experiencing new strategies and materials, the leader explains the how and why of selecting techniques to use in a program. The leader will need to sustain the rapport that was established in the beginning and vary the choice of activities, remembering that no single technique will be effective in all situations.

Frequent and informal evaluation by participants can help keep the professional development program on track. Simple rating scales to provide information on the perceived value and usefulness of sessions should help the leader decide on modification in planned implementation. Feedback at the end of each session might be a two-way street, with both staff developer and teachers exchanging suggestions for improvement. This in turn would result in followup at the next group session. Evaluation in this context, then, becomes an integral and responsive part of the professional development implementation.

Conclusion

Of all the advances in professional development, the refocusing of attention on the role of the teacher as professional is likely to have the greatest impact. School administrators have the potential to play a pivotal role in actualizing programs that will support the professional growth of teachers and, in turn, the quality of educational opportunities offered to students. After all, "the key to school change is a knowledgeable professional in every classroom. That is why

school districts need to reinvest in professional development" (Harste & Carey, 1999, p. 8).

References

ciarhaClyde, J., Condon, M., Daniel, K., & Sommer, M. (1993). Learning through whole language: Exploring book selection and use with preschoolers. In L. Patterson, C. Santa, K. Short, & K. Smith (Eds.), *Teachers are researchers: Reflection and action* (pp. 42–50). Newark, DE: International Reading Association.

Courtland, M. C. (1992). Teacher change in the implementation of new approaches to literacy instruction. In J. Vacca (Ed.), *Bringing about change in schools* (pp. 30–36). Newark, DE: International Reading Association.

Courtland, M. C. (1993). *Towards a holistic model of staff development for language arts teachers.* Unpublished manuscript, Lakehead University, Thunder Bay, Ontario, Canada.

Duke, D. (1993). Removing barriers to professional growth. *Phi Delta Kappan, 74*(9), 702–704, 710–712.

George, J., Moley, P., & Ogle, D. (1992). CCD: A model comprehension program for changing thinking and instruction. In J. Vacca (Ed.), *Bringing about change in schools* (pp. 49–55). Newark, DE: International Reading Association.

Gove, M., & Kennedy-Calloway, C. (1992). Action research: Empowering teachers to work with at-risk students. In J. Vacca (Ed.), *Bringing about change in schools* (pp. 14–22). Newark, DE: International Reading Association.

Graves, D. (1992). Portfolios: Keep a good idea growing. In D. Graves & B. Sunstein (Eds.), *Portfolio portraits* (pp. 1–12). Portsmouth, NH: Heinemann.

Harste, J. C., & Carey, R. F. (1999). *Curriculum, multiple literacies, and democracy: What if English/language arts teachers really cared?* Presidential address of the 89th Annual Convention of the NCTE.

Henk, W., & Moore, J. (1992). Facilitating change in school literacy: From state initiatives to district implementation. In J. Vacca (Ed.), *Bringing about change in schools* (pp. 44–48). Newark, DE: International Reading Association.

Hubbard, R., & Power, B. (1993). Finding and framing a research question. In L. Patterson, C. Santa, K. Short, & K. Smith (Eds.), *Teachers are researchers: Reflection and action* (pp. 19–25). Newark, DE: International Reading Association.

Lieberman, A. (1995). Practices that support teacher development. *Phi Delta Kappan, 76,* 591–596.

Mraz, M. (2000). The literacy program selection process from the perspective of school district administrators. *Ohio Reading Teacher, 34*(2), 40–48.

Murphy, J. (1993). What's in? What's out? American education in the nineties. *Phi Delta Kappan, 74,* 641–646.

Olson, M. W. (Ed.). (1990). *Opening the door to classroom research.* Newark, DE: International Reading Association.

Pahl, M., & Monson, R. (1992). In search of whole language: Transforming curriculum and instruction. In J. Vacca (Ed.), *Bringing about change in schools* (pp. 6–12). Newark, DE: International Reading Association.

Patterson, L., Santa, C., Short, K., & Smith, K. (Eds.). (1993). *Teachers are researchers: Reflection and action.* Newark, DE: International Reading Association.

Patterson, L., & Shannon, P. (1993). Reflection, inquiry, action. In L. Patterson, C. Santa, K. Short, & K. Smith (Eds.), *Teachers are researchers: Reflection and action* (pp. 7–11). Newark, DE: International Reading Association.

Renyi, J. (1998). Building learning into the teaching job. *Educational Leadership, 55*(5), 70–74.

Rycik, J. (1986). *Teachers' perceptions of supervision of reading instruction.* Unpublished manuscript, Kent State University, Kent, OH.

Vacca, R. T., & Vacca, J. L. (1996). *Content area reading* (5th ed.). New York: Harper Collins.

Vacca, R. T., & Vacca, J. L. (1999). *Content area reading: Literacy and learning across the curriculum* (6th ed.). New York: Longman.

Vacca, R. T., Vacca, J. L., & Bruneau, B. (1997). Teachers reflecting on practice. In J. Flood, S. B. Heath, & D. Lapp (Eds.), *Handbook for literacy educators: Research on teaching the communicative and visual arts* (pp. 445–450). Newark, DE: International Reading Association.

CHAPTER TEN

Assessment of Reading Programs

Barbara A. Kapinus

A room full of teachers works to develop tasks for a large-scale assessment. As the teachers talk at their tables, the discussion includes questions about what will work, what is important for students to know or do, how challenging the activities should be, how to allow for creativity while providing direction and focus, how to provide for regional and cultural differences, and how to design classroom activities and environments that promote the learning and achievement they hope the assessment will tap. When they leave the workshop, these teachers will take new insights back to their classrooms. Not only their classroom assessments, but also their instruction will change.

This scene illustrates the potentially beneficial link between assessment and instruction. Educational assessment, whether done in the classroom or on a large scale, has one ultimate purpose: to support effective teaching and learning. This purpose is accomplished by documenting the individual accomplishments of students and looking at how groups of students are performing in order to determine student progress and the success of instructional approaches, programs, school organization, and state and local policy.

During the past decade, some important trends in reading assessment have affected both individual assessment and large-scale assessment. This chapter outlines those trends with which administrators and supervisors should be familiar, offers guidelines for establishing an assessment program, and highlights some issues related to reading assessment:

◆ Large-scale assessment trends
◆ Classroom assessment
◆ Putting together a coherent program

Classroom and large-scale assessment are addressed separately, since the purposes and processes of each, while ultimately focused on the goal stated above, differ in some important ways. Classroom assessment directly informs instruction and should be useful to students, parents, and teachers, all of whom can be involved in directly promoting the reading achievement of individual students. Large-scale assessment, on the other hand, must inform the public and policy makers who are not as interested in specific instructional implications of the results for individuals but rather in whether the overall curriculum and school programs are effective. Large-scale assessment is usually tied to public accountability and must be rigorously, publicly defensible to a degree far greater than classroom assessment. As a consequence of these different orientations, there are different constraints, at least at present, on the types of activities that can be used in each type of assessment, although there have been efforts during the last decade to use the same types of activities for both types. At present, the best way to relate and at the same time differentiate the two types of assessment is a system of related but not identical assessment tools, such as performance tasks on large-scale assessment that probe skills demonstrated in classroom through projects and portfolios. Such a system should address the multiple purposes and audiences of assessments through the use of multiple assessments.

Large-Scale Assessment Trends

The role of large-scale assessment has changed dramatically in the past 10 years. A major impetus for that change has been the standards movement. It is important to remember when setting and using high standards for education improvement that the standards should:

◆ be established with input from informed education stakeholders, including teachers, parents, policy makers, community leaders, and education leaders.
◆ provide focus for instruction, thereby giving all students access to a rigorous curriculum.
◆ promote deep understanding that supports application and problem solving in the content areas rather than rote learning of simple skills and isolated facts.
◆ link and guide improvement efforts throughout education systems, including policy, administration, instruction, assessment, and teacher professional development.

As education policy makers have attempted to implement standards-focused education reform, there has been an increase in the use of large-scale assessments for accountability. In some cases, the assessments that have been implemented have promoted increases in the rigor of curriculum, the effectiveness of instruction, and the access of less-privileged students to rich learning. In other instances, heavy reliance on assessment as the major tool of the standards movement has resulted in misuses that include basing high-stakes decisions such as promotion on one test score and drawing unsupported conclusions about program success or individual achievement from limited test-based data.

In some situations, large-scale assessments do not promote the improvements intended but limit curriculum, trivialize instruction, and hold disadvantaged students and their teachers accountable based on limited data and with limited resources. This is an unfortunate reality for many administrators and teachers, one that ultimately will need to be changed at a policy level.

In general, newer assessments are characterized by:

- a focus on outcomes or goals
- increased authenticity or congruence with real-world reading and sound instructional activities
- increased complexity of assessment tasks and procedures
- increased involvement of teachers in all stages of assessment, including development, scoring, and reporting

Each of these characteristics reflects an improvement in assessment but has both advantages and disadvantages for schools and teachers. These mixed effects are sometimes due to the novelty of an approach that is not yet fine-tuned. It is important to weigh all the consequences and implications of these characteristics of new assessments when designing an assessment system for a school or district, choosing or developing district and school assessments, or participating in some of the larger assessments at state and national levels.

Focus on Outcomes or Goals

Many of the newer large-scale reading assessments focus on the goals of education rather than the enabling skills necessary to reach these goals. Moreover, these goals tend to be broad and complex. For example, one goal from the state of Maryland is "Students will construct, extend, and examine meaning when reading for literary experience, to be informed, and to perform a task." Focusing on complex goals leads to complex, challenging assessment tasks such as this:

> Using the information from the two passages you just read, write an article for your school newspaper on environmental concerns. Relate the scientific and historical aspects of environmental issues to current environmental issues that are global, national, or local. You will draft your article today, and tomorrow you will share your draft with a peer and prepare a revised draft.

Assessments using rich tasks that reflect the more general goals of schooling provide infor-

mation about the achievement of those goals by groups of students, but they have limited utility for individual diagnosis. This is not a new development. There has long been a caveat, usually ignored, against drawing conclusions about individual students' specific instructional needs based on the results of large-scale assessments such as norm-referenced tests. However, teachers and parents are sometimes dissatisfied with the amount of individual student information provided by newer assessments, especially in light of the increased amount of student time such assessments require. This leads to pressure to report individual scores and to over rely on those scores as sources of information about individual reading achievement.

Another aspect of focusing on goals is that students' achievement is measured relative to standards for performance. In some states, the standards have been set purposely high to indicate high expectations for all students. These high standards represent a commitment to providing the best, most challenging education to all students. They also have sparked intense discussions on how to allow for cultural differences and yet hold high expectations for diverse populations of students. In some ways, a standard for all can be seen as both more fair and more enfranchising for students who, in traditional assessments, would not be expected to perform well because of their exceptional status or diverse backgrounds. However, high standards need to be accompanied by a deep conviction that all students can reach those standards and a commitment to supplying the necessary resources and learning opportunities to support that achievement.

Increased Complexity of Assessment Tasks

Large-scale reading assessments are beginning to include complex tasks. Students might be asked to read longer, more complex passages drawn from a variety of genres, including functional and workplace materials. Students might also be asked to respond in diverse ways, such as constructing open-ended responses or providing rationales for selections on multiple-

---

GENERIC RUBRIC FOR READING ACTIVITIES*

Note: The scoring criteria are applied as cued for or required by the activity. Not every activity cues for all the possible behaviors described in the generic rubric. Thus the scoring guide for specific activities can stop at different points.

0 = No evidence of construction of meaning.

1 = Some evidence of constructing meaning, building some understanding of the text. Presence of defensible, and possibly some indefensible, information.

2 = A superficial understanding of the text, with evidence of constructing meaning. One or two relevant but unsupported inferences.

3 = A developed understanding of the text with evidence of connections, extensions, or examinations of the meaning. Connections between the reader's ideas and the text itself are implied. Extensions and examinations are related to the text, but explicit references to the text in support of inferences are not present. When more than one stance is possible, the response may remain limited to one stance.

4 = A developed understanding of the text with evidence of connections, extensions, and examinations of meaning. Connections between the reader's ideas and the text are explicit. Extensions and examinations are accompanied by explicit references to the text in support of inferences. When possible, the response indicates more than one stance or perspective on the text; however, only one stance is substantially supported by inferences to the text.

5 = A developed understanding of the text with evidence of connections, extensions, examinations of meaning, and defense of interpretations. Connections between the reader's ideas and the text itself are explicit. Extensions and examinations are accompanied by explicit references to the text in support of inferences. When possible, the response indicates more than two stances, all substantially supported by references to the text.

6 = A complex, developed understanding of the text with evidence of connections, extensions, examinations of meaning, and defense of interpretations. Connections between the reader's ideas and the text itself are explicit. Extensions and examinations are accompanied by explicit references to the text in support of inferences. Responses indicate as many stances as possible based on the activity, all substantially supported by references to the text. These responses reflect careful thought and thoroughness.

---

* Maryland State Department of Education, Maryland School Performance Assessment Program

Figure 10.1

choice items. The drawbacks to such complex, constructive tasks are the time required for students to respond to them and the time and cost necessary for scoring them.

Many recently developed assessments do not use short, simple excerpts of texts. They employ texts that have been drawn from the real world: magazines, announcements, and directions. These texts are carefully screened for possible bias as well as age appropriateness. They are longer than the one-paragraph "textlets" used on older assessments. The use of these longer texts increases the need for students to be fluent. Students who read accurately but very slowly are not likely to finish reading the passages in time to answer all the questions.

Scoring. The open-ended questions used on recently developed assessments do not have simple right or wrong answers. Scoring of responses is based on several characteristics, not just the text information that the student provides. The scoring guide in Figure 10.1 shows one approach to scoring students' responses to reading.

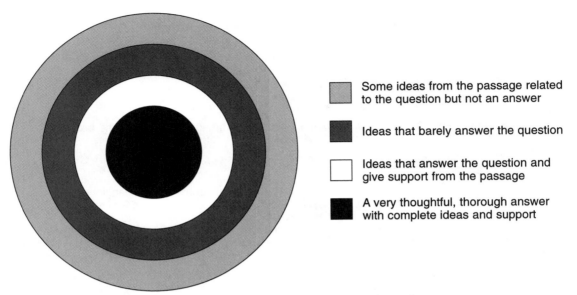

Figure 10.2. Guide for Discussing Qualities of Good Responses

Although other guides include different factors or do not include some of these aspects, there are important similarities across most scoring guides for extended written responses to open-ended reading questions. They usually examine several aspects of students' responses, such as accuracy, thoroughness of rationale, and references to the passage, and they focus on students' interactions with the text—interactions that can take many forms and can be from several possible perspectives: characters in the text, the author, or an outside critic.

In preparing students to respond to the open-ended questions scored by these types of guides, teachers need to help students understand what makes a good response and give students opportunities to explore a range of ways of responding to questions about reading. One teacher developed a chart similar to the one in Figure 10.2 in order to guide discussions with her students about the quality of their responses.

Portfolios. Attempts have been made to modify portfolio approaches in order to use them on a large scale. The challenges of doing this have proved almost insurmountable. There are several concerns related to the use of portfolio-based information for the purpose of large-scale assessment. One is that schools and teachers might base their notions of classroom portfolio assessment on the model used for the larger assessments and thereby limit the possibilities for portfolios in the classroom. A second, related concern is the tension between the need for teachers to develop their own understanding and use of portfolios over time and the public's demands for timely accountability. Another persistent problem is achieving comparability and consistency in portfolio assessment activities and scoring. There is a tension between the leeway allowed teachers and students in classroom portfolio assessment and the demands for publicly defensible large-scale assessment information. Schools and districts embarking on the use of large-scale portfolio assessment need to include time for teachers to understand the use of portfolios in contexts beyond the classroom and to be a part of the planning and development process.

Authenticity

Some of the assessments being developed for state and national assessments are being designed with a clear commitment to reflecting good instruction and real-world reading activities. On the National Assessment of Educational Progress (NAEP) in Reading, students might answer questions about directions for writing a resume and then actually prepare a short resume using the directions. On one form of the Maryland School Performance Assessment, a task integrated science, social studies, reading, and writing and required that students read two articles, take and organize notes, and write a report that would be part of a health fair at the local mall. In Indiana, educators have piloted complex problem-solving tasks that asked students to do research, organize information, and present a possible solution to a real-world problem such as the water shortage in some parts of the country. Students find these more authentic tasks engaging and challenging. Teachers find that they support generative classroom activities that require a wide range of thinking, creativity, and personal involvement on the part of students.

However, the use of these authentic tasks has raised some issues.

◆ What is really authentic for students?
◆ Can we afford the time that these tasks are taking?
◆ Can we generalize about student performance based on tasks that are highly bound by context?

Defining Authenticity. It is important to realize that some tasks might be very related to the real world but not related to students' current experiences and developmental levels. For example, one large assessment piloted a task that asked fourth grade students to pretend they were park rangers and then to write a letter to their boss about a poem they had read. While it is important for students to have realistic audiences for their writing, the audience in this case was not appropriate on two counts. First, few of the fourth graders knew what a park ranger did, much less how such a person would write when addressing a boss. The task was not authentic given the experiences of fourth graders. Second, the task itself was not really very authentic; few park rangers write letters to their bosses about poems they have read. This task was a good

example of efforts to use authentic, real-world tasks gone awry.

Teachers working on the development of assessments continue to struggle with the problem of what is authentic. We need some way to elicit and assess responses to literature, but in the real world we seldom answer other people's questions about what we read except for the general "What was it about?" and "Did you like it?" or "Was it like the author's other books/ stories/poems?" Teachers and measurement staff on several assessment projects are struggling with the problem of how to develop assessments that are at the same time authentic, sound, and challenging.

Finding Time. The amount of time required for students to complete authentic performances is an issue that has been raised by teachers in some instances of performance assessments. Although more complex assessment tasks are engaging for students and reflect good instruction, they take time from other instructional activities that teachers might have chosen and students might have needed.

Generalizing the Results. The degree to which we can generalize about performance is a critical issue. Although reading a long passage and responding with more authentic tasks reflects real-world reading, it reflects only one small type of reading, about only one topic. A student might do significantly better in a different context, reading about a different topic. For example, a student might be given a passage on ecology, a topic of high interest to the student because of family discussions and projects. That student might perform very well on that reading task but show far less proficiency when asked to read a passage about village life in Russia. Consequently, interpretation of and generalization from individual data on newer large-scale assessments must be done with a great deal of caution.

Increased Involvement of Teachers in All Stages of Assessment

Past large-scale assessments were usually developed by measurement experts and commercial testing institutions and had little teacher input except perhaps for some review of items. Some recent assessments have been developed by teachers. In Maryland and Kentucky, for example, teachers have taken part in the discussion of what to assess and how to do it. They have designed the tasks, developed the scoring guides, chosen exemplary student responses, scored responses, and helped to draft and deliver reports on the results of assessments. From identifying the outcomes to be assessed, to speaking at the press conference on assessment results, teachers have had a voice in these assessments. This involvement has had two important results.

First, the discussions and assessment production and scoring activities provide staff development in the form of opportunities to reflect on and articulate what is important in curriculum, instruction, and student achievement. Teachers have the opportunity to build clearer understandings of what they want to accomplish in their classrooms, how they might accomplish these goals, and how they will determine whether they and their students are successful.

The second result of teacher involvement in all the phases of the development and use of assessments is that teachers who have been involved have a better understanding of the assessments and their purposes. With that understanding often comes support for the assessments and improved instruction. Teachers are not as likely to see assessment as something that is done to them, but rather as a tool for looking at their own effectiveness.

Classroom Assessment

Some of the same trends evident in large-scale assessment are also found in current approaches to classroom assessment. It is not always clear which comes first, but it seems that while some large-scale assessments are trying to capture the goals and approaches used in innovative, successful classrooms, classrooms are also being improved by the implementation of innovative assessments. For example, more traditional teachers working on development of or in preparation for innovative large-scale assessments

reported that they were beginning to reflect on their own classroom practices in instruction and assessment, and often modified their approaches to reflect the assessment and in turn the innovative teaching and thinking about education on which the assessment was based. When these teachers provided information on the assessments or worked on additional forms of the assessment, they shared insights based on their classroom experiences that were relevant to improving the design and content of large-scale assessments. That is, the improvement of instruction and assessment in the classroom is linked to improvements in large-scale assessment. Consequently, it is not surprising that the trends in classroom assessment are similar to those in large-scale assessment.

Authenticity

Classroom assessments are becoming increasingly authentic as instruction focuses more on what readers need to be able to do in the real world. In addition, teachers are using separate assessment exercises less and less and instead are using the products and observations of regular classroom activities to assess students' achievement. Teachers are also sharing the responsibility for assessment with students. The following interview questions and the answers of a primary student who is struggling to improve demonstrate this shared responsibility.

1. *What does someone have to do to be a good reader?* They have to write good. Good readers make good sentences. Good readers make mistakes and they fix them.
2. *How have you improved as a reader this nine weeks?* I go back to the beginning and start again. I try to read to the end. I think about the reading.
3. *What reading goal will you set for yourself for the next nine weeks?* I'll try to sound out the hard things I can't read.

—On a bulletin board of Forest Edge Elementary, Fairfax, Virginia, January 1989

Questions like these can document increased understanding of the reading process and growing ownership of their reading on the part of students.

Complexity

As teachers use a wider variety of assessment tools in their classrooms and as they assess more complex aspects of reading, they are challenged to bring these elements together. Managing a classroom system of assessment can be as challenging as managing a statewide system. A classroom assessment system might include the following:

- Interviews of students about their progress
- Interviews of students about their reading preferences
- Observations of students discussing their reading
- Students' reflections on their discussions
- Reading response logs
- Samples of work picked by the teacher, the students, or both
- Special projects
- Students' reflections on their progress and their goals
- Notes on interviews with parents
- Notes from parents about students' reading habits or discussions at home

Managing all of these and weaving them into a coherent, meaningful description of the student as a reader is a challenge. One approach is the use of portfolios. The use of classroom portfolios is rapidly growing in popularity. However, there is also a great deal of misunderstanding about portfolios, as with many new popular movements. Teachers often believe that collecting students' work in some physical receptacle is the critical feature of using portfolios. Portfolios should allow for students and teachers to discuss and negotiate understandings of progress; in the classroom this conversation leads to the establishment of mutually accepted goals. This discussion and the focus on improvement over time are essential ingredients in a portfolio approach in the classroom.

The process of examining progress with respect to goals and revising or reestablishing goals is at the core of portfolio use. Teachers need to have clear, challenging goals for their students that provide benchmarks for considering progress. For example, the following is a set of benchmark descriptors for an early stage of "developing reader." It was piloted by teachers in a multistate project, the Primary Level Assessment System. The descriptors are based on materials used in the Upper Arlington schools in Ohio.

- Selects appropriate reading material with some support.
- Begins to keep a list of books read.
- Retells and discusses text with teacher support.
- Comments upon patterns, characters, plot, and setting with prompts. May compare or contrast his/her experiences with story.
- May make connections with the literature.
- Makes predictions using book language and story elements.
- Self-corrects most miscues that interfere with meaning.
- Able to problem-solve new words in a variety of ways: rereading the sentence, phrase, or preceding work, by analogy, sounding out, and so forth.
- Reads in multiple-word phrases.
- Beginning to read for longer periods of time on his/her own.
- Views self as a reader.

In using portfolios, teachers must be aware of their goals and keep those goals as a focus if they are to ensure students a reliable assessment of real progress. Without such focus, portfolios can support aimless education, unfocused activity, and even capricious evaluation.

Parents as Collaborators

Schools are becoming increasingly committed to forging partnerships with parents in the task of helping students become literate. Teachers are asking parents to provide information on home reading habits and discussion. When they meet with parents, they share portfolios or work samples, demonstrating specific areas of growth rather than reporting only numbers and scores as the course of evaluations. Parents bring to conferences with teachers as wide a range of backgrounds as their children bring to classrooms. However, there are many ways to involve parents in assessments and to inform them of the instructional program and its goals at the same time (see Chapter 14).

Constructivist Learning and Activities

Some classroom assessments are beginning to reflect a move toward constructivist classrooms where teachers and students are partners in the processes of learning and assessing. Teachers in these classrooms use assessment approaches that increase the understanding of students and themselves. For example, students might be asked to culminate a unit in geography by writing a reader-friendly article about the country or area studied and explaining what characteristics of their text they believe will help their readers understand the ideas of the article. Such an activity allows students to apply their knowledge of reading, writing, and geography in complex and creative ways. The teacher also learns about the students' understanding of reading, writing, and geography from the activity.

Impact of Standards on Classroom Assessment

The focus on outcomes that characterizes standards-based education can be both an aid and an impediment in classroom assessment. Teachers need to hold in check a tendency to employ only the question formats used on large-scale assessments; instead, teachers should allow students to demonstrate growth in a variety of ways. They need to be sure they are assessing all possible areas of reading growth, including areas that cannot be easily assessed on a large scale, such as improvements in the amount and range of self-selected reading.

Putting Together a Coherent Program

Assessment based mainly on commercial materials such as basal tests or norm-referenced tests is being replaced by newer tools and approaches more closely connected to good teaching and the ultimate goals of reading instruction. Not only are the characteristics of assessment changing, but so is the process by which assessments are developed. More interested parties, from students and parents to business leaders, are involved in the design of newer assessments. This means that the process of establishing or improving an assessment system for schools and districts requires time and resources as well as careful planning. An effective system must evolve; it cannot be put in place overnight. The purposes and characteristics of each part of the system, from classroom-based evidence of growth to indicators of program effectiveness, must be considered in building a related network of tools and approaches for assessment.

Using Assessment Data for Decision Making

Even the best of assessments, whether large scale or classroom based, are useful only if they provide relevant, reliable information for making sound educational decisions. Administrators and teachers need to question the data from assessments. For example, improvement in overall reading scores in a school can mask ongoing problems with groups of students who are not making progress. When school data on student achievement is disaggregated by economic, gender, or cultural groups or by previous achievement, patterns sometimes emerge that indicate problems such as the following.

- ◆ Students from certain cultural or economic backgrounds may not be making gains in reading achievement.
- ◆ Students who are already high achievers might account for most of the gains a school shows, while struggling readers might be actually losing ground, or vice versa.

Teachers need to ask similar questions of data from classroom assessments. Again, impressive performance by students who began the year with advanced skills and knowledge might mask a lack of progress on the part of other students.

Detection of patterns in student achievement and making inferences based on those patterns in order to plan programs and instruction are activities that administrators should share with teachers and teachers should share with students. Explaining to parents both school and classroom decisions on scheduling, programs, materials, and instruction based on assessment data can promote parental support and involvement.

Communicating with Parents and Policy Makers

Being proactive in sharing assessment information with parents and policy makers is essential to implementation of an effective, schoolwide assessment program. Communication about the types of assessments used, their purposes, and their results promotes confidence in schools and teachers. Keeping stakeholders informed helps to maintain support from outside the school for the flexibility to develop and implement the best assessment system for a school. It is also important to communicate what strategies are being used to improve students' achievement. Finally, it is imperative that students know the purposes and results of assessments. This makes them aware of goals, areas of strength, and where they need to grow in reading achievement.

Conclusion

Above all, assessments should offer insights into the goals of education and ways to reach those goals for educators at all levels, whether at the national level or in the classroom. These insights must be developed by each person. They cannot be simply handed down by policy makers or administrators. This means that an approach like portfolios cannot be set in place quickly through a district or state mandate. A cookbook for assessment is no more appropriate than a cookbook for instruction. Teachers need to be decision makers and problem solvers in assessment as well as teaching.

Teachers are not the only people who need to understand reading assessment. Educational leaders at all levels need to engage all the parties involved in education—students, parents, teachers, administrators, and policy makers—in the process of reflecting on the alignment of education goals, instruction practice, and assessment approaches. A deep understanding and clarification of these areas on the part of individuals is necessary for successful evaluation. That increased knowledge cannot be simply transmitted but must be generated by individuals over time, experiences, and conversations. Administrators can and must provide the time, opportunities, and encouragement for the development of understanding necessary for successful assessment in reading programs.

Resources

Asp, E. (2000). Assessment in education: Where have we been? Where are we headed? In R. S. Brandt (Ed.), *Education in a new era* (pp. 123–157). Alexandria, VA: Association for Supervision and Curriculum Development.

Barrentine, S. J. (Ed.). (1999). *Reading assessment principles and practices for elementary teachers: A collection of articles from* The Reading Teacher. Newark, DE: International Reading Association.

Brandt, R. (Ed.). (1998). *Assessing student learning: New rules, new realities.* Alexandria, VA: Association for Supervision and Curriculum Development.

Bredekamp, S., & Rosegrant, T. (1992). *Reaching potentials: Appropriate curriculum and assessment for young children* (Vol. 1). Washington, DC: National Association for the Education of Young Children.

Elmore, R. F., & Rothman, R. (1999). *Testing, teaching, and learning.* Washington, DC: National Academy Press.

Glazer, S. M., & Brown, C. S. (1993). *Portfolios and beyond: Collaborative assessment in reading and writing.* Norwood, MA: Christopher-Gordon.

Harp, B. (Ed.). (1993). *Assessment and evaluation in language programs* (Abridged ed.). Norwood, MA: Christopher-Gordon.

Heald-Taylor, G. (1989). *The administrator's guide to whole language.* Katonah, NY: Richard C. Owen.

Herman, J. L., Aschbacher, P. R., & Winters, L. (1991). *A practical guide to alternative assessment.* Alexandria, VA: Association for Supervision and Curriculum Development.

International Reading Association. (1995). *Reading assessment in practice: A book of readings.* Newark, DE: International Reading Association.

Marzano, R. J., & Kendall, J. S. (1998). *Implementing standards-based education.* Washington, DC: National Education Association.

McTighe, J., & Ferrara, S. (1998). *Assessing learning in the classroom.* Washington, DC: National Education Association.

Meyer, C. A. (1992). What's the difference between authentic and performance assessment? *Educational Leadership, 49*(8), 39–40.

Rhodes, L. K., & Shanklin, N. L. (1993). *Windows into literacy: Assessing learners, K–8.* Portsmouth, NH: Heinemann.

Stiggins, R. J. (1998). *Classroom assessment for student success.* Washington, DC: National Education Association.

Tierney, R., Carter, M. A., & Desai, L. E. (1991). *Portfolio assessment in the reading-writing classroom.* Norwood, MA: Christopher-Gordon.

Valencia, S. W., Hiebert, E. H., & Afflerbach, P. P. (Eds.). (1993). *Authentic reading assessment.* Newark, DE: International Reading Association.

Valencia, S. W., McGinely, W., & Pearson, P. D. (1990). Assessing reading and writing. In G. G. Duffy (Ed.), *Reading in the Middle School* (pp. 124–146). Newark, DE: International Reading Association.

PART IV

Interconnections

A reading program's richness comes from its diversity of components and students. In order for it to work effectively, it must work together with all facets of the school and community to create and improve literacy. This section of the book provides leaders of literacy with the necessary tools to create a fully effective program that attends to the diversity of students and the communities in which they live.

Chapter 11 looks at writing, its connection to reading, and its importance for literacy achievement today. This chapter includes ideas for facilitating writing and offers exemplary practice guidelines, based on current research, for strengthening writing in schools. Key components of sound writing instruction and ideas for different types of writing are also offered.

Chapter 12 addresses ways to make technology available to reading personnel and students. It identifies the skills that reading personnel should have to promote effective literacy programs, and it offers guidelines for acquiring such competencies. It also looks at the benefits of technology in delivering traditional literacy skills and in developing a new literacy for acquiring content knowledge.

Alongside special initiatives for developmentally average students are programs for those with unique backgrounds and special needs. Given that more and more children from diverse ethnic and linguistic cultures are entering our schools each day, Chapter 13 addresses current trends and issues related to diversity in the classroom. This chapter offers theoretical models for working with these diverse populations and practical ways of addressing their needs on a day-to-day basis.

Chapter 14 describes outreach initiatives for elementary and secondary parents and the community. Urban-suburban differences are addressed, as are community-driven and federally funded programs such as America Reads. The chapter includes topics to share with parents and ideas for creating successful partnerships between school districts and colleges and universities.

Chapter 15 focuses on students who find learning to read and write difficult and those who are in special education programs. This chapter reviews the literature on traditional and current approaches (pull-out and in-class models) that deal with special populations. It describes new early intervention programs such as Reading Recovery, Success for All, Early Steps, and Early Intervention in Reading. It also presents a list of questions to ask to determine the value of a program for students with special needs.

This last section of the book suggests that important links or interconnections to different programs, initiatives, and populations are essential for a reading program's success.

CHAPTER ELEVEN

Promoting Writing with Reading and Learning

Karen Bromley

Stacey, a fourth grade teacher, will move to fifth grade in September because she feels the pressures of new state assessments in reading and writing. Stacey says,

> I see what it does to my kids who are afraid they'll be held back if they don't pass the test. I feel like I've lost my freedom as a teacher and I must teach "on-demand" writing. It doesn't leave time for writing workshop or teaching the writing process. In fifth grade there's no test and I can do thematic

instruction and integrate writing with science and social studies. I can practice what I believe about good teaching.

Jim, an elementary school principal, says,

> We have more transfers out of fourth and eighth grade in our district where state tests are mandated than we've ever had. Teachers are feeling the pressure and opting out of teaching to the test. They don't want to be judged or compared according to their kids' scores.

In school districts around the country, principals report higher than normal openings in grades where students must write as part of new tests in reading, science, social studies, and math.

Louise, Coordinator of Curriculum and Professional Development for Stacey's district, says high standards and new assessments are a challenge for administrators and curriculum supervisors. At issue is not just helping those at grade levels with mandated tests. Helping all teachers feel competent and confident to teach writing and integrate it into reading and the content areas is a daunting task. Louise says,

> The new assessments have changed the focus of who is accountable. They are more complex than previous tests and we all have to realize that fourth, eighth, and twelfth grade teachers can't do it alone. In my district, the assessments have forced communication among K–12 teachers about literacy. We now have to use a common language. For example, everyone must know what "expository writing" is and we must all understand the characteristics of each genre of writing. We have to "converge" first before we can be creative and "diverge" with that knowledge.

One of Jim and Louise's problems is providing time in each building and at the district level for conversations, planning, and curriculum development in writing. Another problem administrators and supervisors face is maintaining the responsibility at all K–12 grade levels for teaching reading and writing, not just in language arts but in science, math, and social studies.

Added to the challenge of higher standards and new assessments, many states and school districts encourage or require the explicit and systematic use of phonics and related word skills in beginning reading instruction (Coles, 2000). Some school districts limit teachers' professional development programs to those that embrace phonics and omit whole language theory. Holistic approaches to literacy, while backed by a "thorough and comprehensive body of research" (Daniels, Zemelman, & Bizar, 1999), are criticized by politicians who believe they need quick solutions to fix failing schools and provide an edu-

cated workforce. Jim and Louise's school boards and state have remained neutral in these "Reading Wars" that engage many educators and policy makers. Their districts support a holistic view of reading that includes the use of writing process and direct teaching of skills and strategies in authentic contexts. Jim and Louise believe they and other administrators and curriculum supervisors need to maintain a balanced view of literacy instruction that integrates reading, writing, and learning.

Key Ideas for Administrators and Supervisors

This chapter identifies seven key ideas to help administrators and supervisors like Jim and Louise promote writing with reading and learning:

1. Know the reading-writing-learning connection and its limits.
2. Agree on long-range writing goals for all students.
3. Identify components of sound writing instruction.
4. Agree on a common curriculum and vocabulary.
5. Stay up-to-date with the literacy field and provide responsive professional development.
6. Form a community of writers and be a model.
7. Educate and involve parents as partners in writing instruction.

For each of these key ideas, the chapter provides:

◆ Ideas and resources for collaborating with teachers and parents to implement change
◆ Ways to achieve sound literacy curriculum and teaching practices that connect writing with reading and learning

The Reading-Writing-Learning Connection

One of Jim and Louise's most difficult challenges is helping teachers, many of whom are not writers and have not had coursework in writing, be competent and confident writing teachers. They believe that administrators and supervisors, as instructional leaders, need sound knowledge of the reading-writing-learning connection and writing process.

How are reading and writing related? Reading and writing are interactive and complementary processes; in the real world, they function together. Both readers and writers must know word meanings and spelling. Readers read what writers write. For a reader, the reading-writing interaction involves constructing a writer's message. For a writer, it involves alternating roles as reader and writer. A writer is usually a reader—often reading others' work before writing. Writing about something read can give the writer a deep appreciation both of what was read and how it was written. Writers read their own work as they draft, revise, and edit. Students continually alternate roles as readers and writers as they move back and forth between the two to interpret and use language to learn.

How does writing promote learning? Writing involves the eye, the hand, the head, and the heart. Through writing, students reinforce information to be learned. Writing is a tool for thinking that allows students to connect ideas and information about things they already know, and it allows for the creation of new knowledge. Writing gives students concrete evidence of their feelings, observations, and actions, and it lets them revisit and review these ideas. By writing, students can explore the known and the new, and they can manipulate language to communicate with themselves and others.

While reading and writing overlap, they are also separate, and their integration does not automatically lead to learning (Shanahan, 1997). Adding writing to the reading curriculum does not necessarily mean students will improve in reading. Because the two processes are so connected, it makes sense to integrate them; providing separate instruction in each makes sense because they are not mirror images of each other. Direct instruction in the skills and strategies of each process is necessary for students at all levels. For example, third graders may need explicit instruction in creating good leads and conclusions, and tenth graders may need instruction in the use of their senses and precise vocabulary to create imagery in their writing. Sometimes this kind of direct instruction is isolated from reading, but it can also be provided through real literature. For example, third grade teachers and their students can read and compare the work of authors like Pam Conrad, Seymour Simon, and Arnold Lobel, and teachers can model lessons using this literature to show students how these authors write leads and conclusions. Tenth grade teachers and students can read the poetry of Edgar Allen Poe or Emily Dickinson, and teachers can model lessons with this literature to show students how these writers evoke images.

Shanahan (1997) reminds us that "Improved learning is only likely to be the result if reading and writing are combined in appropriate ways" (p. 14). One of those ways is through thoughtful, integrated instruction that also includes direct explanation, instruction, and practice. When students read and write in the content areas of science, social studies, and math about ideas that are important to them, they process ideas and information more deeply and have a better chance of remembering that material than by just listening or reading.

Long-Range Writing Goals

Initially, administrators like Jim and Louise and teachers like Stacey need to know what the integration of reading and writing is meant to accomplish. One way to do this is to agree on long-range writing goals for students. Sanacore (1998a) reminds us of the importance of promoting a lifelong love of writing. He cites several reasons, including the pleasure writing brings individuals as they record their experiences, the reflection it affords, and its therapeutic function. This affective goal makes a sound basis for building the cognitive goals of a sound writing program: fluency, competence, and independence.

The International Reading Association (IRA) has developed standards for reading professionals (1998) that many educators find helpful when developing goals for a writing program. Standards are principles or ideals for learning that are agreed upon by a group of professionals. The IRA standards for reading specialists, coordinators, and administrators stipulate that educators should have a "comprehensive understanding" of how to teach students "planning strategies appropriate for particular kinds of writing; to draft, revise and edit their writing; and the conventions of standard written English needed to edit their work" (pp. 16–17). These guidelines can frame discussions with K–12 teachers to establish school or district writing goals. When all teachers are included in the creation of writing goals for students, the result is a shared vision for all students. Teachers are more likely to be guided in their teaching by that shared vision if they have a voice in its creation.

Some districts assemble a committee of administrators, supervisors, parents, teachers, and students to determine writing goals. A group like this might decide it is important to develop writers who possess, for example, the following skills.

- Fluency—to write easily, legibly, and quickly enough to communicate with an audience, whether it be oneself or others.
- Competence—to write accurately and proficiently in a variety of forms or genres for different purposes and audiences.
- Independence—to choose and enjoy writing, and possess the necessary writing skills and strategies to be able to write on one's own with a minimum of help and support.

These writing goals require knowledge of the writing curriculum, which includes the genres or types of writing and the writing process: planning, drafting, revising, editing, and publishing for an audience. A writing curriculum also includes the conventions of writing: spelling, punctuation, grammar, format considerations, legibility in handwriting, and ease in keyboarding.

The writing goals discussed previously assume a definition of writing that includes writing by hand with pen or pencil and writing electronically with a keyboard. Today, new technology standards and the rapid growth of technology and the Internet require that writing goals include electronic literacy as a way of writing and learning (Conyers, Kappel, & Rooney, 1999; DuPont, 2000; Rafferty, 1999; Thomas & Knezek, 1999).

Components of Sound Writing Instruction

In past decades, writing instruction has shifted from a focus on skills and the written product to a focus on writing process, and most recently to a balanced approach that embraces both process and product. How can administrators and supervisors address these changes and help teachers invite students to write, enjoy writing, learn as writers, and write well in a range of forms for a variety of purposes and audiences? One important way is for administrators and teachers to identify together what they consider the components of a sound writing program, for example as depicted in Figure 11.1 (Bromley, 1999). Each of the components in the figure is discussed below.

Standards and Assessments That Guide Instruction. Critics of national standards and high-stakes testing point out drawbacks and threats to both teachers and students, such as de-democratization of teaching (Hoffman, 2000), mediocrity in learning, narrowed curriculum, and technocratic teaching (O'Hanian, 1998). Nevertheless, standards and tests are a reality in most states. Many administrators and supervisors of literacy programs see new mandates as guidelines and a place to begin conversations about accountability in teaching and learning. They use standards and assessments as an opportunity to help teachers shape better teaching of writing and literacy to ensure learning for all students (Strong, Silver, & Perini, 1999).

Large Blocks of Time for Writing, Reading, Discussion, and Sharing. Isolated skill instruction can be accomplished in short segments of time, but integrated instruction focused on meaningful learning with application in authentic contexts requires larger blocks of time. For example, using a workshop approach to teaching writing and reading includes such things as mini-lessons; work time for planning, writing, and revising; conferring with peers, response groups, and the teacher; share sessions and publication celebrations (Atwell, 1998; Calkins, 1994; Graves, 1994).

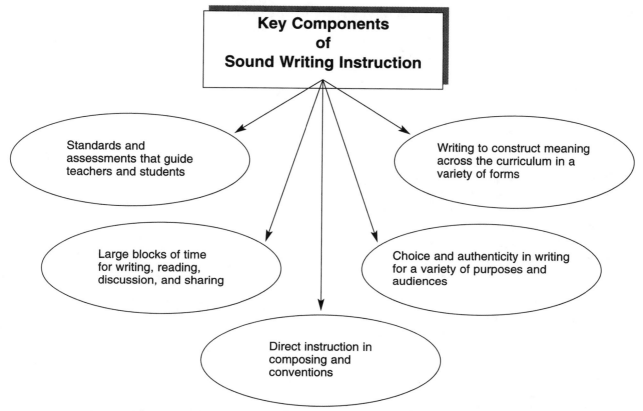

Figure 11.1. Identifying Key Components of a Writing Program

Direct Instruction in Composing and Conventions. Good teachers of writing know that students need direct and systematic instruction in writing as well as time to write (Routman, 1996). Embedded in integrated instruction should be opportunities for lessons, guidance, and practice that allow students to become accomplished writers.

Choice and Authenticity in Writing for a Variety of Purposes and Audiences. Writing for lots of different reasons and audiences builds fluency, competence, and independence. K–12 students need opportunities to become proficient writers on the Internet and with word processors as well as with traditional paper and pencil or pen. Extending literacy beyond traditional print should be a significant part of a strong writing program.

Writing to Construct Meaning Across the Curriculum in a Variety of Forms. K–12 students should write in every genre to show what they have learned and to build new knowledge in science, social studies, math, and other content areas. For example, tenth grade students can use poetry in social studies to relate the agony of war as they study world conflicts, or second graders can write persuasive letters to a community leader about the need for a hiking and biking trail along a local river.

Once components like these or a similar sound framework for a writing program are identified, school faculty and district administrators can plan opportunities for the professional growth of teachers, administrators, and supervisors, and for curriculum development as well as the education of parents about the school's writing program.

A Common Curriculum and Vocabulary

Louise's idea of adopting a common language goes hand-in-hand with agreeing on a writing curriculum. She knows that as supervisor of her district's writing program, she and her teachers must share a vision for the content of the curriculum before they can all support and implement it effectively. One important aspect of a writing curriculum is the genres or types of writing everyone will teach. Typically, a K–12 writing curriculum includes four types of writing: expository, persuasive, descriptive, and narrative (see Appendix A). Most good writing in everyday life contains elements of each of the four types. For example, a well-written newspaper article about a national park may be expository in style overall but include descriptive imagery, a narration of the park's history, and a persuasive style to influence readers to visit the park. Teaching the four types of writing separately makes sense, but the ultimate goal is for students to use elements of the four types together to produce well-crafted writing.

As well as identifying the types of writing to teach, Louise and her teachers must find other common ground. They have to resolve what at first appears to be huge differences between on-demand writing required in state assessments and process writing that most teachers have taught for several years. Louise captures the similarities and differences in a question and answer format for her teachers (see Appendix B). Used at professional development workshops, this handout helps Stacey and other K–12 teachers plan for ways to include on-demand writing and process writing in all content areas of the curriculum.

Current Practice and Professional Development

Jim and Louise say that staying current with new practices and trends in education is difficult. Even more challenging is remaining current in specific areas such as writing. One of the best ways they stay informed is through their professional organizations. Many administrators and supervisors of literacy programs belong to the following organizations and read the journals they publish, which include articles and studies about research and practices in teaching writing:

- International Reading Association (IRA) (www.reading.org)
  - *The Reading Teacher* (for elementary teachers)
  - *Journal of Adolescent and Adult Literacy* (for middle and high school teachers)
  - www.readingonline.org (an electronic journal for K–12 educators)
- National Council of Teachers of English (NCTE) (www.ncte.org)
  - *Language Arts* (for elementary teachers)
  - *English Journal* (for middle and high school teachers)
- Association for Supervision and Curriculum Development (ASCD) (www.ascd.org)
  - *Educational Leadership* (for K–12 educators)

Jim believes he needs to be knowledgeable about current research and theory in writing so he can support his teachers and make informed decisions about his school's literacy program. Besides reading journals and visiting the previously mentioned websites, one of the things he does is listen to and observe his Early Literacy Team Leader, a reading specialist who is trained in Reading Recovery and writing process and who focuses on K–3 literacy. Jim's district has identified one reading specialist in each elementary school as an Early Literacy Team Leader. The district's four team leaders attend conferences and workshops to stay up-to-date with current literacy practices. They in turn spend a half-day teaching Reading Recovery practices to struggling students and a half-day in classroom support. They teach model lessons, co-teach lessons with classroom teachers, observe and respond to teachers, provide materials and ideas, co-plan strategies for guided reading and writing, assess students, and provide training on topics teachers request. Jim attends this training because it helps him better understand literacy instruction and how his teachers are implementing best practices in writing.

Louise also believes in the power of responsive staff development. Louise's district has identified a Literacy Specialist and Coach for K–8 teachers who does professional development training on topics and problems teachers project as concerns for the next three years. Louise says,

> Teachers go back to their classrooms, where they implement ideas and do action-research for several weeks before they come back and share. They bring stories, student work, and examples of what they have done. Together we critique and celebrate successes and "failing forward," which means we acknowledge when things don't work quite right but we celebrate the fact that something's been tried.

Louise believes "Professional development shouldn't be an event; it should be a continuous journey."

One problem both Jim and Louise acknowledge is that some reading specialists don't see themselves as literacy leaders. Jim says, "There is some discomfort with being too directive with others, and the team leaders don't want to be viewed as administrators. We've been working on that with leadership training for our team leaders and other reading specialists." According to Louise, "Some of our reading teachers don't realize how important their leadership is. Any style is OK—but they must be the experts and leaders in their field. They must be willing to go into a classroom, try something, and if it doesn't get them where they want to be, they must know how to approach it differently next time." Louise uses *Habits of Mind* (Costa & Kallick, 2000) in district professional development with reading specialists and classroom teachers.

A Community of Writers

Louise says another challenge is getting teachers and principals to write. She believes that to teach writing well, teachers must be writers themselves, and many aren't. At the beginning of workshops in content-area writing, she and her reading specialists ask participants, "How did you become an effective writer?" This self-assessment usually results in the acknowledgement by many teachers that they don't write and don't believe they write well. In the ensuing dis-

cussion, teachers voice their need to learn how to write and teach writing better.

One of the ways Louise gets teachers to write is by having them examine the state assessments, then create "parallel tasks," and finally write exemplary responses. When they look at the tests, teachers learn the kinds of reading and writing skills the tests require, and then they apply this knowledge as they design similar kinds of questions. In supportive and collaborative groups, when teachers write responses to their own tasks and use rubrics to evaluate their writing, they begin to analyze the assumptions they hold about what good writing is and what it takes to be a good writer.

Louise's advice to her teachers is to be a model and write for and with students: "We should be saying to students, 'Let's learn together how to study and fix the writing problems we have.' Write the assignments yourselves that you give kids and share your writing with them. Find areas in your own writing to improve and use these examples as models." In this way, teachers form a community of learners and writers as they teach, write, and learn themselves.

Another way to form a community of writers is through study groups. Louise and other supervisors and administrators find that teachers are eager to learn and improve their practice in these small, voluntary groups that form to read and discuss a professional book. Typically, teachers choose the book and the district purchases and distributes copies. Groups often meet once a week for 30–45 minutes before school to discuss two or three chapters at a time and enjoy coffee, tea, bagels, and muffins. From these discussions, some teachers form small support groups for their own writing. Study groups can subtly and positively influence teacher knowledge and practices in teaching writing.

Parents as Partners in Writing Instruction

Sanacore (1997, 1998b) reminds supervisors and administrators about the importance of listening to parental concerns and educating them about what is being taught. Both he and Routman (1996) say educators must be proactive in responding to parental concerns about skill development. Showing parents that their concerns are valued and that your writing program reflects a balanced approach that includes both on-demand and process writing where basic writing skills are taught within a meaningful context across the curriculum will do much to promote school credibility and decrease or eliminate the incidence of school criticism. Sanacore suggests involving parents in curriculum development by making them members of curriculum committees.

Sanacore (1997) urges administrators and supervisors to reach out to parents in a variety of ways. Parents who know and understand the rationale behind a spelling or writing program are probably much more inclined to support it at home and with other parents. Sanacore mentions newsletters, presentations at PTA organizations and curriculum nights, coffee klatches, parent-teacher conferences, and invitations to informally observe and discuss classroom practices. Creative educators have found additional ways to enrich parents' understanding of literacy programs. For example, newsletters posted on school or district websites or Internet chat sessions can explain the literacy program to parents with computer access.

Parents can be a vital resource for a school's writing program. Stacey has found that many parents are eager and willing to share their perspectives about writing and the different kinds of writing they do in their jobs and careers. When parents share varied examples of real-life writing, they can highlight for K–12 students the ways writing serves people in the world of work. Moreover, they can give students reasons for learning to be good writers.

Conclusion

Stacey, Jim, and Louise know that there is not just one way to teach literacy. They know that a literacy program will be a strong one if it is balanced and responsive to the concerns of all its constituents. They use higher standards and new assessments as a place to begin conversations about integrating writing with reading. They

know collaboration among students, parents, teachers, administrators, and supervisors is a sound way to educate, plan, and implement a literacy program that promotes writing with reading and learning. They know that through writing, K–12 students can learn in science, social studies, math, and other curriculum areas as they engage in on-demand tasks and writing process. They know that writing can be "a powerful catalyst for learning" (Jenkinson, 1988).

Appendix A: Types of Writing in K–12 Writing Programs

Expository Writing. Writing to explain, inform, make factual information clear, or tell how a process happens. Students do this kind of writing most often.

Elements:

- ◆ A main idea clearly stated or implied.
- ◆ Information that supports and develops the main idea.
- ◆ A clearly ordered sequence of facts and details.
- ◆ A specific audience in mind.

Examples:

- ◆ Messages
- ◆ Invitations
- ◆ Announcements
- ◆ Directions
- ◆ Paragraphs
- ◆ Explanations
- ◆ Reports
- ◆ Learning logs

Persuasive Writing. Writing to convince or persuade. It is done to change the opinion of others or influence someone's actions.

Elements:

- ◆ An opinion clearly stated.
- ◆ Supporting facts and examples as evidence.
- ◆ Logical and orderly arguments.

- Vivid and specific vocabulary.
- Language and tone appropriate for the target audience.

Examples:

- Advertisements
- Product descriptions
- Sales pitches
- Tributes
- Travel brochures
- Letters
- Essays
- Editorials
- Book reviews

Descriptive Writing. Writing that develops images by using precise sensory words and phrases. It is used in expository writing to present facts clearly (e.g., the life cycle of a butterfly) and in persuasive writing to present and support an opinion (e.g., the need for a hiking trail along the riverbank in a community).

Elements:

- Precise, vivid vocabulary that describes accurately.
- Sensory images (sights, sounds, smells, tastes, textures).
- Effective use of comparisons (e.g., metaphor, simile, personification).
- Clear images or pictures that have unity and focus.
- Organization and logical sequence.

Examples:

- Sentences and paragraphs that are parts of a story, report, essay, advertisement, or letter
- Poems
- Biographical sketches
- Processes (How a _____ Works)
- Procedures (Our Trip to _____)
- Essays
- Editorials
- Reports
- Letters

Narrative Writing. Writing that tells a story or gives an account of events. It can be fiction or nonfiction and can be a retelling, new version, sequel, or original account.

Elements:

- An introduction and conclusion.
- Plot or sequence of events told in order.
- A character, setting, or event to care about in the first sentence
- A conflict or problem to solve.
- Setting that makes sense and helps the story.
- Vivid, exact words.
- Theme that everyone understands and can relate to.

Examples:

- Autobiographies
- Biographies
- Stories
- Story summaries
- Nonfiction accounts
- Plays
- Journals
- Learning logs
- Letters
- Reports
- Book character conversations
- Sequels or new chapters or episodes

Appendix B:
Questions and Answers About On-Demand Writing*

1. *What is on-demand writing?*

   On-demand writing is time-restrictive writing. It is the writing process in an accelerated and compacted form. There are four steps to the on-demand writing process:

   —Planning
   —Writing
   —Editing
   —Publishing

2. *Why should educators be concerned about on-demand writing?*

   - On-demand writing is the type of writing most adults engage in on a daily basis. If schools are in the business of preparing students for life, it makes sense that the writing curriculum focus on developing this skill.

- ◆ The increased on-demand writing expectation found on all state assessments encourages us to examine how to develop student skill and fluency in on-demand writing. All state exams ask students to respond to challenging questions by writing coherent, well-developed, logical answers that are supported with content-area facts or text details in a restricted time. In other words, students' writing skills are being put to the test of time.

3. *What are some examples of on-demand writing?*

- ◆ In the classroom: short responses to literature and content texts; content-area assignments in social studies, science, and math; assignments for homework and classroom assessment purposes.
- ◆ On the state exams: short-response questions, extended responses, thematic essays, document-based questions, and scaffolded questions.

4. *How is the on-demand writing process different from the writing process?*

- ◆ In on-demand writing, the first copy the writer produces is usually the final copy. The restriction of time promotes a linear writing process that requires the writer to prioritize tasks as follows: (1) planning, (2) writing, and (3) editing. The time restriction allows little "wiggle" room with the process of on-demand writing.
- ◆ True implementation of the writing process includes recursive steps that require ample time for students to:
  —Plan
  —Produce several drafts
  —Conference with critical friends and the teacher
  —Revise
  —Edit
  —Share published work

5. *Does this new emphasis on on-demand writing mean teachers should stop teaching the writing process?*

Absolutely not! It is important to emphasize that on-demand writing is a version of the writing process. It is very important that students have ample time to learn about the art of writing through the steps of the writing process. In fact, this is the best preparation for on-demand writing! However, students should not be required to use the writing process with all classroom assignments. Many assignments lend themselves to teaching and practicing the on-demand writing process, for example, short responses to literature and content-area assignments. If ample time is given to modeling the thinking and organizing needed for on-demand writing, student writing skill and fluency in on-demand writing can improve.

6. *How can we help students become proficient on-demand writers?*

There are many ways to improve student ability to produce coherent, well-developed, logical writing in a brief time period. Among them are:

- ◆ Teach and model the writing process through the use of think-alouds, write-alouds, and critiques of exemplars. Regular practice with the writing process helps students learn the art of writing.
- ◆ Help students:
  —Understand the purpose of the writing task.
  —Select the best planning or organizing structure.
  —Learn how to use the structure in their writing.

Our ultimate goal should be to move students toward independence in selecting and using a few useful planning or organizing structures. It is critical that students understand the graphic organizer as a logical precursor to effective writing. Clever and cute graphic organizers do not always support logical and thoughtful writing. Ideally, a K–12 writing program provides a sequential and developmentally appropriate continuum of instruction in several basic graphic organizers.

◆ As a class, regularly examine the differences and similarities between on-demand writing and the writing process.

◆ Help students plan for and assess their own writing and the writing of others by having them use rubrics you create together. The state assessments provide one model for developing such rubrics.

*Created by Louise Cleveland

Acknowledgments: We extend special thanks to Jim Fountaine, Principal, Union-Endicott Schools, Endicott, New York, and Louise Cleveland, Coordinator of Curriculum and Professional Development, Vestal Central Schools, Vestal, New York, for generously sharing their ideas and insights.

References

Atwell, N. (1998). *In the middle: New understandings about writing, reading, and learning.* Portsmouth, NH: Heinemann.

Bromley, K. (1999). Key components of sound writing instruction. In L. Gambrell, L. M. Morrow, S. Neuman, & M. Pressley (Eds.), *Best practices in literacy instruction* (pp. 152–174). New York: Guilford.

Calkins, L. (1994). *The art of teaching writing.* Portsmouth, NH: Heinemann.

Coles, G. (2000). Direct, explicit and systematic: Bad reading science. *Language Arts, 77,* 543–545.

Conyers, J. G., Kappel, T., & Rooney, J. (1999). How technology can transform a school. *Educational Leadership, 56*(5), 82–85.

Costa, A. L., & Kallick, B. (2000). *Habits of mind.* Alexandria, VA: Association for Supervision and Curriculum Development.

Daniels, H., Zemelman, S., & Bizar, M. (1999). Whole language works: Sixty years of research. *Educational Leadership, 57*(2), 32–37.

DuPont, S. (2000, March). Hard hitters! Hardware without headaches for the 21st century. *Instructor,* 88–93.

Graves, D. H. (1994). *A fresh look at writing.* Portsmouth, NH: Heinemann.

Hoffman, J. (2000). The de-democratization of schools and literacy in America. *The Reading Teacher, 53,* 615–623.

International Reading Association. (1998). *Standards for reading professionals, revised.* Newark, DE: Author.

Jenkinson, E. B. (1988). Learning to write/writing to learn. *Phi Delta Kappan, 69,* 712–716.

O'Hanian, S. (1998). *One size fits few.* Portsmouth, NH: Heinemann.

Rafferty, C. D. (1999). Literacy in the information age. *Educational Leadership, 57*(2), 22–25.

Routman, R. (1996). *Literacy at the crossroads.* Portsmouth, NH: Heinemann.

Sanacore, J. (1997). Guidelines for successful reading leaders. *Journal of Adolescent and Adult Literacy, 41,* 64–68.

Sanacore, J. (1998a). Promoting the lifelong love of writing. *Journal of Adolescent and Adult Literacy, 41,* 392–399.

Sanacore, J. (1998b). Responding proactively to criticisms of literacy-learning practices. *Journal of Adolescent and Adult Literacy, 41,* 574–579.

Shanahan, T. (1997). Reading-writing relationships, thematic units, inquiry learning: In pursuit of effective integrated literacy instruction. *The Reading Teacher, 51,* 12–19.

Strong, R., Silver, H., & Perini, M. (1999). Keeping it simple and deep. *Educational Leadership, 56*(6), 22–24.

Thomas, L. G., & Knezek, D. G. (1999). National educational technology standards. *Educational Leadership, 56*(5), 27.

CHAPTER TWELVE

Leading and Learning with Technology

Shelley B. Wepner and Lucinda C. Ray

In reading supervisor Linda Trent's school district, reading specialists use technology to support and enhance their teaching. Trent believes the specialists' instructional style will influence classroom teachers to follow their lead. She is convinced that the literacy of today and tomorrow assumes the ability to use both technology and traditional print media to communicate, access information, and learn.

Trent works closely with the district's technology coordinator to create an infrastructure for her eleven reading specialists. They each have five computers in their classrooms for students' individualized instruction. For demonstration lessons, each reading specialist also has a mobile computer station complete with a video projection system, speakers, and a printer. Technology specialists are available in each building to troubleshoot and assist with technological challenges.

Trent makes technology a priority for the reading specialists. She organizes workshops at regular intervals throughout the year to develop their skills. They must demonstrate their competencies with keyboarding, computer vocabulary, desktop navigation (find files, copy disks, use the control panel), web searching, word processing, and database management. She also has each school's technology specialist work with the reading specialists to maintain the district's web page on the reading program. She and her reading specialists communicate almost daily through email and instant messaging. They use the district's electronic student records to enter and discuss anecdotal observations, informal assessment results, and the success of programs, materials, and strategies.

Her most recent venture with a team of two reading specialists has been the creation of an interschool teleconferencing hour in which remedial students participate in book talks between schools. These reading specialists have observed that their students are especially motivated to read and discuss the books assigned for the book talks. She intends to have all of her reading specialists bring this pilot project to the regular classrooms within the next year. The two reading specialists who experimented with teleconferencing will mentor the other reading specialists in the district. Trent has used similar approaches over the years to develop the high caliber of technology-using reading specialists.

This administrator's leadership with technology is the result of a time-consuming and painstaking process of learning for herself and her colleagues. Notwithstanding the perceived enormity of such an undertaking, there are certain content topics and process methods that help leaders of literacy move their schools and districts forward. This chapter discusses:

◆ What reading personnel need to know about technology
◆ Making technology available to students
◆ Ways to get started
◆ Creating a professional development plan

What Reading Personnel Need to Know About Technology

Navigating technology is similar to operating a car. When we buy a car, we usually don't read the comprehensive owner's guide cover to cover.

We simply cannot remember, and usually are not interested in remembering, all the details of the car's mechanical operation. Instead, we keep the manual in the glove compartment and use it as the need arises. At the same time, we try to learn about the options that come with the car so that we can drive it with all the creature comforts. Years of experience with driving enable us to know enough about the basics of operating a car that we can drive a new vehicle almost immediately.

Much of this approach to driving a car extends to operating a computer. Years of experience with computers enable us to move from one brand of machine to the next, and from one computer upgrade to another, with a fair amount of ease. We use manuals and guides for information and tips about the unique features of a new platform or a new model, but seldom do we read them cover to cover.

Those new to navigating technology are similar to those new to driving a car in that certain levels of knowledge, skills, and practice are essential for developing independence with the machine. This section highlights basic technological knowledge and skills needed in three major areas: hardware and basic desktop commands, application programs, and electronic communication.

Knowledge of Hardware and Basic Desktop Commands

Our knowledge of computer hardware includes our ability to work with a central processing unit, monitor, printer, keyboard, and mouse. It also means working with modems, disk drives, speakers, microphones, scanners, digital cameras, and video projection devices, especially if we are responsible for or called upon to demonstrate software or Internet sites to students.

Navigating a computer desktop involves knowing how to start and shut down a system; how to find, open, copy, print, close, and save files to both the hard drive and storage media such as ZIP or floppy disks; how to install, open, and close programs; how to keep multiple programs in temporary memory; and how to use the operating system's control panel to adjust color, modify the design of a desktop, and change the date and time.

Knowledge of Application Programs

Application programs are the electronic tools of the trade. Word processing programs such as Microsoft Word enable us to write with greater fluency, especially if we are facile with options such as format and font, and commands such as cut, paste, and copy. Multimedia tools such as PowerPoint and HyperStudio help us to present ideas effectively and to help students do the same. Database management programs such as Microsoft Access help with class lists and student assignments; electronic spreadsheets such as Microsoft Excel help with grade calculations. Knowing how and when to use curricular applications for their tutorial, drill and practice, and exploratory features for specific age and ability groups helps us work with students more effectively.

Knowledge of Electronic Communication

Communication commands, concepts, and software connect teachers and students to other people, places, and ports of information. Knowing how to use a web browser (for example, Netscape Navigator or Internet Explorer), how to send email, how to use listservs, and how to search for websites are vital for successful instruction and leadership in our field. Electronic communication generally falls into two broad categories: asynchronous, which is analogous to traditional written communication, and synchronous, which is analogous to traditional oral communication.

Asynchronous Communication. Asynchronous communication involves a time lag of some length. The sender and receiver work independently, and each often waits to receive a message before composing and sending one. The communication style is therefore linear. It most typically occurs in writing, although voice messages also belong in this category. Examples of asynchronous communication include email, key pals, distance learning, on-line instruction, and web publishing.

Email is the most common form of asynchronous electronic communication. Its delivery time is fast, and the receiver can choose when or whether to respond. Besides speed, a benefit of email is that one can communicate easily and cheaply with people in remote parts of the world. This easy and fast access motivates students to compose, read, and write who otherwise resist reading or writing much of anything at all in a traditional sort of assignment. Key pals, or electronic pen pals, are typically students who use email to correspond with students in other schools.

Distance learning and on-line instruction are the electronic versions of the correspondence courses of the past. Whether course content is provided through video, over the Internet, or in some combination, electronic media make it possible for people who are physically unable to meet in a traditional classroom to participate in a learning experience and a learning community.

Web publishing is a formal way of reporting on learning. It resembles the sharing of information in a journal article or term paper, but there are powerful differences. First, web publishing allows for a much broader audience. Knowledge is not just delivered to one person but rather is shared widely. Second, information that is published on a website can be enhanced with multimedia and usually cross-referenced to other material. These hyperlinks, created intentionally between one's knowledge and other sources, are indicators of the way technology enables learners to connect their knowledge with related ideas and resources.

These technological options offer access to new or additional resources for learning, both for teaching and learning. Teachers involved in professional listservs (asynchronous group email) and email with colleagues have an ever wider pool of ideas, recommended books, and tips about where to find good information on a particular topic. They may discover websites that have good maps or lesson plans to supplement a curricular unit.

Synchronous Communication. Synchronous communication happens in "real time"; the communication act is experienced simultaneously by sender and receiver. It is similar to speech, even if the actual message is textual. Examples of synchronous communication include on-line chatting, instant messaging, teleconferencing, and electronic whiteboards.

On-line chatting and instant messaging enable two or more people to enter text into an electronic space at the same time. Participants compose and post ideas in the same way a conversation flows at a dinner party. If there are more than two participants (chat), a unified conversation can easily diverge into several threads of dialogue that coexist in the common space, much as two groups at a table break off into separate conversations.

Teleconferencing enables real-time oral conversations between widely dispersed participants. While teleconferencing offers a visual component, its use is somewhat restricted because it requires specific facilities. Electronic whiteboards enable participants to view, comment on, or annotate material. They enable dispersed groups working together on a presentation or project to see and edit that project together, rather than sending drafts or versions around for review and revision.

Making Technology Available to Students

Students benefit from technology because it delivers traditional literacy skills and content knowledge in an interactive medium. Second, technology challenges students to develop electronic literacy to build their communication skills and their own knowledge base.

Developing Students' Traditional Literacy Skills

CD-ROM software and web-based applications help students learn traditional literacy skills and content knowledge across curricular areas (Wepner & Ray, 2000). These applications are especially useful when they are aligned with curricular goals and state standards. It is just a matter of sifting through CD-ROM software programs

to locate the specific applications that will help students with the needed skills. A variety of commercial companies provide databases on CD-ROM and on the Internet that match the specific content of curricular software with national or state curriculum standards. Websites·such as the California Clearinghouse (http://clearinghouse.k12.ca.us) provide software reviews to help guide choices. Preview centers exist across the country in area education agencies, universities, and other publicly accessible sites where educators can review software before it is purchased. Moreover, most software companies offer 30–60-day preview policies to allow schools to return inappropriate software purchases.

Linda Trent recently created an after-school club through which a group of reading specialists and students of varying ages and abilities review software and websites together and rate them according to specific characteristics. She uses this club to develop an annotated bibliography of software and websites. The software bibliography includes information about location, platform compatibility, network capabilities, and the number of copies available within the district. The website bibliography is divided into sites that contain electronic books, sites about specific authors, and sites that focus on specific skills.

Developing a New Literacy

As students learn to communicate globally, use electronic research and presentation tools, and conduct on-line research, they are developing a new literacy with technology that helps them acquire content knowledge. Communicating globally through electronic media is increasing students' interest in and use of the language arts of reading and writing. Key pals connect students with contexts and issues that teachers previously had to fabricate on bulletin boards or evoke in filmstrips or videos. Many websites exist that are specifically designed for teachers who are looking for collaborative projects with schools all over the world, or for book discussions or curricular projects with students from such schools. These real-world communication opportunities stimulate nonwriters to create text and nonreaders to rush to school to read an email posting.

Electronic research and presentation tools facilitate nonlinear searching for information and offer writers new strategies for organizing ideas and presenting information. Students are challenged to find and establish specific connections between ideas that are coherent and cognitively effective. Our challenge is to keep ahead of, or at least on par with, students so that we feel comfortable working collaboratively with them to share ideas and techniques.

Conducting on-line research has become a necessary skill for accessing information. Learning to search with Boolean operators is no longer an esoteric skill in the realm of the computer scientist, but rather a lifelong literacy skill. A decade ago, it was the teacher's responsibility to help students learn to use a card catalog and to locate what information might be available on a topic. In the information age, teachers need to help students access and then learn to sift through the huge amount of information available on-line and to establish sophisticated selection and evaluation skills.

Even though many students may be facile with surfing the web or accessing information, they need to apply research criteria and standards to on-line sources. Giving credit to one's sources, staying within the limits of current copyright laws, and verifying the credibility and authority of a site are skills students need to learn to apply to on-line materials in the same way that they learn to apply them to print materials.

Dealing With Access Issues

School districts must grapple with important equity issues. How widely is technology really available to all students? What policies has your district put in place to ensure that all students have an equal opportunity to learn to use technology and to make use of that learned skill during and after school hours?

The digital divide should end at the doorway of each school, whether it is a pre-school or a high school, an inner-city multiracial school or a suburban college preparatory showcase school.

Technology should be as available in a classroom as in a computer lab, in a marine biology class as in a remedial reading class. Does each location have the same high-speed Internet connection? Does each have the same proportional number of computers with the same processor speeds and peripheral devices? If not, why not?

Is technology in all of these locations being used to advance curricular achievement? Or do some sites continue to use software as a reward for early finishers (i.e., high-achieving students) or as a babysitter for students unable to participate in collaborative classroom work? Does your district choose to wink at the reluctance of some of the professional staff to embrace technology rather than to recognize that this reluctance restricts the opportunities for their students?

Reading professionals who are committed to the integration of technology into all areas of the curriculum need to take an active role in the distribution of computer hardware, software, training, and Internet access throughout the schools in the district. The following can serve as guidelines for these committed educators:

♦ Determine whether there are computer labs, computers in each classroom, or laptop computers available for students and teachers to check out.

♦ Tour the local public and college libraries in your area to make sure that students within your schools are learning the routines they will need to access material at these locations.

♦ Volunteer to serve on local committees that make decisions about what kinds of research tools (CD-ROM databases, subscription services, on-line catalogs, software, Internet access, or filtering software) are chosen for each site.

♦ Monitor the sign-up procedures for student computer use in each facility to ensure that all students have equal access to the learning, research, and communication tools that technology offers.

♦ Help your district or school establish "acceptable use" policies to communicate with students about appropriate use of technology and to communicate with parents about your school's commitment to their children's safety and responsibility in using technology.

Technology, like any other instructional tool, is valuable only when it is available consistently, fairly, and effectively for all learners. This includes students with special needs.

Technology for Inclusion

In 1997, the federal government passed important amendments to the Individuals With Disabilities Education Act (IDEA) affecting the nation's 5.8 million students with special needs, including both learning disabilities and physical disabilities. This legislation requires that all children with disabilities have available to them a free, appropriate public education that emphasizes special education and related services designed to meet their unique needs and prepare them for employment and independent living. (See Chapter 15 for additional information about special needs students.) Under IDEA, specific considerations must be made for certain groups of disabled children, many of which involve technology. For example, Individual Educational Program (IEP) teams must consider the communications needs of children and the use of assistive technology for those who require it.

Technology can provide access to reading materials that regular students use in paper form. For example, students with low vision may need screen enlargers to magnify the type. Some students with motoric disabilities may be unable to hold a book or pencil but can perform capably with software and alternative keyboards, switches, or other input devices. For some students, the cognitive load of a full page of text may be overwhelming, while software that can divide the same material into smaller chunks of information may enable them to process it.

A variety of assistive devices are available to provide access to the kinds of standard software that have been discussed thus far:

◆ Special keyboards for students with limited hand or arm mobility
◆ Screen enlargers for students with low vision
◆ Switches, head pointers, and puff and sip devices for students with severe motor restrictions

◆ Voice-activated menus for low vision or blind users
◆ Text-to-speech features that enable students to hear what they write
◆ Word-prediction word processors to speed the writing task for students who have motor restrictions that make composing text a painfully slow task

Some software companies develop programs that are specifically designed to remediate special learning needs. For example, some programs focus on students' auditory perception, discrimination, and processing—skills essential in the acquisition of phonemic awareness and phonics skills. Some software programs train students to develop cause-and-effect skills necessary to control devices such as wheelchairs. A useful book on assistive devices and programs is *Computer Resources for People With Disabilities* (Alliance for Technology Access, 2000).

Providing access to and knowledge of electronic skills and resources requires committed leadership, especially from literacy educators. The next section highlights steps to take to acquire the expertise needed to bring about such change.

Ways to Get Started

A simple set of statistics will clarify how quickly technology is being assimilated. In 1998, computers with Internet connections were in more than 90% of schools and more than 40% of fourth through twelfth grade classrooms (Becker, 1999; Schlager, 2000). As of 2000, 57% of the nation's classrooms have direct access to the Internet. Moreover, 65.2% of classroom teachers use the Internet for teaching (Stephens, 2000). The ever-increasing presence of technology in the schools and its ever-growing use by teachers make clear the compelling need for leaders in literacy education to be aware of how technology use affects teaching and learning. Ironically, the problems with the quantity and quality of technology use are the same problems that existed years ago: access, professional development, and time. Our advice in the next few sections for getting started, or for helping someone else get started, is similar to advice given years ago. Important differences, however, are the level of sophistication of technology available and its greatly increased availability.

Get Yourself Involved

In order to advocate for the use of technology, you need to appreciate its value and use it frequently enough to be aware of technology's integral role in the lives of students. After all, most companies have a website. Local bus schedules and school bulletin boards are accessible on websites. Print, radio, and television ads include website addresses.

Use the K-W-L instructional framework (Ogle, 1986) to find out what you *know,* what you *want* to learn, and what you have *learned* and still need to learn. Then, look for assistance from colleagues, friends, and family. Attend workshops and courses, especially those offered by your school districts, universities, and professional organizations. Observe others using technology. Find a buddy you trust to introduce you to some of the rudimentary skills. Obtain a software package such as one of the many versions of Mavis Beacon Teaches Typing (1999) to help with keyboarding skills or an electronic book such as Just Grandma and Me Deluxe (1997) to work with interactive features that require using the mouse to see hidden actions and activities.

Look to universities for technology support and tutoring. The technology field has become so specialized that, as you seek assistance, you should identify the kind of expert you need: web expert, machine expert, software expert, systems expert, or research expert. Acknowledge that you need access, training, and time to really become proficient with technology. Be certain to get training every year, not only to learn about the latest technologies and accompanying application packages but also to fill in the gaps of what you still need to learn.

The goal should be that technology is almost an invisible part of the curriculum. The focus should be not so much on technology itself but its use as a resource for learning, data collection and analysis, and communication. If our teach-

ers see that we are doing this for ourselves and for them, they in turn will do it for their students.

Part of our ability to deliver professional development to our teachers requires an awareness of what our school districts and schools, and neighboring schools and districts, expect from students. Informal needs assessments help us find out what is available in support, personnel, resources, and professional development, and what is actually happening in the classrooms, the labs, and the community. Observations, conversations, interviews, and email with contacts within and outside the district help us gather information. It is then possible to use existing resources from our school districts, schools, and community agencies to help get started. See the Appendix to this chapter for a list of recommended resources.

Identify Significant Others Who Can Help You Move Forward

Find an expert teacher or technotutor in your school or district who can teach teachers the skills needed for working with technology. Technotutors are teachers with certain areas of technological expertise who make office calls to tutor faculty on, for example, creating web pages or searching the World Wide Web. Teachers know to contact a technotutor hotline for their queries, and a technotutor with the appropriate expertise gets assigned.

Work with others from both pre-K–12 and higher education interested in pursuing technology projects. For instance, computer coordinator Joan Farnsworth (2000) approached a local university to start a mentoring project with pre-service teachers. These pre-service teachers, as part of their field experience requirements in a methods course, used email to be telementored by a teacher in Farnsworth's district to develop lessons that they ultimately taught.

Professors of reading and language arts methods courses pair their students with classes of students in local school districts. For example, Roe (2000) paired her students with seventh graders in a middle school to discuss literature selections that both groups were reading. The partners communicated about the selections through regularly scheduled email exchanges. The university students used this assignment as an opportunity to apply the literary analysis and reading strategies learned in the methods courses. Sullivan (1998) had her university students use email with fifth grade, special needs students to share ideas about selections from children's literature. The university students had the fifth graders think about literary elements found in the books (character development, foreshadowing, and tension) and make comparisons with events in the story and their own life experiences. The fifth grade teacher helped students to prepare their responses through oral discussion groups and then had the students compose their responses on a word processor before sending them as an email message.

Creating a Professional Development Plan

A professional development plan for the teaching staff needs to be crafted similarly to the way we plan instruction for students. For instance, a combination of whole class, small-group, and individual instruction, with ample time set aside for practice and feedback, should be planned. The competencies that teachers need to develop (Strong, Wepner, Furlong, & Wartenberg, 2000) include the ability to:

♦ use and apply CD-ROM software for word recognition and vocabulary, reading development, writing, and content learning
♦ use basic desktop and electronic applications for data management and the expression of ideas
♦ communicate electronically with others through asynchronous and synchronous modes
♦ use the web to conduct on-line research as a reference tool and an instructional tool
♦ mix and match CD-ROM software, communication tools, and Internet tools for lesson and unit development

These competencies help teachers meet the standards prescribed by the International Society for Technology in Education (2000b), which identi-

fy what teachers should be able to do in their classrooms.

Teachers will be motivated to become proficient with technology when they see that technology use is easy and worthwhile to do. One incentive for teachers is to see the impact of technology on students' enthusiasm for learning. Another incentive is the creation of annual goals that teachers must accomplish, usually through a Professional Improvement Plan. The goals should be realistic and need to be created with the principal so that they are part of a teacher's annual evaluation. Grade level or content teachers can get together to decide what they can reasonably accomplish with the resources available.

A buddy system can be created for teachers to help each other. Teachers who are active users of technology can use faculty meetings or professional development sessions to demonstrate what they are doing in their classrooms and to provide positive peer pressure. Tapping national resources such as the Presidential Award for Reading and Technology, co-sponsored by the International Reading Association and The Learning Company (http://reading.org/happening/awardtech.htm), helps to reward those involved with inspiring technology initiatives.

Access to troubleshooting is essential, whether it is a school-based person, a hotline, or someone from the community (e.g., a retired person) who can help. As with any change, it is important to celebrate steady, slow, and continuous progress, rather than push for an overnight overhaul of pedagogical practice.

Conclusion

Our leadership as professionals depends on our ability to be on the cutting edge of what is current in the field, not just with technology but in all aspects of literacy. As we change, we need to bring others along so we are in charge of determining how our students are taught. As we encounter issues of equity and use, we need to take the time to address them so that we determine technology's availability. As we expand our definition of literacy to include electronic tools, we need to share our knowledge with our colleagues. We need to grow with technology the way we do with other new developments in our field, especially during this era of standards-based education and high-stakes testing, so that we can continue to steer our programs and constituencies with near-perfect vision.

Appendix: Recommended Resources

An excellent resource for establishing competencies is *National Educational Technology Standards for Students: Connecting Curriculum and Technology* (International Society for Technology in Education, 2000a). This guide identifies standards at each level, including English language arts, for both pre-service teachers and pre-K–12 students, which help determine what we need to know for the students that we teach, whether in pre-K–12 or teacher education.

Books, magazines, professional journals, and websites also offer information and insights about technology's influence on learning. *Growing Up Digital* (Tapscott, 1998) talks about the shift in learning paradigms resulting from the growth of the Internet, particularly from linear to hypermedia learning, and from instruction to construction and discovery (Rhodes, 2000). The monograph *Log On or Lose Out: Technology in 21st Century Teacher Education* (American Association of Colleges for Teacher Education, 2000) addresses issues related to teaching and technology, including ethical and social use, commercialization in the classroom, and assessment.

Books

Books for Beginners. Que Publications (http://www.mcp.com/publishers/que) has a series of *Complete Idiot's Guide* books for beginners, for example, *Complete Idiot's Guide to the Internet* (Kent, 2000). IDG Books (http://www.dummies.com) has a series of *Dummies* books, for example, *Netscape Communicator 4.5 for Dummies* (Hoffman, 1998).

Books for Teaching. *Linking Literacy and Technology: A Guide for K–8 Classrooms* (Wepner, Val-

mont, & Thurlow, 2000) shares ideas, options, and opportunities for using technology for literacy instruction in the classroom. *Teaching With the Internet: Lessons From the Classroom* (Leu & Leu, 1997) offers ideas about how to effectively integrate the Internet into the classroom. *Quick Guide to the Internet for Education* (Provenzo & Gotthoffer, 2000) is a handbook of facts and ideas for using the Internet. *New Kids on the Net: Internet Activities in Elementary Language Arts* (Burgstahler & Utterback, 2000) includes over 80 ready-to-use language arts worksheets with Internet activities.

Magazines and Journals

MacWorld (http://macworld.zdnet.com), *PC Magazine* (http://www.pcmag.com), *T.H.E. Journal* (http://www.thejournal.com), and *Technology and Learning* (http://www.techlearning.com) offer information about a variety of technologies that can be used in the classrooms. On-line journals such as *Reading Online* (http://www.readingonline.org) offer ideas and information for using technology for literacy development. This electronic journal, published by the International Reading Association, contains peer-reviewed articles and columns about the electronic classroom, international perspectives, and the new literacies.

Websites

Education World (http://www.education-world.com), created by a group of educators, offers teachers a place to get articles, lesson plans, ideas for thematic units, lists of resources, and links to other websites. The site http://www.4teachers.org, created for and by teachers, includes lessons for integrating technology and teacher-made sites of class projects.

Tech Knowledge (http://www.pbs.org/techknowledge), presented by the Public Broadcasting System (PBS) Adult Learning Service, offers on-line professional development for K–12 teachers. Web-based modules contain project lessons and demonstrations that have been videotaped in working classrooms. It offers teachers access to other teachers who are using technology in their classrooms. PBS also has a website (http://www.pbs.org/uti/begin.html) that is a beginner's guide for using and understanding the Internet.

AOL@School (http://www.school.aol.com), created by America Online, offers a variety of age-appropriate educational websites and special safety tools. A group of educators selected the sites that are included for each of the separate portals (site or service that offers a broad array of resources and services such as email, forums, search engines, and on-line shopping malls) in grades K–2, 3–5, middle school, high school, and teachers and administrators. It also includes a suite of on-line tools such as encyclopedias, dictionaries, and a calculator.

Also, be aware of the research that supports the use of technology for learning (e.g., Hasselbring, Goin, Taylor, Bottge, & Daley, 1997; Labbo, 1996; Shiah, Mastropieri, & Scruggs, 1995) as well as the undercurrents of skepticism that question technology's merits (e.g., Armstrong & Casement, 2000; Healy, 1998). This helps you become an informed consumer and decision maker as you get more and more involved.

References

Alliance for Technology Access. (2000). *Computer resources for people with disabilities* (3rd ed.). Alameda, CA: Hunter House.

American Association of Colleges for Teacher Education. (2000). *Log on or lose out: Technology in 21st century teacher education.* Washington, DC: American Association of Colleges for Teacher Education and the ERIC Clearinghouse on Teaching and Teacher Education.

Armstrong, A., & Casement, C. (2000). *The child and the machine: How computers put our children's education at risk.* Beltsville, MD: Robins Lane Press.

Becker, H. J. (1999). *Internet use by teachers: Conditions of professional use and teacher-directed student use. Teaching, learning, and computing: 1998 national survey.* Irvine and Minneapolis: University of California at Irvine and University of Minnesota, Center for Research on Information Technology and Organizations.

Burgstahler, S., & Utterback, L. (2000). *New kids on the net: Internet activities in elementary language arts.* Needham Heights, MA: Allyn and Bacon.

Farnsworth, J. (2000). *A collaboration between preservice and inservice teachers using telecommunications to facilitate the use of instructional technology.* Unpublished doctoral dissertation, Widener University, Chester, PA.

Hasselbring, T. S., Goin, L., Taylor, R., Bottge, B., & Daley, D. (1997). The computer doesn't embarrass me. *Educational Leadership, 55*(3), 30–33.

Healy, J. M. (1998). *Failure to connect: How computers affect our children's minds—for better and worse.* New York: Simon and Schuster.

Hoffman, P. (1998). *Netscape Communicator 4.5 for dummies.* New York: IDG Books Worldwide.

HyperStudio [Computer software]. (1999). Torrance, CA: Roger Wagner Publishing.

International Society for Technology in Education. (2000a). *National educational technology standards for students: Connecting curriculum and technology.* Eugene, OR: Author.

International Society for Technology in Education. (2000b). *National educational technology standards for teachers.* Eugene, OR: Author.

Internet Explorer [Computer software]. (1999). Redmond, WA: Microsoft.

Just Grandma and Me Deluxe [Computer software]. (1997). Cambridge, MA: Broderbund/The Learning Company.

Kent, P. (2000). *Complete idiot's guide to the Internet.* Indianapolis: Que Publications.

Labbo, L. D. (1996). A semiotic analysis of young children's symbol making in a classroom computer center. *Reading Research Quarterly, 31,* 356–385.

Leu, D. J., Jr., & Leu, D. D. (1997). *Teaching with the Internet: Lessons from the classroom.* Norwood, MA: Christopher-Gordon.

Mavis Beacon Teaches Typing [Computer software]. (1999). Novato, CA: The Learning Company.

Microsoft Access [Computer software]. (1999). Redmond, WA: Microsoft.

Microsoft Excel [Computer software]. (1999). Redmond, WA: Microsoft.

Microsoft Word [Computer software]. (1999). Redmond, WA: Microsoft.

Netscape Navigator [Computer software]. (1999). Mountain View, CA: Netscape Communications.

Ogle, D. (1986). K-W-L: A teaching model that develops active reading and expository text. *The Reading Teacher, 39,* 564–570.

PowerPoint [Computer software]. (1996). Redmond, WA: Microsoft.

Provenzo, E. F., Jr., & Gotthoffer, D. (2000). *Quick guide to the Internet for education.* Needham Heights, MA: Allyn and Bacon.

Roe, B. D. (2000). Using technology for content-area

literacy. In S. B. Wepner, W. J. Valmont, & R. Thurlow (Eds.), *Linking literacy and technology: A guide to K–8 classrooms* (pp. 133–158). Newark, DE: International Reading Association.

Rhodes, E. M. (2000). The impact of technology on how we learn: Implications for teacher education. In *Log on or lose out: Technology in 21st century teacher education* (pp. 69–73). Washington, DC: American Association of Colleges for Teacher Education and the ERIC Clearinghouse on Teaching and Teacher Education.

Schlager, M. (2000). Communities of practice as catalysts for a revitalized teaching profession. In *Log on or lose out: Technology in 21st century teacher education* (pp. 202–208). Washington, DC: American Association of Colleges for Teacher Education and the ERIC Clearinghouse on Teaching and Teacher Education.

Shiah, R.-L., Mastropieri, M. A., & Scruggs, T. (1995). Computer-assisted instruction and students with learning disabilities: Does research support the rhetoric? *Advances in Learning and Behavioral Disabilities, 9,* 161–192.

Stephens, L. (2000). *Internet usage in public schools* (4th ed.). Denver, CO: Quality Education Data.

Strong, M., Wepner, S. B., Furlong, M., & Wartenberg, A. (2000). Philosophical dilemmas in undergraduate and graduate literacy programs. In *Literacy at a new horizon: The twenty second yearbook. A peer reviewed publication of the College Reading Association* (pp. 131–145). Commerce, TX: College Reading Association.

Sullivan, J. (1998). The electronic journal: Combining literacy and technology. *The Reading Teacher, 52,* 90–93.

Tapscott, D. (1998). *Growing up digital.* New York: McGraw-Hill.

Wepner, S. B., & Ray, L. (2000). In S. B. Wepner, W. J. Valmont, & R. Thurlow (Eds.), *Linking literacy and technology: A guide to K–8 classrooms* (pp. 76–105). Newark, DE: International Reading Association.

Wepner, S. B., Valmont, W. J., & Thurlow, R. (Eds.). (2000). *Linking literacy and technology: A guide to K–8 classrooms.* Newark, DE: International Reading Association.

CHAPTER THIRTEEN

Literacy Development for Culturally Diverse Populations

Junko Yokota and William Teale

The literacy development of diverse learners warrants close attention by school administrators and supervisors. One concern is that despite the increasing ethnic and cultural diversity in our classrooms, the teaching force is composed predominantly of middle-class Anglo-Americans (Hoffman & Pearson, 2000). Another concern is that differences in the literacy achievement between mainstream students and their peers of diverse backgrounds are evident by the early elementary years and increase as students move through the grades. Although ethnic, cultural, or linguistic variances are not automatic determinants of academic performance, there is much evidence that these factors are often part of the profile of students who have low levels of school success and limited literacy achievement (Au, 1993, 1998a; Hoffman & Pearson, 2000; Pallas, Natriello, & McDill, 1989). Blaming low achievement on diversity abdicates the responsibility for teaching all students. What we need is to understand such variances and consider how best to support the literacy development of students from diverse backgrounds.

Administrators and supervisors play a critical role regarding how issues of diversity are addressed in the classroom. Being well informed about the various issues surrounding the education of students from diverse populations allows administrators and supervisors to take a leadership role in the decisions that must be made. This chapter discusses:

- ◆ Types of diversity
- ◆ Models of addressing diverse populations of students
- ◆ Cultural identity and beliefs
- ◆ Educational implications

Types of Diversity

When discussing students who are different from the mainstream population, we frequently identify three types of diversity: ethnic, cultural, and linguistic. A brief description of each type of diversity is provided next. These descriptions are followed by a summary of understandings about each of these types of diversity that are helpful to educators.

Ethnic Diversity

Ethnicity basically refers to ancestral roots. More importantly, ethnicity is the core by which people often share a sense of belonging to a group. Ethnic group membership implies a shared history that affects the way in which people live today (Gollnick & Chinn, 1990). It is usually best to identify ethnicity as specifically as possible. For example, students should be referred to as being Japanese, Cuban, or Navajo rather than broadly categorized as Asian, Hispanic, or Native American. One issue to keep in mind is that the acceptable name for some ethnic groups is based on highly individual preference. For example, people of Mexican descent living in the United States may prefer to be called Mexican American, Hispanic, Latino or Latina, or Chicano or Chicana.

Cultural Diversity

Culture is defined as a system of values, beliefs, and standards that guides people's thoughts, feelings, and behavior. Culture is not static; it is a dynamic process by which people make sense of their lives. Cultural understanding is learned and shared by members of the cultural group (Au, 1993). Values and behaviors shared by cultural groups are adapted by subgroups and individuals, but often there is a common basis from which these values and behaviors stem. The boundaries by which cultures are defined are sometimes based on ethnicity, religion, philosophy, geographical region, or other common ground.

Linguistic Diversity

Two types of linguistic diversity can be identified: multilingualism and dialect differences. Multilingualism refers to the ability to speak more than one language. Dialect differences are variations within one language. Linguistic factors like these often play a critical role in school learning because uses of language by different groups of people can result in miscommunication due to differences in interpretation. When mainstream rules of communication are imposed on all, students from nonmainstream backgrounds often feel a sense of denial because language is so much a part of one's identity.

Models of Addressing Diverse Populations of Students

Understanding these different types of diversity is important foundational knowledge that can help educators develop ethnosensitivity, a critical disposition for having success in reaching diverse populations. Although it may be unintentional, most mainstream U.S. educators have been made to believe that the cultural and linguistic norm of their background is to be maintained, and they interpret the actions and speech of their students according to that norm (Farr, 1991). Such ethnocentrism needs to be replaced by an ethnosensitivity that takes into account an understanding that all students are competent in the language and culture in which they were raised. When students possess a cultural background or linguistic pattern that is different from that of the mainstream, it should not be considered a deficit but, rather, a difference (Au, 1993;

Farr, 1991). For many students of diverse backgrounds, there is often a mismatch between the experiences they have in their homes and the experiences they have at school (Rueda, 1991). It becomes problematic when these differences conflict with what is expected in schools and are interpreted by educators as deficits to be overcome. A priority need, then, is to eliminate prejudices against such variation and bring about the understanding that cultural and linguistic variation is natural. Understanding the naturalness of variance is only a first step; the next important one is to recognize the value that variance offers.

Beyond an understanding of the types of diversity, it is helpful to consider various models for how culturally diverse populations can be addressed in schools. Numerous models have been proposed, and terms used to describe these models are varied, but we have chosen to use the terms identified by Au (1993): transmission model and social constructivist model.

Transmission Model

Transmission models are based on the belief that all students learn in the same manner, absorbing knowledge that is transmitted to them. The emphasis in this model is on learning skills in small units, presented in a predetermined sequence. The belief here is that learning the parts leads to understanding the whole; learning a sequence of skills leads to ability to read and write. This belief is put into practice when students are taught to read by first learning the letters of the alphabet, then letter-sound correspondence, then combining sounds until they make words, and gradually combining a few words to make sentences. The underlying philosophy of this approach is that students cannot learn to read unless they progress successfully through each step of this process. Tasks are assigned to the students, often in the written form of worksheets or workbooks focused on isolated skills. There is a sense of organization and orderliness; all students are given the same set of instructions and the same tasks to be completed. The reason students complete assignments may be because they were instructed to do

so by the teacher, and they are complying (Langer, 1991). Students in the transmission model tend to view reading and writing as skills that are required for the purpose of advancing in school; they often do not make the connection of the role of literacy development to their lives.

Transmission models tend to reflect the teacher's background experiences, which are often largely based on mainstream values. It is not surprising that the transmissions are better received by students who are from a background similar to the teacher's. Students of diverse backgrounds, however, may feel the imposition of the dominant group's expectations, or they may not be able to interpret the transmission as intended. When failure for literacy learning occurs in this situation, sometimes the remedy has been to place students in highly structured remedial programs. The problem is compounded as students get a heavier dosage of what they have already experienced as failure.

Often believing that such students lack ability or experience, teachers focus on teaching "the basics." Students of diverse backgrounds report a high degree of "transmission teaching" (Nieto, 1992/2000), despite the fact that such a focus on transmitting the basics denies students the time and opportunity to engage in higher-level thinking (Au, 1998a). Strickland (1994) identified the pros and cons of focusing on teaching basic skills. When performance on standardized tests improved, students felt empowered; however, the limitations of such a focus also meant that students hit a ceiling, "not knowing how to use that information, how to learn on their own, to think for themselves, solve problems, and critique their own work and the work of others" (Strickland, 1994).

Social Constructivist Model

The social constructivist model is based on the understanding that all learners come to school with literacy knowledge of some type, but the kind of literacy knowledge and the way in which the learner develops literacy will differ from student to student (Erickson, 1991). In the most basic sense, "constructivism" (e.g., the works of Dewey, Piaget, Vygotsky) in literacy learning refers to the understanding that meaning is created through the interaction of reader and text.

Learners in the social constructivist model are active participants in constructing their own learning, based on their own backgrounds and interests. Students set their own goals and determine their own paths for literacy learning. The teacher's role is to guide and to provide support for students so that they may successfully pursue their literacy acquisition. This support includes instruction and mini-lessons in specific areas of literacy development.

Literacy is seen as embedded in social contexts. Learners are aware of the many functions of literacy and how it connects to their everyday lives and to their backgrounds. The instruction the teacher provides is contextualized and meaningful to students.

A classroom employing the social constructivist model is one in which the teacher creates an ethos that is supportive and nurturing, and students take ownership of their learning. The teacher provides students with opportunities to make choices about planning and carrying out their own learning and acts as a facilitator in assisting and guiding students in their own search for making the learning experiences personally meaningful. Au (1998b) defines students' "ownership" of their own literacy as valuing it enough to have a positive attitude about literacy, choosing to make literacy a part of their lives even outside of school, and being engaged in the process. A visitor to such a classroom may find the active student participation to be rather disorganized. However, structure and organization are found in the variety of reading and writing activities occurring and in the materials being used by students.

1. Why does the social constructivist model work for students of diverse backgrounds? The social constructivist model defines literacy learning by considering how people think and construct knowledge in the various social contexts in which literacy is used. Because of their variety of social and cultural experiences with literacy prior to schooling, students of diverse backgrounds inevitably have varying understandings of "literacy" and ways of thinking about literacy. The social constructivist model endorses literacy instruction that takes such backgrounds into consideration, makes connections, and builds literacy based on the backgrounds students already have (Langer, 1991). Specific reasons the social constructivist model is particularly well suited to students of diverse backgrounds include:

◆ Students can select some of their own reading material.
◆ Students can write and speak on topics of their choice.
◆ Students have the opportunity to select some of the types of literacy activities in which they wish to participate.
◆ Literacy-related skills are contextualized in meaningful ways.

When students of diverse backgrounds have choices regarding their reading materials, topics for writing and speaking, and literacy activities, the opportunity to tap into their individual backgrounds becomes an option. It is then more likely that students will be able to make meaningful connections between their backgrounds and literacy learning in schools. In a discussion of the best ways to educate African American learners at risk, Strickland (1994, pp. 331–333) suggests that literacy learning should:

◆ start early and continue throughout life
◆ be used to make meaning out of our world
◆ take place through active involvement and use
◆ be influenced by one's language and cultural background
◆ be influenced by social context

These recommendations endorse the social constructivist model as appropriate.

2. What precautions should be taken when employing the social constructivist model for students of diverse backgrounds? Clearly, the social constructivist model has many advantages for students of diverse backgrounds, as well as for mainstream students. Nevertheless, there are potential pitfalls that should be avoided when employing the model. Students from mainstream families acquire the basic codes of literacy at home and put them into practice at school. However, students who have acquired their literacy from a code other than standard English may need explicit instruction to acquire the skills expected. In order to have lifetime access to the opportunities of the culture of power, all students must be able to communicate in standard English. Explicit instruction is often the most effective and efficient method of explaining how and why things work the way they do (Spangenberg-Urbschat & Pritchard, 1994). Explicit instruction may seem to conflict with the role of teachers as facilitators. But a facilitator meets the needs of students, and students cannot be held accountable for knowledge that has never been made available to them. This does not imply that direct instruction of skills in isolation is advocated. Delpit (1988) cites Siddle in stating that direct instruction mini-lessons taught in the context of meaningful activities are most effective.

Although emphasizing the process of learning is quite valuable, there is also a need to emphasize product; ultimately, it is the product that society will judge (Delpit, 1988). Often, the standards of mainstream culture are used to make these judgments. A teacher will assume different roles in helping students achieve these end goals, sometimes acting as facilitator and guiding students in their own personally meaningful learning, and at other times offering explicit instruction.

Most literacy-related components of the social constructivist model are supportive of diversity in learners. However, not all activities appropriate for the mainstream population within the constructivist model should also be assumed to be appropriate for the diverse population. For example, Reyes (1991) studied the use of dialogue journals and literature logs in a sixth grade bilingual classroom. Although the students were able to communicate effectively with their teacher, gains in mastering the conventions of standard English writing were not made as rapidly as could be accomplished through direct instruction. Such activities should not necessarily be dropped as inappropriate; instead, they should be altered to fit the differing needs of diverse students.

Another example of the differing roles for teachers who teach diverse students is the need for explicit teacher assistance when students are unable to make choices on their own (Reyes, 1991). An example cited by Au (1993) is that of a student who is asking for help in selecting a library book and is told by the teacher to continue looking alone. The student's subsequent failure to find an appropriate book is interpreted as a lack of motivation. Selecting a book is viewed as needing less guidance than some other choices to be made. For example, children are generally given much guidance on how to select the proper foods in order to have a balanced meal; parents would not consider allowing a child to eat only sweets all day but would insist on the child making more nutritious choices. A student who is having difficulty making a book selection is analogous to our entering a foreign restaurant for the first time, being offered any choice on a multipage menu in a foreign language, and trying to select a meal among dishes we have never tasted. Most adults would ask for assistance from someone with more knowledge about the choices presented. The "expert" then would offer assistance by making a few recommendations along with explanations of each item. Choosing becomes more manageable with such guidance.

Likewise, children who have limited background in making personal book selections should be encouraged to seek the assistance of those they perceive as having the expertise and experience in making such choices. When the school curriculum offers opportunities for students to discuss authors and illustrators and to share personal book recommendations, students are likely to consider these factors and more successfully make choices when faced with selecting a book independently (Hiebert, Mervar, & Person, 1990).

Self-Examination of Cultural Identity and Beliefs

Too often, teachers from the mainstream view themselves as being "American"—without a "culture"—and believe that only "others" have a "culture" (Schmidt, 1999). This belief is problematic in many ways. First, lack of recognition of their own cultural grounding makes it impossible for teachers to fully understand the implications of their students' cultural identity. Also, the notion that one is "American" and that cultures belong to "others" shows an attitude of accepting the notion that people who have strong cultural identities are not quite American. In the process of cultural self-identification, teachers should take time for self-reflection about their attitudes and beliefs, as well as for engaging in discussions of the topic with others. Then, teachers can consider how their personal background, beliefs, and attitudes affect their teaching and their relationships with their students (Schmidt, 1999; Willis & Lewis, 1998; Xu, 2001).

Educational Implications

The discussion of an appropriate model for the literacy education of diverse populations has important implications for classroom climate and educational activities. First, educators can acknowledge diversity as a factor that can enrich students' literacy development. Second, although many similarities and parallels exist between literacy development for mainstream populations and students of diverse backgrounds, there must be an understanding that some differences exist as well. An attitude of willingness to understand these differences will be reflected in the effectiveness of instruction.

Guidelines for Practice

The following paragraphs discuss eight specific ways in which the literacy needs of diverse student populations can be effectively met. Classroom examples are included.

1. Create a culturally responsive language and literacy community. A culturally responsive classroom environment provides an ethos that is conducive to advancing students' literacy learning while recognizing and supporting diverse backgrounds. When students of diverse backgrounds live in a different world at home

than that which exists in the school, they must change from one world to another when going between the two settings (Phelan, Davidson, & Cao, 1991). Au (1993) suggests that students will better be able to manage this boundary crossing if they become active and constructive participants in their literacy instruction.

A classroom that has a culturally responsive language and literacy environment is one in which there is an ethos of support, cooperation, and collaboration. All languages and dialects spoken by students are respected and, when possible, represented in the materials and activities available to students. Most importantly, all students feel safe and equal as members of a community. This implies the need for creating a stronger sense of belonging than "tolerance" offers. Being an equal member of a community implies relationships that are reciprocal and family-like. Group members make an emotional investment in the learning successes as well as the difficulties of each member.

2. Connect student background to literacy instruction. This statement is true for all students, but it is especially important to recognize the background knowledge and experiences of culturally diverse students because this background may be perceived by others as irrelevant or deficient. There are two aspects to connecting student background to literacy instruction and activities. First, there is a need to make connections between literacy materials and activities to the background knowledge and experiences of students, since it is more likely that print materials encountered in schools relate to the background knowledge and experiences of the mainstream population. Educators could include materials that relate to the backgrounds of diverse students, and they could make the connections of other materials more explicit. An example of such a connection is found in the book *Molly's Pilgrim* (1983) by Barbara Cohen. Molly is a recent immigrant from Russia and, prior to Thanksgiving, is assigned to make a Pilgrim doll at home to bring to school. This very American holiday and the concept behind it are made applicable to Molly's heritage when her mother makes a Russian pilgrim doll that represents her own journey to America in search of freedom. Creating such connections between school instruction and students' background makes learning more personally important.

The second aspect of connecting students' background to literacy instruction goes beyond the initial connection made and extends to literacy growth. Literacy-related activities should have a basis in the cultural background held by the child. Students should be encouraged to make personal connections and personal responses to their reading. Encouraging students to tell stories from their own backgrounds can be one way to accomplish this. Books that are strongly rooted in culturally based experiences can provide good reading material as well as serve as the springboard for speaking and writing experiences. *Family Pictures* (1990) by Carmen Lomas Garza is a bilingual book reflecting a Mexican American family's experiences. Other books that pair well with this one are *The Relatives Came* (1985) by Cynthia Rylant, about an Appalachian family's reunion, or *Bigmama's* (1991) by Donald Crews, about an African American family reunion. After reading the variety of books on family gatherings, students could interview family members, tell or write about their own family experiences, and even create their own family album of remembered family gatherings. *Leon's Story* (1997) by Leon Walter Tillage is a narrative account of a young African American boy growing up in the segregated south. When students read this book they come to realize that personal life stories can be engaging and powerful. Students can learn to value the contributions of oral histories and the histories of their own communities. If their stories of family and community are valued in school, students develop pride and a sense of self-empowerment in contributing to the classroom the stories from their own backgrounds (Willis & Lewis, 1998).

3. Recognize the first language and add English as another language. Three positions regarding language policies are eradication, appreciation of dialect differences, and biloquialism (Fasold & Shuy, 1970). Advocate biloquialism. Teach mainstream linguistic patterns as an addition to what

students already have in their linguistic repertoires, rather than as a replacement. This "additive approach" recognizes the worth of the first language and adds standard English as another language for communication. The value of continuously maintaining the first language should be made clear to students. Students also need to understand that effective communication in the language of the mainstream is important for success in many situations. Some believe that diversity in dialect should be accepted; others argue that this denies some students access to the language of power (Delpit, 1988).

Students entering school with a language other than English as their first language may find that English is the exclusive language developed in school. In such cases, the native language does not become developed in a formal sense. Consequently, students may never learn to improve that first language to the extent of using it effectively for full communication in their adult lives. A point for consideration: What happens before the student becomes proficient enough for English to be the language in which content learning can take place?

Bilingual education is an enormous field of study by itself. There is much researched and written on the topic; however, because these issues go beyond the scope of this chapter, they will not be discussed here. The main issue that educators need to keep in mind is that whenever possible, students should be supported in continuing to learn their first language (Snow, Burns, & Griffin, 1998). For further reading about children acquiring a second language, see McLaughlin (1992) and Tse (2001).

Most of all, it is important to keep in mind that language is a significant part of people's sense of self. How linguistic diversity is viewed by the school shapes the attitudes students accept about their own language.

4. Give students opportunities to talk and establish an oral communicative competence. Students need opportunities to engage in meaningful language use in order to develop competency in oral communication. Oral language competency can serve as the basis through which all learning can take place. In order to develop communication skills, students need opportunities to listen and to talk in a variety of contexts for a variety of reasons. Some students, particularly those with linguistic diversity, need extra time to phrase their thoughts before feeling prepared to express them through speech. Teacher feedback should focus primarily on the content of what was said, with selective feedback on how it was said. Scaffolding can provide temporary frameworks for students as they build their levels of competence (e.g., Cummins, 1989; Watts-Taffe & Truscott, 2000).

The ability to communicate orally allows students to connect to one another and to become a part of the classroom community. In *The Trouble Is My English*, Fu (1995) recalls her experiences as a foreign student in a graduate English department; she listened and read, but she did not often join in the conversations in class. When she entered a doctoral program in reading and writing instruction at the University of New Hampshire, she found herself pulled into the community of learners who sought to engage her as a member—one who would respond, express opinions, question, and laugh with the group. What Fu found was that her professors and classmates validated her talk, and she no longer felt an outsider to class discussions. This kind of engagement in talk helps students feel empowered in their ability to communicate, encouraging them to practice and thereby develop competency.

5. Provide assessment that accurately reflects students' strengths and weaknesses, focusing on literacy achievement and expecting students to be successful. Ladson-Billings (Willis & Lewis, 1998) calls for a focus on academic achievement, with teachers and students expecting success. Assessment, then, should provide feedback that leads to successful achievement. However, traditional assessment practices do not necessarily reflect the true strengths and weaknesses of students from diverse populations. They may instead lead to teachers' locating problems in the students, and even to labeling and segregation. This results in a "gatekeeping" function of allowing some to have entry into educational experiences but not others. In addition, it

promotes a tracking system in which students, once labeled as in the low group, tend to stay in that track for the rest of their school careers. When administrators and supervisors look at their own schools, they should see if the percentage of students of diverse backgrounds who are in remedial programs parallels the ethnic balance of the school as a whole or if there is a disproportionately large number of such students in those programs.

There is also a need to consider advocacy-oriented assessment that locates the problems in the social and educational context, instead of in the students, and seeks to change the instructional situations (Allington, 1991). One example of the need for assessment to match student background is evident from a study by Applebee (1991). He cites statistics that indicate students tend to fare better on testing that reflects their particular ethnic background. For example, when responding to a question on Langston Hughes's poetry, 53% of the African American students, 35% of the white students, and 27% of the Hispanic students answered the question correctly. When students appear to give a wrong response, teachers should try to determine how the student arrived at that response and gain insight into the student's thinking (Watts-Taffe & Truscott, 2000).

6. Establish strong home, school, and community connections. The importance of a strong connection between home, school, and community is virtually without debate. However, a misconception is that when the home and community differ from the mainstream population, there is little interest or willingness for home or community involvement. Rather, there are factors that inhibit the participation of homes and communities of diversity. When these factors are addressed, and the reasons for their hesitation dispelled, then families and communities find themselves very actively involved in their neighborhood schools. Moll (1992) talks about the notion that all families have "funds of knowledge" that they can contribute to the educational enterprise of the school. What Moll and his colleagues discovered in their work with Latino families was that these funds of knowledge often

go unrecognized because they are often nontraditional sources of knowledge, such as that pos-
sessed by migrant workers or the woman who is
the local *curandera,* or folk healer. When these
funds of knowledge are invited into the school
community, home-school connections improve
dramatically because the contributions of formerly disenfranchised families are recognized.
Furthermore, typically, parents and the community are asked to provide support for the instructional program in ways identified by the school.

When Keenan, Willet, and Solsken (1993)
invited community participation, they changed
the focus so that the school looked for ways to
change and support families. They identified
four ways in which such change can occur: dis-
covering parents' talents and teaching capabilities, overcoming fears of difference, trusting curriculum to emerge through conversation, and
constructing equitable relations with parents.
Schmidt (1999) discusses the following ways to
strengthen family involvement: avoid educational jargon, encourage families to provide
insights about their children, share student work,
encourage families to visit the school, and
encourage families to share their knowledge of
the community. Schmidt also encourages teachers to help families understand the culture and
structure of the school, and understand whom to
call in various situations.

In Japan, nearly all mothers are members of
parent/teacher organizations and operate an
extensive volunteering network. The same mothers, when coming to the United States, are usually not involved in PTAs. Causes cited for not
being involved include a sense of not belonging
due to cultural and linguistic barriers, a lack of
understanding about how American schools
operate, and not being solicited for assistance.
When asked about their interest in being
involved in their children's schools, the mothers
expressed interest and willingness, provided that
the barriers cited be removed (Yokota, 1988).
Goldenberg and Gallimore (1995) found Latino
immigrant parents tended to regard formal education as the way to social and economic mobility, and they tended to support the efforts of their
children's literacy learning when it was made
explicit to them. Ada, Campoy, and Zubizarreta

(2001), based on their program called "Transfor-
mative Family Literacy," identified specific principles for engaging Latino parents in family literacy. These principles include:

- Parents are the first and most constant educators of their children.
- Parents' home language is a valuable resource
for children's oral language and cognitive
development.
- Parents are valuable allies for children's emotional and social development.
- Parents need to experience the pleasure and
relevance of reading in order to be more inclined to share books with their children.

Picture books are an accessible medium for all
parents. As parents and children share their
thinking, their writing, stories, and self-confi-
dence grow (Ada, Campoy, & Zubizarreta, 2001,
p. 178).

**7. Include multicultural literature as reading
material in the classroom and as a catalyst for
discussions of diversity.** Multicultural literature, when culturally authentic, offers insights
into how cultures function. "Culturally conscious" literature reflects cultural groups through
values, perspectives, language, and artifacts of
the group depicted (Sims, 1982). Students from
the cultures represented feel a sense of self-
esteem as they see their lives reflected in literature. Through reading, students from other cultural groups can gain insight into cultures and
their values and beliefs. Regardless of their backgrounds, all students will gain from the broad-
ening of the literary cannon to include multicultural literature that reflects a diversity of views.

Applebee (1991) conducted a survey of the
literature being read in high schools that indicated that students were required to read basically the same works by white, male Anglo-
Saxons that were required nearly a hundred
years ago, when literature was seen as a vehicle
to reduce diversity and promote a common set
of values. However, if literature is to be regarded as having power not only to influence the
values of individuals but also to "redirect the
course of society as a whole" (Applebee, 1991),
the need for diversity of literature is clearly

stated. Rosenblatt's (1938) belief that literature provides access to the feelings, beliefs, and values that help individuals make choices in developing their personal philosophies also calls for the dignification, through inclusion in the curriculum, of the literature that reflects the lives of diverse students.

When including multicultural literature in the classroom, some considerations are important to keep in mind (Yokota, 1993):

◆ Include multicultural literature in all aspects of the curriculum.
◆ Include a diversity of cultural groups, ethnic, linguistic, etc.
◆ Include a balance of genres: folklore, poetry, historical fiction, informational, contemporary fiction, biography, and picture books.
◆ Include a balance of books set in other countries and of diverse groups in the United States.

Literature in a language other than English holds an important place among books made available to students of diverse backgrounds. When bilingual books and different language versions of books are made available to students who are bilingual, they see both of their languages represented and have the opportunity to comparatively study the two languages. Translated literature, originally published in a non-English language, offers a different opportunity. It presents a culture and language natively depicted by people from the original country of publication and also allows the English translation to make it available to a wider audience. Readers may be able to read a book that originated in the country of their own heritage, or from the heritage of their classmates.

Multicultural literature can also serve as a catalyst for discussions of diversity. Often, multicultural literature has characters facing the same issues that students of diverse backgrounds face. Through such literature, students of diverse backgrounds and students from the mainstream population can vicariously experience these lives. One book that naturally leads into discussions of what characters of diverse backgrounds face is Sonia Levitin's *The Golem and the Dragon Girl* (1993). Laurel Wang's Chinese heritage and

Jonathan's Jewish heritage seem to be very different backgrounds. Initially, readers may notice the many ways in which these two cultures experience contrasting beliefs; however, many parallels exist: Saturday Chinese school/Hebrew school, great grandfather's spirit/golem, the influence of elderly relatives, and the ways in which both Laurel and Jonathan realize the meaning of their heritage. Through literature of this type, readers have the opportunity to discuss issues regarding how diversity affects the lives of characters.

An example of how linguistic diversity is viewed by speakers of more than one language is found in Laurence Yep's *The Star Fisher* (1991). The Chinese-born mother repeatedly tells her American-born children to "speak only Chinese" in the home. She supports their success in learning English at school but fears that her children will not retain their family's home language. The mother expresses concern that as the children's English improves, their Chinese will diminish, and she will no longer be able to communicate effectively with her own children. This does not arise from lack of desire to learn English on the mother's part, but rather from fear of losing higher levels of verbal communication between parent and child. This fear is very real and valid not only in this story but also among bilingual people today. For example, the first author of this chapter has been raised with Japanese as her first and home language but with English as her school and adult language; this affects communication with her mother on some difficult issues because their stronger language is not the same.

This perspective of bilingualism, as presented in *The Star Fisher,* is one that adult readers will understand. On the other hand, students who read this book may instead empathize with the children who are told they must always speak to each other only in Chinese when they would prefer to use the language of school instruction. Students may also relate to what it is like to have parents rely on children when English communication for the parents is difficult. Educators reading books such as Yep's *The Star Fisher* will find themselves empathizing with the characters' dilemma, rather than wondering at each conference time: "Why can't a parent who has lived in this country for so many years communicate at a child's conference in English?"

Discussion can help illuminate a book's theme, broaden perspectives, and deepen understanding. When students of diverse backgrounds identify with a book, it may allow them to feel empowered in discussions. But discussions can also be met with hostility, resistance, and surface prejudices that author Toni Morrison calls "willful critical blindness." Students of diverse backgrounds may feel silenced in such cases. In other cases, students of the mainstream may become patronizing or may make responses they believe to reflect tolerance but that reveal a lack of sincere understanding (Harris, 1994; Rogers & Soter, 1997). Earlier, we discussed the power of talking with peers, and we do not negate that here. While literature discussions with peers are a powerful way to come to new understandings, the role of a teacher cannot be overlooked. A perceptive teacher can sensitively mediate discussion when it appears to go in directions that are problematic.

8. Provide extensive professional development opportunities and support in issues related to ethnic, cultural, and linguistic diversity. Ongoing staff development is necessary to support educators who are working to meet the literacy needs of students of diverse backgrounds. When student backgrounds differ from the educators' backgrounds, there is need for additional support in learning about these differences and how to best support literacy learning in each case. Teachers also need access to appropriate materials that connect to experiences of diverse students. Good instruction is good for all students, and good instruction is based on the quality of planning and reflection teachers give to their instruction. To that end, Watts-Taffe and Truscott (2000) developed a questionnaire to promote the practice of reflection and to serve as an impetus for change. In addition to taking time for self-reflection, teachers benefit from opportunities to engage in discussion about issues facing students of diverse backgrounds. Resources and opportunities for growth are critical in order for teachers to act upon their desire to provide culturally relevant instruction. An ongoing support group offers teachers a regularly scheduled time to discuss the issues they may individually be pondering in their separate classrooms.

Conclusion

Administrators and supervisors should advocate an open discussion about issues of diversity among teachers, parents, and students. Many of the responses to the challenge of educating diverse children tend toward what may be called a technical approach, one that sees this as an issue of transmitting to such children the background knowledge, vocabulary, and skills related to phonemic awareness, comprehension, phonics, and so forth that they are lacking. Such an approach essentially operates from a deficit model. We hope that this chapter has demonstrated that although children benefit from extra attention and extra instruction, a deficit approach that so often characterizes attempts to work with diverse children does little to help them learn to read and write; often it contributes to a lack of engagement in literacy and ultimately to high numbers of school dropouts. Instead, approaches that foreground the diversity and differences of children and regard these differences as resources stand a better chance of engaging such children and raising their literacy skill.

One issue that administrators and supervisors can profitably consider is how various policies and mandates affect the literacy learning that goes on in classrooms. The interpretation of state legislation or district mandates may leave little room for negotiating the implementation of such decisions. Therefore, those who are in positions of influencing such policy making and implementation need to have a thorough understanding of literacy development that is responsive to diversity (Hiebert, 1991). Au (1998b) calls for leaders to speak out on issues for which there exists a research-based theoretical stance on how to best meet the literacy development needs of students of diverse backgrounds. Without such voices, political forces can bring about consequences that will affect students and teachers, consequences based not on research or evidence related to the learning or achievement of diverse students but on politics.

Many of the recommendations made in the other chapters of this book are true for students of diverse backgrounds as well. Recommendations for improving the literacy learning of students of diverse backgrounds are specifically geared to meet their needs. However, many of the principles are also applicable to mainstream students and can be helpful to all students, regardless of their background. It should be noted that although all students deserve the best literacy instruction possible, at present there is a notable difference in the quality of instruction offered (Allington, 1991). The additive stance (Cummins, 1986) implies that the home language and culture are not replaced but broadened, so that students will be able to function in the home and their ethnic community as well as in the mainstream culture. Ladson-Billings (Willis & Lewis, 1998) notes the importance of teachers understanding more than what and how to teach diverse students. Teachers must realize why it matters, and they must make a commitment to offer all students the best instruction possible. This commitment goes beyond the call for "tolerance" or "social justice"—it implies that emotional investments are made in supporting the literacy success of each student.

References

Ada, F., Campoy, F. I., & Zubizarreta, R. (2001). Assessing our work with parents on behalf of children's literacy. In *Literacy assessment of second language learners*. Boston: Allyn and Bacon.

Allington, R. L. (1991). Children who find learning to read difficult: School responses to diversity. In E. H. Hiebert (Ed.), *Literacy for a diverse society: Perspectives, practices, and policies* (pp. 237–252). New York: Teachers College Press.

Applebee, A. N. (1991). Literature: Whose heritage? In E. H. Hiebert (Ed.), *Literacy for a diverse society: Perspectives, practices, and policies* (pp. 228–236). New York: Teachers College Press.

Au, K. H. (1993). *Literacy instruction in multicultural settings*. Fort Worth, TX: Harcourt Brace Jovanovich.

Au, K. H. (1998a). Constructivist approaches, phonics, and the literacy learning of students of diverse backgrounds. *National Reading Conference Yearbook, 47,* 1–21.

Au, K. H. (1998b). Social constructivism and the school literacy learning of students of diverse backgrounds. *Journal of Literacy Research, 30,* 297–319.

Cohen, B. (1983). *Molly's pilgrim.* New York: Lothrop, Lee and Shepard.

Crews, D. (1991). *Bigmama's.* New York: Greenwillow.

Cummins, J. (1986). Empowering minority students: A framework for intervention. *Harvard Educational Review, 56*(1), 18–36.

Cummins, J. (1989). *Empowering minority students.* Sacramento: California Association for Bilingual Education.

Delpit, L. D. (1988). The silenced dialogue: Power and pedagogy in educating other people's children. *Harvard Educational Review, 58,* 280–298.

Erickson, F. (1991). Foreword. In E. H. Hiebert (Ed.), *Literacy for a diverse society: Perspectives, practices, and policies* (pp. vii-x). New York: Teachers College Press.

Farr, M. (1991). Dialects, culture, and teaching the English language arts. In J. Flood, J. M. Jensen, D. Lapp, J. R. Squire (Eds.), *Handbook of research on teaching the English language arts* (pp. 365–371). New York: Macmillan.

Fasold, R., & Shuy, R. (1970). Preface to *Teaching standard English in the inner city.* Washington, DC: Center for Applied Linguistics.

Fu, D. (1995). *My trouble is my English: Asian students and the American dream.* Portsmouth, NH: Heinemann.

Garza, C. L. (1990). *Family pictures/Cuadros de familia.* San Francisco: Children's Book Press.

Goldenberg, C., & Gallimore, R. (1995). Immigrant Latino parents' values and beliefs about their children's education: Continuities and discontinuities across cultures and generations. In M. L. Maehr & P. R. Pintrich (Eds.), *Advances in motivation and achievement: Culture, motivation, and achievement* (Vol. 9, pp. 183–228). Greenwich, CT: Jai Press.

Gollnick, D. M., & Chinn, P. C. (1990). *Multicultural education in a pluralistic society* (3rd ed.). Columbus, OH: Merrill.

Harris, V. J. (1994). Multiculturalism and children's literature: An evaluation of ideology publishing, curricula, and research. In C. K. Kinzer & D. J. Leu (Eds.), *Multidimensional aspects of literacy research, theory, and practice. National Reading Conference Year-*

book, 43, 15–27. Chicago: National Reading Conference.

Hiebert, E. H. (1991). *Literacy for a diverse society: Perspectives, practices, and policies.* New York: Teachers College Press.

Hiebert, E. H., Mervar, K. B., & Person, D. (1990). Research directions: Children's selection of trade books in libraries and classrooms. *Language Arts, 67,* 758–763.

Hoffman, J., & Pearson, P. D. (2000). Reading teacher education in the next millennium: What your grandmother's teacher didn't know that your granddaughter's teacher should. *Reading Research Quarterly, 35,* 28–44.

Keenan, J. W., Willett, J., & Solsken, J. (1993). Focus on research: Constructing an urban village: School/home collaboration in a multicultural classroom. *Language Arts, 70,* 204–213.

Langer, J. A. (1991). Literacy and schooling: A sociocognitive perspective. In E. H. Hiebert (Ed.), *Literacy for a diverse society: Perspectives, practices, and policies* (pp. 9–27). New York: Teachers College Press.

Levitin, S. (1993). *The Golem and the dragon girl.* New York: Dial.

McLaughlin, B. (1992). *Myths and misconceptions about second language learning: What every teacher needs to unlearn.* Santa Cruz, CA: National Center for Research on Cultural Diversity and Second Language Learning.

Moll, L. (1992). Funds of knowledge for teaching: Using a qualitative approach to connect homes and classrooms. *Theory Into Practice, 31*(2), 132–141.

Nieto, S. (1992/2000). *Affirming diversity: The sociopolitical context of multicultural education.* New York: Longman.

Pallas, A. M., Natriello, G., & McDill, E. L. (1989). Changing nature of the disadvantaged population: Current dimensions and future trends. *Educational Researcher, 18*(5), 16–22.

Phelan, P., Davidson, A. L., & Cao, H. T. (1991). Students' multiple worlds: Negotiating the boundaries of family, peer, and school cultures. *Anthropology and Education Quarterly, 22,* 224–250.

Reyes, M. de la Luz. (1991). A process approach to literacy instruction for Spanish-speaking students: In search of a best fit. In E. H. Hiebert (Ed.), *Literacy for a diverse society: Perspectives, practices, and policies* (pp. 157–171). New York: Teachers College Press.

Rogers, T., & Soter, A. O. (Eds.). (1997). *Reading across cultures: Teaching literature in a diverse society.* New York: Teachers College Press.

Rosenblatt, L. (1938). *Literature as exploration.* New York: D. Appleton Century.

Rueda, R. (1991). Characteristics of literacy programs for language-minority students. In E. H. Hiebert (Ed.), *Literacy for a diverse society: Perspectives, practices, and policies* (pp. 93–107). New York: Teachers College Press.

Rylant, C. (1985). *The relatives came.* New York: Macmillan.

Schmidt, P. R. (1999). Know thyself and understand others. *Language Arts, 76,* 332–340.

Sims, R. (1982). *Shadow and substance.* Urbana, IL: National Council of Teachers of English.

Snow, C. E., Burns, M. S., & Griffin, P. (Eds.). (1998). *Preventing reading difficulties in young children.* Washington, DC: National Research Council.

Spangenberg-Urbschat, K., & Pritchard, R. (Eds.). (1994). *Kids come in all languages: Reading instruction for ESL students.* Newark, DE: International Reading Association.

Strickland, D. S. (1994). Educating African American learners at risk: Finding a better way. *Language Arts, 71,* 328–336.

Tillage, L. W. (1997). *Leon's story.* New York: Farrar, Straus, and Giroux.

Tse, L. (2001). *Why don't they learn English? Separating fact from fallacy in the U.S. language debate.* New York: Teachers College Press.

Watts-Taffe, S., & Truscott, D. M. (2000). Using what we know about language and literacy development for ESL students in the mainstream classroom. *Language Arts, 77,* 258–264.

Willis, A. I., & Lewis, K. C. (1998). A conversation with Gloria Ladson-Billings. *Language Arts, 75,* 61–70.

Xu, S. H. (2000). Pre-service teachers in a literacy methods course consider issues of diversity. *Journal of Literacy Research, 32,* 505–532.

Yep, L. (1991). *The star fisher.* New York: Morrow.

Yokota Lewis, J. (1988). *Home literacy environment and experiences: A description of Asian American homes and recommended intervention.* Unpublished doctoral dissertation, University of North Texas, Denton.

Yokota, J. (1993). Issues in selecting multicultural children's literature. *Language Arts, 70,* 156–167.

CHAPTER FOURTEEN

Community Outreach and Initiatives

Anthony D. Fredericks

School personnel seeking to establish effective reading programs need to be cognizant of many factors that have an impact on the development and maintenance of those programs. Research suggests that dynamic reading programs emanate from strong leadership within the school as well as from sincere efforts by school personnel to reach out and involve all members of the family and community (Come & Fredericks, 1995; Benjamin & Lord, 1996). In fact, reading programs that seek to establish a strong and positive partnership with parents and other community members are those that promote reading as more than just a school-related subject; rather, students are provided with innumerable opportunities to make reading a very natural part of their lives.

If, as many educators contend, the school is a microcosm of the community it serves, then it seems logical to assume that scholastic affairs, including reading instruction, are a necessary interest of that community. Indeed, there is convincing evidence that when parents and community members are recruited as supporters and promoters of reading instruction and lifelong reading habits, then reading and learning become much more meaningful in children's lives (Cairney & Munsie, 1995).

This chapter will cover:

♦ The background of community outreach
♦ Urban-suburban differences
♦ Topics to share with parents
♦ Intergenerational programs
♦ America Reads
♦ Strategies for community involvement at the elementary and secondary levels
♦ Guidelines for community outreach

Background of Community Outreach

The need to involve all family members in scholastic affairs is supported by logic and a growing body of research that underscores the impact parents and others have on children's literacy development (Neuman, Caperelli, & Kee, 1998; Morningstar, 1999). Although involving the entire family in a school's reading program would seem to be a naturally valuable extension of that program, past practices have not always subscribed to this notion. During the early part of the 20th century, parents were admonished not to get involved in the scholastic affairs of their offspring. Many school personnel believed that the education of students should be left entirely to those formally trained to undertake such a task. Some educators believed that parents would create unneeded conflict for children by imposing inappropriate values or using unsophisticated teaching methods. Unfortunately, this isolationist policy persisted for many years, creating a "we versus them" attitude that, in many cases, threatened the fundamental tenets of American education.

Fortunately, the accumulation of a significant body of data in recent years has resulted in some rethinking for many school personnel. In one longitudinal study of the effects of parental involvement on students' achievement (Johnson & Walker, 1991), there was significant evidence of the positive influence parents had on their children's academic growth throughout the primary grades. However, there is a perception that only the parents of young students need to be targeted for involvement practices and that the parents of students in middle school or secondary school are not appropriate candidates for outreach efforts. This erroneous assumption has hampered or diminished the impact of involvement efforts and isolated one segment of the community from another.

A balanced reading program includes a balanced approach to community outreach. Initiating programs and processes that include both elementary and secondary parents not only assures a well-coordinated effort throughout a school district but also recruits larger numbers of people in support of those efforts. In other words, community outreach should not be isolated to a small segment of the student population; rather, it should embrace, celebrate, and honor all components of the community in a coordinated and multifaceted effort. To do so ensures the strength of the reading program as well as its longevity.

Fredericks and Rasinski (1990a, 1990b) provide convincing evidence that the overall strength of a reading program can be predicated in large measure on the degree of parent and community involvement. Such involvement is structured on three vital elements woven throughout all dynamics of a planned or functioning reading program:

♦ Parent involvement must be an integral part of the program rather than a convenient add-on.
♦ Parent and community involvement must be conducted comprehensively, as an investment throughout the entire school year.
♦ Parent and community involvement must be approached systematically and not as a one-shot effort by a few concerned educators.

The success of effective outreach efforts is often grounded on nine critical criteria (Neuman et al., 1998). These criteria not only serve as markers for a successful program, but they also provide guidelines for the maintenance of the program over time:

1. All members of a family (grandparents, children, parents, siblings) are encouraged to participate in all literacy efforts.
2. A variety of recruitment techniques (word of mouth, newspaper, radio, posters) are employed to get the word out.
3. Parental involvement is a significant factor in curriculum development and planning.
4. Creative scheduling, child care, and transportation options are vital to retention.
5. Experienced teaching staff with expertise in diversity issues is recruited.
6. Monitoring of the program is ongoing and continuous.
7. Both long-term and short-term achievements are recognized and celebrated.
8. The establishment of social networks within classrooms in particular and the school in general is a significant factor.
9. Collaborations with a variety of social agencies establish meaningful partnerships that encourage community involvement.

Urban-Suburban Differences

Significant differences exist between suburban schools, which are typified by highly involved community outreach efforts and high levels of student achievement, and urban schools, typically characterized by low levels of participation and similarly low levels of achievement. Although many schools are utilizing the power of parent participation within and throughout their reading programs, many other schools, most noticeably those in urban or economically deprived neighborhoods, lack sufficient participation. This may be a matter of perception as much as it is a matter of fact. Significant numbers of educators frequently perceive urban families as "hard-to-reach." As stated by Epstein (1992), "The hard-to-reach include those whose physical, social, or psychological distance from the school place[s] extra barriers in the school's or family's path, and make[s] communication and interaction even more difficult than usual" (p. 1145).

To be sure, urban parents, beset by a host of social and economic restraints, compounded by years of benign neglect, offer urban reading supervisors challenges not faced by their suburban counterparts. However, many urban administrators are realizing that they may be neglecting a potent force for their reading program if they systematically exclude parents and the community at large.

It is an unfortunate condition of urban education that class bias and racism remain entrenched in the public school system. Klumpp (1990) states that the number one barrier to successful outreach programs in urban populations is "racism and behavior which is not intentionally racist but has a racist effect" (p. 1). This racism may be reflected in subtle discrimination based on differences in gender, social class, education, and language. As Klumpp states further in her position paper for PTA Project HOPE:

> In terms of outreach to parents, it is immoral to campaign to bring in people who may not be treated with respect and understanding after they get here. It is the responsibility of the school and the parents groups to take any steps needed to make sure that all interactions with parents [are] conducted in an atmosphere of warm acceptance and mutual respect. (p. 1)

An Example of Parent Involvement in an Urban School

Partnerships within an urban school setting can be effective and sustaining. One example of a successful urban literacy program has been documented by Come and Fredericks (1995) at the Pulaski Elementary School in Savanna, Georgia. This school is an innercity school where 95% of the children are minority group members from low socioeconomic backgrounds. In conjunction with the local community and with the support of educators at nearby Georgia Southern University, a family literacy program was established to address the needs of at-risk children. The overall goal of the program was to help develop self-esteem in children at an early age through parental encouragement and support of their literacy development.

The implementation and continuation of the program were founded on five critical and interrelated factors that ensured success:

1. Establishment of the program based on the expressed needs and wishes of parents.
2. The willingness of parents and teachers to promote a spirit of shared responsibility.
3. Parents' active involvement in making decisions and following through on those decisions.
4. Establishment and maintenance of open lines of communication throughout the school year.
5. A long-term commitment to continuous and sustained involvement.

The multifaceted and multidimensional nature of the program was critical to its success. Parents were actively involved in the planning process, parents and teachers worked together to promote the program throughout the community, partnerships with local businesses were established and maintained, and support was solicited from publishers and local bookstores in providing necessary reading materials.

The foundation of the project was a series of community workshops focusing on the value of read-alouds, the value of storytelling in a family environment, book discussion activities, and book extension activities such as bookmaking. Additional components of the project included a book loaning program, schoolwide book exchanges, a cross-age reading program, monthly reading calendars, parent volunteers, various communication tools, and a lending library within the school library. Future outreach plans include an intergenerational reading component, linkages with the adult literacy program, and field trips to the local public library to obtain library cards.

The success of this project—indeed the success of any parental involvement project in an urban setting—stems from the fact that the program is an invitational one. As such, the program is based on a fundamental belief that parents, no matter what their social or economic standing, have the potential for making an educational difference in their children's lives when offered sincere opportunities for becoming important members of the education team. Obviously, this assumes that all parents can and should be part of the school community and that there are multiple ways through which they can demonstrate support of their children's education. Such a posture is a necessary element in any outreach effort, but particularly so for parents and community members in urban settings.

Topics to Share with Parents

The collaborative partnership necessary between home and school is essential if all children are to reap the benefits of literacy training. Equally important is that school and district personnel seeking to establish and maintain those strong bonds address the needs and interests of both elementary and secondary audiences. Critical to that success will be the need to respond to the queries parents at all levels have about the reading program in general and their child's participation in the program specifically.

What follows is a listing of concerns parents often have about the reading curriculum. This list is not intended to be thorough or complete, since each community will have topics and interests that are specific to its particular reading program. You are encouraged to view this list as a starting point for the information you wish to disseminate to parents as well as the outreach efforts you seek to implement. It should be noted that this list represents concerns and questions most often expressed by the parents of both elementary and secondary students.

- How is reading taught in elementary/secondary school?
- What are the reading standards and how will they affect my child?
- What kind of training in reading instruction do teachers have?
- How can we be sure we are getting a quality-based reading program?
- How are students being graded in reading?
- What is "balanced reading"?
- How are assessment outcomes being used to shape the direction of the reading curriculum?
- What materials and techniques are used in the reading curriculum?
- Is there a reading list for students? For parents?
- How can we support our child's reading growth and development?

- How are children grouped in reading class (high, middle, low)?
- How flexible are the grouping procedures?
- What commercial materials are being used?
- Are there special programs for below-level readers? For above-level readers?
- Is reading emphasized throughout the curriculum?
- Are reading specialists or reading supervisors available for students and classroom teachers?
- What are the expectations of the school or district?
- What should I know about the testing program?
- How is technology integrated into the reading curriculum?
- What can I do?

Communicating responses to these and other parent concerns can be effectively accomplished through regular, systematic, and informative newsletters and friendly letters. Frequent contact with parents alerts them to the value of the connection between home and school and establishes a welcome format that promotes trust and cements mutually agreeable bonds. The key to success lies in the regular and expected distribution of these communication tools for all families—from the primary grades through secondary school. Here are some items used by many teachers in their outreach efforts:

- Welcoming letter to parents at the start of the school year.
- Lists of recommended books for families to share.
- Information sheet on activities and programs at the local public library.
- Letter from the principal or superintendent.
- Telephone "trees" for parents to communicate with each other.
- Email newsletters sent to parents within a class or the entire school.
- Notes on current achievements of students.
- Reproducible letters from commercial publications.

Figure 14.1 is an example of a commercially produced letter that can be duplicated and sent to parents of kindergarten or first grade students.

Intergenerational Programs

One of the most exciting aspects of community involvement centers on intergenerational programs in which children have an opportunity to participate in literacy activities and events with older members of the community. Such events provide children with wonderful insights into reading as a lifelong activity, an activity for all ages, and an activity that knows no limits of time, age, or circumstance. The result is not only a greater appreciation of reading by students, but also an equally important appreciation of community members and the role of reading in their lives. The result is children and adults who are able to share a common bond and some common beliefs about education in general and reading in particular.

Rasinski and Fredericks (1991) present an intriguing overview of several different intergenerational projects for consideration by schools and teachers. These projects usually fall into one of two categories: (1) community members come into the classroom to share books, read favorite stories, or participate with students in any number of literacy activities (e.g., plays, puppet shows, readers theater); (2) students participate in group or individual trips into the local community. The advantage of the classroom activities is that they allow children to interact with adults of the community in a supportive and friendly environment, and children begin to understand the impact of reading in many individuals' lives. The planned and regular visits to businesses or group homes can offer valuable opportunities for students to learn about life in the community and to develop related literacy skills. An example of this type of program is when students are paired with residents of a local nursing home. Visits to the home allow children to read to the residents, share school experiences, learn about the "good old days," and converse in a friendly and meaningful way. Extensions of this kind of project can include the initiation of a pen pal program with the residents, taking and recording oral histories of the senior citizens, and developing appropriate journal activities over an extended period of time. The result is not only a sensitivity to the problems

---

SAMPLE LETTER FOR PARENTS

Word Fun

Dear Parents:

In school we are learning about the sounds that letters make and how those sounds can be put together to form words. This is a very important skill for all children because it helps them learn about all the sounds in the English language and how some of those sounds can be combined to make words. Most important, children learn that one sound or two sounds or more can be put together to create words. As children learn about the sounds in words, they begin to understand the wide variety of sounds there are.

You can help your child learn about word sounds with some of the activities and games below. As always, keep the emphasis on fun—be sure your child knows that making sounds and learning about sounds can be a playful and enjoyable way to spend a couple of minutes with you.

As you read a book or story with your child, look for some words that begin with the same letter—for example, two words that begin with "b," or two words that begin with "m." After you've read the story, ask your child a question such as "What sound do you hear at the beginning of these two words from the story—"boy" and "bird"? or "What sound do you hear at the beginning of these two words from the story—"man" and "many"? Just ask your child for the sounds at the beginning of each word—not the names of the letters.

Play a "word pair" game with your child. With your child, locate objects in or around your house that begin with the same sound. For example—"I see a table and a tree." Or "I see some green grass." Or "I see a carpet and a cat." Invite your child to note the matching beginning sound for each pair of words.

As you read a book with your child, invite her or him to listen for words that begin with a pre-selected sound. For example, you might say "Today, let's listen for words that begin with the 's' sound." Or "As we read this story, let's listen for words that begin with the 't' sound."

Introduce your child to rhythm by having her or him clap to the beat of a favorite song or tune. You may want to begin with a song your child is very familiar with (for example, "Happy Birthday").

Spending time with your child is important. Your contributions are important to your child's future reading success.

Sincerely,

Adapted from *The Complete Phonemic Awareness Handbook: More Than 300 Playful Activities for Early Reading Success*, by A. D. Fredericks, 2001, Crystal Lake, IL: Rigby. Used by permission of the author.

Figure 14.1

and conditions experienced by older people, but also an appreciation of literacy as a vehicle to learn more about a segment of the community.

America Reads

Efforts to expand and extend the reading program into the community exist at many different levels. Local efforts, however, can be strengthened and supplemented via governmental programs that offer resources and expertise that can add immeasurably to all outreach initiatives. America Reads, initiated in the late 1990s, challenges people from all walks of life to assist children in learning to read. It is directed at establishing strong partnerships between educators, media outlets, parents, librarians, business people, college students, religious groups, and senior citizens. As of this writing, more than 300 organizations and groups across the country have banded together to organize book drives, train tutors, provide necessary child care, publish reading materials, and support parents in an effort to improve children's reading achievement.

The America Reads program is founded on six interrelated goals:

- Inspiring families to read together at home.
- Asking childcare providers to read daily to children.
- Encouraging teachers to use research-based methods.
- Recruiting college students and others to tutor children.
- Engaging businesses to involve employees.
- Uniting communities to form strong partnerships.

See Chapter 15 for additional information about America Reads.

Strategies at the Elementary and Secondary Levels

Perhaps the most significant concern of administrators and reading supervisors deals with the methods and models proven effective in stimulating, promoting, and maintaining parent and community involvement. This section will address those methods educators have traditionally used, the data educators need to establish a viable home and school connection, and an effective model that insures positive parent participation.

Assessing Traditional Methods

Over the years, teachers have communicated with parents through a few established and universal methods. These typically include sending notices home, talking with parents during open-school evenings, and making occasional telephone calls. Other communication tools used universally by teachers include booklets and handbooks, brochures or pamphlets, activity

sheets, progress letters, notes and conferences, reading and shopping lists, courses and workshops, calendars of activities, and home learning kits. What is apparent in reviewing these parental contact methods is that educators have a multiplicity of ways to reach out to parents and involve them in the dynamics of the reading program.

Although we are aware of the plethora of ways to communicate with parents and the myriad types of information traditionally suggested to parents, one major concern remains: What kinds of information do educators need in order to plan, develop, and implement an effective outreach program? Most reading professionals are aware of the variety of ideas, suggestions, and information that could be shared with parents, but they need an operational framework upon which to build a successful outreach program. While most educators have had little or no formal training in how to work with parents, they do, for the most part, have an intuitive knowledge of some communication methods and materials. What is lacking from their repertoire, however, is a systematic and easy-to-use network that facilitates outreach efforts and promotes family involvement as a positive extension of the school reading program.

Creating a New Model

In an exhaustive review of family literacy projects that had been funded by the Barbara Bush Foundation for Family Literacy, Neuman et al. (1998, p. 244) sought answers to four basic questions:

- What attracts participants to family literacy programs?
- What accounts for success from their point of view?
- What are the most salient features of these programs?
- Are there basic principles that can be applied across a broad spectrum of programs?

The results of their work serve as a model for teachers and administrators seeking higher levels of family involvement in the dynamics of their respective literacy programs. The overriding issue in the success of outreach efforts was not the work, time, or effort expended by educators, but rather program aspects deemed most important to families from their perspectives.

1. *Involve participants in planning.* Successful programs are based on a mutual partnership and ownership of all project components. Families are seen as active members, active participants, and active planners throughout the initiation and continuation of a program. In other words, programs are not something done for parents; they are more appropriately done with parents.

2. *Incorporate family-based activities.* The emphasis in successful literacy projects with parents should be diverse and eclectic. Provide parents with multiple activities and opportunities to be with their children—not just in literacy-based activities but in quality sharing-time opportunities as well. Extensions of what a family might do at home should be seen as a positive element in all outreach efforts.

3. *Include ongoing assessment of needs.* Outreach programs risk failure whenever they are predicated on ease of delivery rather than assessed needs. Parents will be more willing to participate in an outreach program when they know that the project is addressing their identified needs more than when the program is being set up at the convenience of the school or teachers.

4. *Create social networks.* Paramount to the success of many involvement projects is the fundamental belief that literacy is learned best within a social context. That social endeavor can help parents feel more comfortable within a project in addition to providing a support structure that encourages and promotes the activity of many. Social networks are seen as crucial to the ultimate success of any effort—in short, parents need to feel that they are valuable members of a total team effort.

5. *Provide integrated services.* Integrated support services are a significant factor in the short-term and long-term success of any project. Programs need to address the multiplicity of issues, concerns, and challenges faced by modern-day families. Divorcing literacy development from the day-to-day needs of parents and their children has been identified as a significant delimiting factor in the success of that effort.

6. *Plan links for future learning and career development.* Establishing linkages with community offerings such as job training, vocational education, technology instruction, and post-secondary coursework are vital to any literacy-based project. A true outreach project is one that involves many components of the local community in a systematic and integrated fashion. In short, parents are able to see extended possibilities not only for their children, but for themselves as well.

In sum, this model provides a workable framework for any reading supervisor or administrator interested in soliciting parent support and participation within the school or district reading program. Its influence lies in the fact that it underscores the cooperative effort needed by both educators and community members for the benefit of all students. Of course, as a model, it does allow for necessary modifications according to the dynamics of individual schools or communities. Whatever its local variations, however, working with parents always requires an investment of time, talent, and energy on the part of many individuals in order to guarantee success.

Creating School and University Partnerships

Reading specialists, reading supervisors, and district administrators seeking to establish coherent and practical outreach programs should consider the services and personnel available at a local college or university. A teacher training institution offers innumerable resources that can activate and energize any parent involvement efforts. Not only can the talents of the institution be tapped, but so too can this partnership help to cement the community bonds necessary for an effective and well-designed reading program.

Following is a list of some types of partnership efforts established between local schools or districts and institutions of higher education. Readers are invited to consider these as possibilities for their local community and as examples of the connections that can be made between educational partners.

- Invite pre-service teachers into the school to present parent programs throughout the year.
- Establish a program in which pre-service teachers can work with small groups of parents (or individual parents) on reading-related activities. A series of after-school parent workshops would be one option.
- Invite pre-service teachers to compose and publish a parent newsletter with lists of recommended books, reading tips and ideas, and ideas on fostering the reading habit at home.
- Work with the local college to dedicate a portion of the district's website to parent involvement. The site can include information about recently released children's books and adolescent literature, summaries of the district's reading assessment, helpful hints, and other pertinent information.
- Invite professors in the education department of a local college to present workshops or seminars to parents on the value of reading to children, selecting appropriate literature, or other parent-related issues.
- Work with education department faculty to organize a parent workshop at the school or to invite a children's author to visit the local area.
- Invite university professors and pre-service teachers to become members of a Parent Reading Advisory Council which helps shape the form and direction of the reading program.

Guidelines for Community Outreach

Without question, a wide diversity of outreach projects and programs can be incorporated into the reading curriculum at both the elementary and secondary levels. Yet, regardless of the type of outreach program planned, several guidelines will help reading educators by offering some practical considerations in planning effective parent and community involvement efforts. Included with each of the following guidelines are some suggested parent involvement possibilities for the classroom, school, or district.

1. Provide daily opportunities for parents and children to share, discuss, and read together. Establish "reading contracts" with school families. Encourage families to read together on a regular basis every day. Ask parents to sign a contract that pledges them to make this a regular family practice. Special calendars can be prepared and distributed so parents can check off appropriate reading times for all family members. Families who read together for a specified number of minutes each month could be awarded special certificates obtained from a local teacher supply store.

Community and neighborhood newspapers are always on the lookout for newsworthy items to put into their pages. Consider drafting a regular column on tips and ideas parents can use in promoting the reading habit at home. This space can also be used to describe literacy-related events happening at school or list recommended children's books.

2. Plan purposeful activities as the heart of the program. Parents must understand the relevance of reading-related activities (reading recipes, assembling a model, and so on) to their children's growth as readers. Develop and design a series of orientation programs for parents new to the school or district. It would be valuable to develop a slide program, a series of brochures, family guides, or other appropriate orientation materials to assist new families in learning as much as they can about purposeful activities in the reading curriculum.

Work with a group of parents to prepare a notebook of vacation activities that can be done in the home or in the community. Games, reading activities, places to visit, and sites to see in the community could all be included. These notebooks could be distributed to all families prior to a vacation period, especially summer.

3. Provide children with regular opportunities to interact with good literature and well-written stories. Establish a lending library of resource materials and books for parents to check out and utilize at home. The local home and school organization can purchase these materials. Also, include a selection of educational games and activities for families to borrow.

Periodically provide parents with various lists of recommended books. Work with the school librarian in distributing lists such as "The Supervisor's Top Ten Hits" throughout the year. Consider disseminating a list of books on child-rearing practices as well as books containing reading-related activities. If possible, plan a few "share-and-discuss" sessions with groups of parents to talk over selected books.

Promulgate the benefits of public library membership to all families. Plan to work closely with the local public library to share information on the wealth of resources and information available to families in the community.

Ask parents and community people to list some of their favorite children's books, either those they read as children or those they are currently reading to their own children. Publish this list on a frequent basis and distribute it to all families.

4. Take into account not only the specific needs of parents but also the day-to-day needs of children. Students' interests, hobbies, and free-time activities can be utilized in promoting the reading habit. Distribute lists of recommended books to parents based on students' interests. Parents would welcome suggested readings on popular hobbies, arts and crafts projects, and playtime activities. For example, families can be provided with book lists on how to create or practice a project or activity along with names of books covering important personalities or discoveries in those particular areas. Encouraging families to share their experiences with other students would also be appropriate.

5. Do not attempt to turn parents into surrogate teachers, but seek to promote and extend the natural relationship between parent and child. Parenthood is not the easiest of occupations. It's one in which tolerance levels may be low and frustration ever present. Any outreach effort must not place undue pressure on parents; rather, it should subscribe to the notion that parent-child interaction time should be unhurried, pleasant for all parties, and tolerant of everyone's feelings.

Set up an exhibit in the local shopping mall, church, synagogue, or similarly public area that includes photos of parents and children reading together, tips for parent participation, and other reading-related activities. Engage children in designing and creating these displays, and include their ideas for sharing the reading experience with the entire community.

Ask parents to keep special diaries or scrapbooks of family-related reading activities. For example, include books they have read and stories discussed, as well as photos of family members reading together. Students can bring these to school for special sharing.

6. Provide parents with a variety of opportunities to support and encourage their children's growth as readers. Utilize the local media in disseminating information on how parents can and should become involved in their school's reading program. Public service announcements distributed to local television and radio stations, letters to the editor of the local newspaper on the value of community and parent involvement in the reading curriculum, or a monthly advice column in the Sunday newspaper can all be effective.

Invite parents and community people to join a reading curriculum council to assist in the selection of new reading materials or to help establish guidelines and directions for the reading program throughout the year.

Establish an open-door policy with the community early in the school year. Parents need to feel comfortable in visiting their children's classrooms or schools. Frequent invitations from the administrator or reading supervisor are an important way of transmitting this philosophy. Also, invite parents and other community leaders to demonstrate their hobbies or favorite reading materials to groups of children. This reinforces the idea that all community members can and should enjoy reading as a lifetime pursuit.

Involve the community in establishing homework policies and practices. Homework continues to be the most traditional method of contact between home and school. By encouraging parental input in the design of an all-inclusive homework policy, schools can insure the support they need.

7. Offer informal community workshops and meetings. Offer parents and other community members a series of informal workshops throughout the year that will focus on various aspects of the reading curriculum. The workshops can address specific components of the school's reading program as well as ways that parents can help support teachers' instructional efforts.

Establish regularly scheduled informal meetings with parents throughout the year. These can be set up as brown-bag lunches with the building principal, a meeting over tea and coffee with the reading supervisor, or a "bring-your-own-dessert" gathering in the evening. The intent of these meetings should not be to provide instruction, but rather to give educators and community people an opportunity to meet informally and discuss common goals and objectives. If these meetings can be held in a neutral location, such as a church or YMCA, parents will be more inclined to come, particularly if the meeting is planned for the convenience of their schedules.

8. Infuse a spirit of shared responsibility into any outreach effort. Gather a coalition of parents, community workers, local business people, and educators to write a series of newsletters on suggested parent involvement ideas. Plan to have these distributed throughout the community in workplaces, office buildings, factories, and community centers.

Don't neglect grandparents and other senior citizens. Many effective volunteer programs have relied on older people to provide innumerable reading services to the school. These can include listening to children read aloud, sharing childhood experiences with reading, and reading popular stories to classes of students.

Conclusion

Community outreach, to be effective, is not a one-shot or short-term project initiated by a school or district to pacify parents or respond to a crisis situation. It is a natural, dynamic, and multifaceted effort by all members of the community to involve families in the literacy development of all children. Its true effectiveness lies in the fact that it is structured and perceived as a very normal and natural outgrowth of the school reading program. Its success is built upon mutual respect and mutual cooperation among all elements of the local community. The creative vision generated when parents, community members, and educators come together for the shared benefit of all children can be the keystone for any and all literacy efforts.

References

Benjamin, L. A., & Lord, J. (1996). *Family literacy.* Washington, DC: Office of Educational Research and Improvement.

Cairney, T., & Munsie, L. (1995). Parent participation in literacy learning. *The Reading Teacher, 48,* 392–403.

Come, B., & Fredericks, A. D. (1995). Family literacy in urban schools: Meeting the needs of at-risk children. *The Reading Teacher, 48,* 566–570.

Epstein, J. (1992). School and family partnerships. In M. Alkin (Ed.), *Encyclopedia of educational research* (6th ed., pp. 1139–1151). New York: Macmillan.

Fredericks, A. D. (2001). *The complete phonemic awareness handbook: More than 300 playful activities for early reading success.* Crystal Lake, IL: Rigby.

Fredericks, A. D., & Rasinski, T. V. (1990a). Involving the uninvolved: How to. *The Reading Teacher, 43,* 424–425.

Fredericks, A. D., & Rasinski, T. V. (1990b). Whole language and parents: Natural partners. *The Reading Teacher, 43,* 692–694.

Johnson, D., & Walker, T. (1991). A follow-up evaluation of the Houston parent-child development center: School performance. *Journal of Early Intervention, 15,* 226–236.

Klumpp, K. (1990, March). *Barriers to successful outreach to parents of diverse populations.* PTA Project HOPE, San Diego, CA.

Morningstar, J. W. (1999). Home response journals: Parents as informed contributors in the understanding of their child's literacy development. *The Reading Teacher, 52,* 690–697.

Neuman, S. B., Caperelli, B. J., & Kee, C. (1998). Literacy learning, a family matter. *The Reading Teacher, 52,* 244–252.

Rasinski, T. V., & Fredericks, A. D. (1991). Beyond parents and into the community. *The Reading Teacher, 44,* 698–699.

CHAPTER FIFTEEN

Special Initiatives for Special Needs

Dixie Lee Spiegel

The first 14 chapters in this book have shown how to develop and administer the very best reading programs. However, even an exemplary program will rarely succeed with all children. Some children come to school at risk for falling behind in literacy for a variety of reasons. Other children have difficulty in attaining full literacy once they enter school. For these special children, special initiatives are needed. This chapter discusses:

◆ Traditional responses to children with special needs, including pull-out remedial reading programs, special education programs, and programs for children with limited English proficiency

◆ Promising interventions that fit well within the framework of more traditional programs

◆ Guidelines through which educators might wish to examine programs either for modification or adoption

Traditional Responses to Special Literacy Needs

In spite of nearly three decades of concerted efforts to wipe out illiteracy, schools in the United States are still graduating too many marginally literate young adults. In addition, the dropout rate, which hovers around 30% in some states, virtually ensures that large numbers of young people are leaving school without even functional literacy. Students attending high-poverty schools (defined as having populations of whom at least 50% are poor) are 57% more likely to drop out of school by the tenth grade than students in low-poverty schools (6–20% poor) (U.S. Department of Education, 1993). Nearly 40% of fourth graders in the United States have not attained the basic level on national assessments of reading (Donahue, Voelkl, Campbell, & Mazzeo, 1999; Wasik, 1998b). Although the scores for lower performing students increased in 1998 for Grades 4 and 8, they decreased for Grade 12 (Donahue et al., 1999). At all three grades for which National Assessment of Educational Progress (NAEP) data are collected, the 1998 reading scores for children in poverty were lower than for students not eligible for free or reduced-price lunch (Donahue et al., 1999). Thus it would seem that traditional responses to children at risk for literacy failure have had limited success. An examination of these traditional programs is in order, to determine the nature of these programs and the degree to which they are meeting the children's needs.

Pull-out Remedial Reading Programs

The most common special placement for children experiencing trouble with literacy is a pull-out remedial reading program. In these programs, children leave their regular classroom and go to the reading teacher's room, where they receive instruction in small groups, usually on a daily basis. Many of these pull-out programs are funded by Chapter 1; data about Chapter 1 and non–Chapter 1 pull-out programs will often be combined in this review.

The extent of Chapter 1 funding provides a sense of the magnitude of special efforts for children with reading problems. Among U.S. public elementary schools, 71% receive Chapter 1 services (U.S. Department of Education, 1993). The 1993–1994 Chapter 1 budget was $6.1 billion (LeTendre, 1991).

One would expect that such an infusion of funds and effort would have positive results. However, most reviews of research have concluded that Chapter 1 programs have had at best a "positive but marginal impact" on achievement (Fagan & Heid, 1991; U.S. Department of Education, 1993). Children in Chapter 1 programs have often made more progress than at-risk children not receiving services, but overall, Chapter 1 children remain behind their grade-level peers. They just don't fall as far behind as children not served (Bean, Cooley, Eichelberger, Lazar, & Zigmond, 1991; Fagan & Heid, 1991; Slavin, 1987). For example, the average gain in reading for Chapter 1 students in 1987–1988 was a modest three normal curve equivalents, or NCEs (Fagan & Heid, 1991). Furthermore, gains shown by spring achievement tests do not appear to last, often disappearing as early as the following fall (Slavin, 1987), with no lasting discernible effects of participation in Chapter 1 showing by junior high school age (Carter, 1984; Kennedy, Birman, & Demaline, 1986). Another depressing finding is that Chapter 1 programs generally are most effective with children with only minor to moderate reading disability (Carter, 1984; Kennedy et al., 1986). In fact, the test scores of children in high-poverty schools actually get worse from primary to later grades (U.S. Department of Education, 1993).

An examination of research about Chapter 1 and pull-out remedial reading programs provides insight into their modest success. When one compares what typically happens in these programs with what we know about effective reading instruction, it is not surprising that children do not progress more rapidly. One important factor is the amount of reading instruction provided. Chapter 1 programs are specifically funded to provide supplemental instruction. Therefore, one would expect that when the amount of instruction in the regular classroom is combined with the amount of instruction in the Chapter 1 classroom, Chapter 1 students would receive more instruction than children not receiving special services. However, observation does not confirm this expectation (Carter, 1984; Johnston & Allington, 1991; Rowan & Guthrie, 1989). Chapter 1 students typically receive only 30 minutes of extra instruction, and these 30 minutes are at the expense of regular literacy instruction in at least 70% of the classrooms (U.S. Department of Education, 1993). Thus, there is not the increased opportunity to learn that is needed for children to make the accelerated progress necessary to catch up with their peers (Allington, 1983).

Research has indicated that other factors related to achievement in literacy are frequently not present in pull-out programs. Instruction often focuses on fragmented skills taught and practiced in isolation (Allington, Stuetzel, Shake, & Lamarche, 1986; Rowan & Guthrie, 1989; U.S. Department of Education, 1993), with little or no attention to transfer to real texts (Allington et al., 1986; Bean et al., 1991). In fact, children in remedial reading programs get few opportunities to practice their strategies with authentic, connected text; instead, they spend their time completing worksheets (Bean et al., 1991).

One would also expect that instruction in small pull-out programs would be individualized so that every child got the program he or she needed. Sadly, little evidence of individualization has been found (Allington & McGill-Franzen, 1989; Allington et al., 1986; Bean et al., 1991). Small groups of students often get a group lesson, and groups at the same grade placement may get the same lesson on a given day, that is, "the third grade lesson." One especially dangerous result of this lack of individualization is that students are often given materials not at their instructional level. Often the material is too hard for them, and they cannot successfully practice strategies they are learning (Johnston & Allington, 1991).

Another aspect of individualization is monitoring and reinforcement of student efforts. This, too, does not seem to occur in many pull-out programs (Allington et al., 1986; Bean et al., 1991). Typically, the monitoring that does take place is feedback on the accuracy of children's responses and not on the appropriateness of the strategies used (Allington et al., 1986; Johnston & Allington, 1991). Even more damaging, responding to the correctness of student responses frequently is given in the absence of direct instruction. That is, all too often direct instruction in

what a strategy is, why it might be useful, and how that strategy is carried out is not provided (Allington & McGill-Franzen, 1989; Allington et al., 1986; Bean et al., 1991). Children are simply given worksheets and workbooks to complete with little or no teacher input. They are told to do a task, but not told how or why.

Another extremely important factor to consider in the success of pull-out programs is the degree to which they are congruent with regular classroom programs. Children targeted for special help through pull-out programs are generally having difficulty learning one literacy curriculum. If they are placed in a pull-out program that offers a different curriculum, these at-risk children are forced to try to learn two (sometimes incompatible) curricula (Allington & Broikou, 1988; Johnston, Allington, & Afflerbach, 1985). Unfortunately, research has not found a high degree of congruence between pull-out programs and classroom programs (Allington et al., 1986; Bean et al., 1991; Carter, 1984; Johnston et al., 1985).

Special Education Programs

Many children with special needs are served through special education programs, typically through pull-out programs in resource rooms. Literacy instruction in special education resource rooms unfortunately mirrors instruction in pull-out remedial reading programs. There is little individualization in either amount or nature of services (Allington & McGill-Franzen, 1989; Haynes & Jenkins, 1986; McGill-Franzen & Allington, 1990; Ysseldyke, Christenson, Thurlow, & Bakewell, 1989). Monitoring of student responses is infrequent and generally limited to marking papers right or wrong (Haynes & Jenkins, 1986). Strategies are seldom explicitly taught, and when they are, children receive few opportunities to practice them in extended, authentic text (Allington & McGill-Franzen, 1989; Haynes & Jenkins, 1986). As in Chapter 1 pull-out programs, congruence is rarely found between special education pull-out programs and the regular education curriculum (Haynes & Jenkins, 1986; O'Sullivan, Ysseldyke, Christenson, & Thurlow, 1990).

Overall, attendance in special education resource rooms does not guarantee that special education children get more reading instruction than regular education students. Some research has found that special education students often receive more reading instruction in their pull-out programs than do Chapter 1 students (Allington & McGill-Franzen, 1989), although other research has found little reading instruction in resource rooms (Haynes & Jenkins, 1986). Observations consistently show that special education children get less reading instruction and opportunity to learn in their regular classrooms than do nonhandicapped children (Allington & McGill-Franzen, 1989; O'Sullivan et al., 1990). Thus, even when reading instruction is taking place in the resource room, the overall reading instruction provided special education students is not greater than or even equal to that of children in regular education settings. Furthermore, Haynes and Jenkins (1986) found that the amount of services scheduled by special education had only a weak relationship to the severity of the child's need. Thus, say Haynes and Jenkins, it is not surprising that children rarely "get out" of special education; at best, comparable services are provided, and comparable services do not allow for accelerated progress.

Research on traditional programs for children with literacy problems is not encouraging. Some children in these programs make normal progress, but as a group they do not catch up with their peers. One possible explanation for the minimal results is the failure of these programs to implement effective instructional practices. Fortunately, some recent early intervention tutorial efforts show great promise, because research shows that served children can catch up, and these programs do provide sound instruction.

Early Intervention Tutorial Programs

Early intervention programs are designed to prevent problems from arising in the first place. Traditional school-based literacy intervention programs, such as most Chapter 1 and special education programs, are often reactive; they respond to the needs of children who have already begun to fall behind in literacy acquisition. Early intervention programs are proactive; they seek to identify children at risk for literacy failure prior to or at the very beginning of formal literacy training, and to work with them before the cycle of failure begins. Children identified as at risk are placed in an intensive one-to-one or small-group program that provides strategy training, immediate reinforcement, and corrective feedback. In other words, these programs utilize effective instructional practices. Four early intervention tutorial programs will be described here: Reading Recovery, Success for All, Early Steps, and Early Intervention in Reading.

Reading Recovery

Reading Recovery, originated by Marie Clay (Clay, 1987) in New Zealand, is the most widespread first grade tutorial intervention program in the United States. The U.S. training and dissemination site is Ohio State University. Reading Recovery teachers complete a rigorous year-long training program with a certified Reading Recovery teacher trainer. The children are selected from the lowest 20% of first graders, based on teacher judgment and performance on the Observation Survey, Reading Recovery's screening measure. Children who have been identified as special education students are eligible (Lyons, 1989, 1991a). Selected children then work with a Reading Recovery teacher on a one-to-one basis for 30 minutes a day in order to improve their "in-the-head processing" during reading and writing (Clay, 1987, p. 49). Emphasis is on the development of metacognition and strategy usage. Children are "discontinued" when they meet two criteria: (1) they are able to work in the middle reading group in their own classroom, and (2) they have developed a self-improving system through which they learn more about reading by themselves every time they read (Clay & Cazden, 1990).

The general Reading Recovery lesson framework has four parts:

1. The child rereads one or more familiar books in order to practice strategy use and gain fluency.
2. The child reads a new book and the teacher keeps a "running record" that describes the child's strategy use with that text.
3. The child writes and then reads a one- or two-sentence message, with assistance as needed from the teacher. The child and the teacher use this message to explore letter-sound relationships.
4. The child reads another new book, which is then used for the first part of the next day's lesson.

During each part of the lesson, the teacher responds to the child's attempts in ways that will strengthen appropriate strategy usage and replace ineffective practices (Pinnell, DeFord, & Lyons, 1988).

Reading Recovery has been the subject of several reviews of research and evaluation studies in the past few years, some completed by researchers associated with Reading Recovery (Askew, Fountas, Lyons, Pinnell, & Schmitt, 1998; DeFord, Tancock, & White, 1990; Lyons, 1991b, 1998; Pinnell, 1989; Pinnell, DeFord, & Lyons, 1988; Pinnell, Lyons, DeFord, Bryk, & Seltzer, 1994) and some by independent outsiders (Hiebert, 1994; Shanahan & Barr, 1995; Wasik & Slavin, 1993). Askew et al. (1998) summarize Reading Recovery national evaluation data, which show that over 400,000 children were served from 1985 to 1997. Of the children who were involved with Reading Recovery long enough to complete the program, 81% were successfully discontinued (i.e., were at or above the achievement of their classroom peers). The data are similar for children participating in Reading Recovery in Spanish (Askew et al., 1998).

One important question to ask about any intervention program relates to the long-term effects of the program. Longitudinal data reported by Pinnell (1989) suggest that at least two-thirds of discontinued children make accelerated progress, are able to perform within the average range for their classes, and continue to make progress for at least two more years after intervention has stopped. Shanahan and Barr's

(1995) rigorous evaluation of Reading Recovery research is less positive about the long-term effects, but they still conclude that once the children attain average achievement, in following years they maintain their advantage over other poor readers (in the comparison groups), but their progress is not quite at the average level for their class.

These data are impressive, especially when one remembers that these children were in the lowest 20% of their classes. However, Reading Recovery is not without its critics. Some researchers (cf., Center, Wheldall, Freeman, Outhred, & McNaught, 1995) have found far less impressive results. Concerns have also been raised about which children are included in the program (Wasik & Slavin, 1993) and in the data analyzed (Center et al., 1995; Hiebert, 1994), the measures used and the form of the data available from Reading Recovery (Hiebert, 1994; Wasik & Slavin, 1993), the cost of the program (Hiebert, 1994; Rasinski, 1995; Shanahan & Barr, 1995), and the limited effect that Reading Recovery may have on the literacy programs within their schools (Hiebert, 1994; Shanahan & Barr, 1995). In general, however, most critics are cautiously supportive of Reading Recovery. For example, Wasik and Slavin (1993) conclude that "the effects of Reading Recovery are impressive at the end of the implementation year, and the effects are maintained for at least two years" (p. 187). Shanahan and Barr (1995) conclude that Reading Recovery students make greater than expected gains, but that the program is not as effective as its proponents have claimed.

Success for All

Success for All (Madden, Slavin, Karweit, Dolan, & Wasik, 1991; Wasik & Slavin, 1993) is a comprehensive, schoolwide program that has been implemented in more than 400 schools in more than 30 states, as well as in Australia, Canada, Israel, and Mexico (Weiler, 1998). The program has many components: a daily 20-minute tutoring session during the social studies or science period for first and second graders who need support; a 90-minute classroom reading program in which first through third graders are regrouped across ages and classes for instruction; frequent assessments and changes in reading group assignment; staff development; a family support team; and a facilitator who helps implement the program (Weiler, 1998).

The tutors in Success for All are trained, certified teachers. In addition to providing one-on-one instruction, the tutors also serve as additional teachers during the 90-minute classroom reading period, thus effectively reducing class size to about 15. Tutors coordinate their efforts with the classroom program but also may teach alternative strategies. Tutors and classroom teachers receive two days of training together at the beginning of the year on the beginning reading program; the tutors have another four days of training on assessment and the tutoring program.

Wasik and Slavin (1993) describe four tenets on which the tutoring program has been developed: (1) Children learn to read by reading text that is meaningful, not isolated bits of print. (2) Systematic phonics instruction is critical. (3) Comprehension, not word identification, is the ultimate goal of reading. (4) Children need to become strategic readers.

Success for All has been evaluated at multiple sites in several states (Slavin et al., 1996b). In her summary of evaluations for Success for All, Weiler (1998) concludes that the program is "effective in enhancing the reading achievement of economically disadvantaged and non-native English speaking students" (p. 1). The benefits are greatest for children scoring in the lower 25% of their classes at pre-testing (Slavin et al., 1996b) and are especially strong for children identified as special education students (Ross, Smith, Casey, & Slavin, 1995). Success for All also has been associated with better attendance, fewer retentions, and fewer placements in special education (Weiler, 1998).

As with Reading Recovery, there is some concern about the lasting effects of Success for All. Slavin, Madden, Dolan, and Wasik (1996a) report that although Success for All students were still scoring higher in reading in the sixth and seventh grades than their matched counterparts in their comparison groups, that difference was diminishing. Venezky (1994) pointed out that only 12.5% of the Success for All students were reading at or nearly at grade level after five years in the program; however, as reported above, these students still outperformed the students in the control groups.

Early Steps

Early Steps (formerly entitled First Steps) is an individual tutoring program for at-risk first graders and has much in common with Reading Recovery (Morris, Tyner, & Perney, 2000; Santa & Høien, 1999). The lowest-achieving first graders are selected and the lesson framework is similar to that of Reading Recovery. However, both Chapter 1 reading teachers and first grade teachers are trained to tutor, with the Chapter 1 teacher working with three or four children daily and the classroom teacher tutoring one child from his or her classroom. Another difference is in tutor training, which is somewhat abbreviated from the Reading Recovery model. Training begins with the trainer explaining the process. Next, tutors observe the trainer via video implementing the process. Then tutors observe the trainer with a child, followed by a debriefing session. Next, tutors implement the process under the trainer's observation, followed by a debriefing session to jointly plan the next lesson. In addition, tutors attend 15 evening inservice sessions, mostly in the first semester. Also, the trainer continues to observe the tutors at work throughout the year and provide feedback. A third difference between Early Steps and Reading Recovery is that Early Steps has more explicit instruction in phonemic awareness.

Early Steps has been implemented at only a few sites, but it has been the subject of several evaluations and the data are encouraging (Morris et al., 2000; Santa & Høien, 1999). When Morris (1993) compared Early Steps students to low-reading first graders from two previous years who had no intervention, more Early Steps children were able to read 75% of the basal primer words than comparison children (50% vs. 7%, respectively). Further, 76% of Early Step students could read the primer text with 90% accuracy at the end of first grade in three of the four schools, and 38% could read at the first grade second half

level. In the Santa and Høien (1999) evaluation of
Early Steps, the control group students received
supplemental practice in reading both familiar
and new books. The Early Steps children outperformed the control group students on all
measures: spelling, word and nonword recognition, and comprehension. Santa and Høien conclude that Early Steps "led to accelerated growth,
particularly for children most at risk for not learning to read" (1999, p. 69). Morris et al. (2000)
found similar results, and again the children most
at risk benefited the most.

Early Intervention in Reading

Early Intervention in Reading is another program in which the most at-risk children are
served, in this case the five lowest-achieving students in a classroom. First grade teachers are
trained through a one-day summer workshop
and inservice training after school to work with
these groups of five for 15 to 20 minutes daily
(Taylor, Short, Frye, & Shearer, 1992; Taylor,
Strait, & Medo, 1994). Early Intervention in
Reading sessions follow a three-day cycle that
begins with the teacher reading a picture book to
the entire class and then a summary of that book
to the Early Intervention in Reading group. Over
the next two days, repeated readings and other
interactions with the book summary help children develop use of context, phonemic awareness, writing and spelling abilities, sight vocabulary, and a working knowledge of phonics. The
teacher uses records of children's strategy usage
to plan lessons. In addition to the small-group
work, each child works for five minutes a day
individually with a trained teacher aide or for
10 minutes in a group of two.

As with Early Steps, Early Intervention in
Reading data show promise. At the end of first
grade, the ability to read at least at the first grade
second half level was seen in 50% of Early Intervention in Reading children, 20% of the control
group of 30 low achievers from other first grade
classes, and 55% of 30 average-ability children in
their own classes (the comparison group) (Taylor et al., 1992). Follow-up data showed that at
the end of second grade, without further intervention, 98% of Early Intervention in Reading

children could read at the second grade level
(Taylor et al., 1994).

A small-group extension of Early Intervention
in Reading was implemented for children ages
7–8 in which children ages 9–10 were used as
cross-age tutors. Taylor, Hanson, Justice-Swanson, and Watts (1997) found that both the tutored
children and their tutors made significant gains
in reading.

Tutor Programs Using Volunteers or College Students

The four programs described above all use tutors
who are professional teachers. Although the four
programs have had promising results, one concern across all the programs to one degree or
another is cost. Hiring certified teachers to tutor
is more expensive than using volunteer tutors or
nonprofessional tutors who are paid a relatively
low wage. With that concern in mind, two programs that use volunteer or college student
tutors are described next: the Charlottesville Volunteer Tutorial Program and America Reads, the
massive federally funded effort to make every
child a reader by Grade 3.

The Charlottesville Volunteer Tutorial Program

The Charlottesville Volunteer Tutorial Program
(Invernizzi, Juel, & Rosemary, 1996–1997; Invernizzi, Rosemary, Juel, & Richards, 1997) uses
community volunteers to tutor first grade children who are at risk for reading failure. Tutoring
is available to second graders when space is
available. The tutors are trained three times a
year for a total of six hours of training. However,
they also receive continuing training and support from a reading specialist who supervises
each tutorial session, giving immediate feedback
to the tutors and modeling appropriate practices
as needed. The specialist uses ongoing assessment of the children's progress to modify the lesson plans that the tutors then implement. The
specialist also meets with the classroom teacher
and Title I teacher twice a month to discuss each
child's progress.

A child is tutored twice a week for 45 minutes in each session. Each tutoring session focuses on reading, writing, and phonics and has four parts. The child rereads familiar books. The child participates in word study, which utilizes a compare and contrast approach to help children focus on the features of words. Next the child writes. Last of all, the child reads a new book.

The criterion for success in the program is the ability to read *Little Bear* (Minarik, 1957) with 90% accuracy in word recognition. *Little Bear* is identified by the authors of the program as "a milestone book for first grade readers" (Invernizzi et al., 1996–1997, p. 308). To date, three years of data on the Charlottesville Volunteer Tutorial Program have been reported (Invernizzi et al., 1996–1997; Invernizzi et al., 1997). These data show steadily improving results over the three years of implementation, especially for children who participated in more than 40 tutoring sessions. Typically these are the children with the most need who were identified first for tutoring. The results for all three years are encouraging, and those for the last year reported are particularly so: 90% of the students who received more than 40 tutoring sessions achieved the criterion for success, as did 73% of those who had fewer than 40 sessions.

America Reads

America Reads is a funding effort announced in 1997 by the federal government. Its goal is that all children in the United States will be successful readers by Grade 3. A primary component of America Reads is the use of one million volunteers or federal work-study college students in the schools to help children who are at risk for failure in reading (Wasik, 1998a, 1998b). Neither the America Reads Challenge Grant nor its governing body offers guidelines for the actual programs that might be used by these tutors or the training they would receive. As a result, extreme variation exists across the programs funded. Wasik (1998a) summarizes this variation:

> Some [programs] have very well developed training programs for tutors; others do not. Some of the programs have written materials for the tutors to follow; other programs rely mostly on oral dissemination of information. Some have student materials; most do not. . . . What has occurred is that many programs are being implemented across school districts with little evidence of their effectiveness (p. 2).

Published evaluations of the effectiveness of America Reads programs are sparse and only recently forthcoming, since the initiative is relatively new. Part of the problem is the lack of an evaluation requirement as part of the America Reads initiative. Fitzgerald et al. (2000) decry this missing component of the legislation and stress the importance of including flexible requirements for evaluation in national efforts such as America Reads.

Fitzgerald et al. (2000) summarize evaluation efforts from three America Reads sites. All sites had the following characteristics.

1. The tutoring program, including its evaluation, was designed by university education faculty with expertise in the teaching of reading and writing.
2. The program coordinator at each site was an individual with a master's degree and experience as a reading teacher.
3. The sites were at elementary schools identified as serving students eligible for Title I funds or as having students with low reading scores on the average, or both.
4. Children were tutored individually two to three times a week for 35–40 minutes a session. The tutoring supplemented rather than replaced classroom reading instruction.
5. The lessons included rereading familiar text, word study, writing, and reading a new book.
6. The tutors received intensive training.

Using different evaluation designs, all three sites showed positive results. The children made significant progress or scored better than the comparison and control group students in word recognition (Site 1 and 3), letter identification (Site 1 and 3), letter sound knowledge (Site 3), oral retelling of what was read (Site 2), probed comprehension (Site 2), writing (Site 2), concepts about print (Site 2), and instructional reading level (Site 3) (Fitzgerald et al., 2000).

Guidelines for Special Needs Reading Programs

This review of existing programs has presented both good news and bad news. The bad news is that traditional programs often have only limited success. The good news is that new initiatives in early intervention show much promise, probably because they implement effective instructional practices. The very good news is that traditional programs are amenable to change and modification. They can be made better. Research about effective instructional practices, both within the developmental reading program and in programs for at-risk children or children who have already fallen behind, can inform these modifications, just as they have informed the development of the early intervention programs described in this chapter. The questions that follow have been extracted from that research, and their discussion is presented here in the hopes of providing educators a lens through which to view their current special reading initiatives or through which to select a program.

Real Reading

1. Is reading instruction focused on comprehension of connected text, not on the fragmented study of isolated skills? Real reading involves comprehension of connected text for authentic purposes. We teach children to read in order that they can do real reading, so that they can read to find information they need, entertain themselves, and broaden their understanding of the world.

Clay and Cazden suggest a persuasive rationale and a clear guideline:

> For all children, the larger the chunks of printed language they can work with, the richer the network of information they can use, and the quicker they learn. Teaching should dwell on detail only long enough for the child to discover its existence and then encourage the use of it in isolation only when absolutely necessary. (1990, p. 207)

2. Do children spend time reading? Practice may not make perfect, but in reading practice, spending time reading does have a positive relationship with achievement (Anderson, Wilson, & Fielding, 1986). It is through practice that learners try out new strategies, develop fluency, and begin to experience the rewards of reading.

Opportunity to Learn

3. Do students have the opportunity to learn? Students have the opportunity to learn when time is both allocated to and actually provided for a task, and when students are on task or engaged.

4. Are the goals of instruction clear to both students and teachers? When the goals of instruction are clear to the learners, they focus on the tasks at hand. For example, poor readers are often given tasks that focus on accurate decoding, not comprehension, whereas good readers are given comprehension-based tasks (Allington, 1983). Therefore, it is not surprising that some poor readers may view reading as pronouncing words correctly, not comprehending (Gambrell & Heathington, 1981) or that they cannot express the purposes of the activities they are completing (Johnston et al., 1985). Conversely, if the goals of instruction are not clear to teachers, they too may focus on other issues. Research by Allington et al. (1986) concluded that teachers often do not have clear goals for individual students, nor do they have long-term plans for their students.

Curriculum Coordination

5. Is the special reading program congruent with the classroom reading program? The teachers of special programs and the teachers of classroom programs need to coordinate their efforts so that struggling readers are not trying to learn two curricula when they are already having trouble learning one. Research on both Title I and special education settings in the 1980s and early 1990s rarely found congruence between either pull-out or in-class models and the regular classroom.

6. Are learners given materials at their instructional level? When a reader can decode with approximately 95% accuracy and comprehend about 70–90% of what was read, that individual is said to be reading at the instructional level. This is the level at which the learner is challenged but not overwhelmed (Morris, Shaw, & Perney, 1990), the level at which the learner can profit from instruction.

7. Is instruction individualized? In spite of lower student-teacher ratios than in regular classrooms, most special initiative classrooms show little individualization. But individualization is important. Handerhahn (1990) found that the most successful Reading Recovery teachers were those who used greater variability in strategies. When Pinnell, Lyons, DeFord, Bryk, and Seltzer (1994) compared the traditional Reading Recovery model with a variation in which Reading Recovery teachers worked with groups of children rather than with individuals, results clearly favored the traditional model, and in fact this individualization was deemed essential. Wasik and Slavin's (1993) review of five one-to-one tutoring models for Grade 1 found impressive positive and lasting effects for tutoring when compared to traditional remedial models.

Direct Instruction

8. Is direct instruction a part of the program? Through direct instruction, a teacher explains, models, or discusses what is to be learned, why it is important, and how to apply what is learned. Direct instruction acknowledges that many children cannot infer strategies, their importance, or the situations in which they might be used (Adams, 1990; Ehri & Wilce, 1985). Direct instruction is especially important for children targeted for special initiatives because children from low-income families (Calfee & Piontkowski, 1981) or minority backgrounds (Delpit, 1988) have been found unable to discover reading strategies without some guidance.

9. Are children's attempts to make meaning of text monitored and reinforced? Through monitoring and reinforcement, teachers reassure students when they are using strategies appropriately and make suggestions for alternatives when ineffective strategies are used. Work by DeFord, Tancock, and White (1990) and Lyons (1998) confirms that a critical factor is "teachers' ability to make spontaneous effective decisions that provide sustaining feedback and to provide prompts that simplify the demands of the task" (Pinnell et al., 1994, p. 36).

Program Content

10. Are children taught strategies and how to transfer strategies to new situations? Strategies are complex "in-the-head" processes (Pinnell, 1989, p. 166) and are consciously selected to solve a problem. Skills, on the other hand, are taught as entities of value in themselves and are used without thought, in a reflexive manner. Children who are taught to use strategies become successful readers more quickly than those who do not receive strategy instruction (Share & Stanovich, 1995). For strategies to be useful, they must be taught in such a way that learners can generalize the usefulness of the strategy beyond the immediate context (Johnston et al., 1985). For this to happen, a real-world use for the strategy must be clearly delineated.

11. Is writing an integral part of the program? This is especially important for a beginning reading program because of the reciprocal nature of reading and writing for developing an awareness of the sound-symbol relationship of the language (Clarke, 1988; Clay & Cazden, 1990; Invernizzi et al., 1997; Pikulski, 1994). When emergent writers try JKLT for *chocolate*, they are breaking words down, isolating sounds, attempting to match letters with sounds, and blending it all back together again. This playing with sounds to spell helps learners in the task of playing with sounds to read.

12. If this is a beginning reading program, is phonemic awareness part of the curriculum? Phonemic awareness is a *consciousness* of sounds as entities that can be blended and taken apart and manipulated. Phonemic awareness includes the ability to *use* sounds. It is different from *knowing about* sounds, which may be what is taught in a traditional phonics program.

From her massive study of beginning reading, Adams (1990) concluded that familiarity with the letters of the alphabet and phonemic awareness "are very strong predictors of the ease with which a child will learn to read" (p. 7). Clay and Cazden (1990) suggest that phonemic awareness is an outcome of learning to read and write rather than a prerequisite for learning to read. It is by using sounds, by "trying them out" in reading and writing, that children develop phonemic awareness. Iverson and Tunmer (1993) compared a traditional Reading Recovery program with a modified version that included explicit instruction in phonemic awareness. The students in the enhanced phonemic awareness version of Reading Recovery needed fewer lessons than those in the traditional program to reach discontinuation ("graduation"). Santa and Høien (1999) found similar positive effects for phonological instruction in their evaluation of Early Steps, especially for the children most at risk for failure. Pikulski's (1994) review of five effective remedial programs identified attention to phonemic awareness as an important factor.

Quality of Instructional Personnel

13. Are children most at risk taught by the best teachers? Sadly, research indicates that in many initiatives for special needs children, often the children are not taught by the most effective teachers. Stanovich (1986) warns of the Matthew Effect: Learners who need the most and best instruction too often get the least and the worst (Allington & McGill-Franzen, 1989; Cooley, 1993). One salient example of the Matthew Effect is the common practice of using federally funded aides, who may not be certified teachers, to work with poor readers (Johnston & Allington, 1991). Another example is the tendency for students from advantaged backgrounds to attend schools rich in resources while those from disadvantaged backgrounds attend schools with limited resources (Carter, 1984). At-risk children must be given the best, not just what is available or left over.

Research has shown that extensive training is important for teachers and tutors who serve our most at-risk children (Pinnell et al., 1994; Shanahan, 1998). Without such training, and sometimes even with it, teachers may interpret new ideas through old lenses and change is minimized at best, or worse, results in distortions of intended practice (Chall, 1983; Sarason, 1990). Studies that have systematically manipulated the amount and duration of Reading Recovery training consistently have shown that more training is associated with better effects (Lyons, 1991a; Pinnell et al., 1994). Wasik and Slavin's (1993) review of tutoring programs also concluded that tutoring is more effective when certified (i.e., more highly trained) teachers are used rather than paraprofessionals. Chapter 1 data support this conclusion: In high-poverty schools, in which we have been least successful in closing the achievement gap, Chapter 1 programs rely heavily on instruction from teacher aides, 80% of whom do not have bachelor's degrees (U.S. Department of Education, 1993).

Accelerated Progress

14. Will this program help children who have fallen behind make accelerated progress? For children who have fallen behind, traditional programs such as Chapter 1 programs, preschool intervention programs like Head Start (Scott-Jones, 1992), or special education are not helping them close the gap. Although in some instances programs have helped children who have fallen behind to make normal progress, normal progress is not enough. They need to make accelerated progress in order to catch up with their peers. Therefore, equivalence of services is insufficient. Children with only the same opportunities to learn as their peers who are on grade level cannot make accelerated progress. O'Sullivan and colleagues (1990) ask: "Does it make sense, at the elementary school level, that the same amount of time is spent in reading instruction time for students who are good readers as for students who are poor readers?" (pp. 144–145). Allington (1994) warns that slowing down the pace of instruction actually makes it less likely that struggling readers will ever catch up.

Conclusion

Special needs children must have special initiatives, and "special" should mean the very best. From research on effective literacy education, we know many of the factors related to literacy success. From research on traditional intervention programs, we know that many programs do not implement effective practices. Literacy administrators, supervisors, and teachers need to ensure that our at-risk children receive the instruction they need to make accelerated progress. Fortunately, the first grade intervention programs highlighted in this review are a big step in this direction.

References

Adams, M. J. (1990). *Beginning to read: Thinking and learning about print.* Cambridge, MA: MIT Press.

Allington, R. L. (1983). The reading instruction provided readers of differing reading abilities. *Elementary School Journal, 83,* 548–559.

Allington, R. L. (1994). The schools we have, the schools we need. *The Reading Teacher, 48,* 14–29.

Allington, R. L., & Broikou, K. A. (1988). Development of shared knowledge: A new role for classroom and specialist teachers. *The Reading Teacher, 41,* 806–811.

Allington, R. L., & McGill-Franzen, A. (1989). School response to reading failure: Instruction for Chapter I and special students in grades 2, 4, and 8. *Elementary School Journal, 89,* 529–542.

Allington, R. L., Stuetzel, H., Shake, M., & Lamarche, S. (1986). What is remedial reading? A descriptive study. *Reading Research and Instruction, 26,* 15–30.

Anderson, R. C., Wilson, P. T., & Fielding, L. G. (1986). *Growth in reading and how children spend their time outside of school* (Tech. Rep. No. 389). Urbana: University of Illinois, Center for the Study of Reading.

Askew, B. J., Fountas, I. C., Lyons, C. A., Pinnell, G. S., & Schmitt, M. C. (1998). *Reading Recovery review: Understandings, outcomes, and implications.* Columbus, OH: Reading Recovery Council of North America.

Bean, R. M., Cooley, W. W., Eichelberger, R. T., Lazar, M. K., & Zigmond, N. (1991). In-class or pull-out: Effects of setting on the remedial reading program. *Journal of Reading Behavior, 23,* 445–464.

Calfee, R. C., & Piontkowski, D. C. (1981). The reading diary: Acquisition of decoding. *Reading Research Quarterly, 16,* 346–373.

Carter, L. F. (1984). The Sustaining Effects Study of compensatory and elementary education. *Educational Researcher, 12,* 4–13.

Center, Y., Wheldall, K., Freeman, L., Outhred, L., & McNaught, M. (1995). An evaluation of Reading Recovery. *Reading Research Quarterly, 30,* 240–263.

Chall, J. (1983). *Stages in reading development.* New York: McGraw-Hill.

Clarke, L. E. (1988). Invented spelling versus traditional spelling in first graders' writings: Effects of learning to spell and read. *Research in the Teaching of English, 22,* 281–309.

Clay, M. M. (1987). Implementing Reading Recovery: Systemic adaptations to an educational innovation. *New Zealand Journal of Educational Studies, 22,* 35–58.

Clay, M. M., & Cazden, C. B. (1990). A Vygotskian interpretation of Reading Recovery. In L. C. Moll (Ed.), *Vygotsky and education: Instructional implications and applications of socio-historical psychology* (pp. 206–222). New York: Cambridge University Press.

Cooley, W. (1993). The difficulty of the educational task: Implications for comparing student achievement in states, school districts, and schools. *ERS Spectrum, 11,* 27–31.

DeFord, D. E., Tancock, S., & White, N. (1990). *Teachers' models of the reading process and their evaluations of an individual reader: Relationship to success in teaching reading and judged quality of instruction* (Report No. 5, MacArthur Foundation). Columbus, OH: Ohio State University.

Delpit, L. D. (1988). The silenced dialogue: Power and pedagogy in educating other people's children. *Harvard Educational Review, 58,* 280–298.

Donahue, P. L., Voelkl, K. E., Campbell, J. R., & Mazzeo, J. (1999). *NAEP 1998 reading report card for the nation and the states. Executive summary.* Washington, DC: U.S. Department of Education.

Ehri, L. C., & Wilce, L. S. (1985). Movement into reading: Is the first stage of printed word learning visual or phonetic? *Reading Research Quarterly, 20,* 163–179.

Fagan, T. W., & Heid, C. A. (1991). Chapter I program improvement: Opportunity and practice. *Phi Delta Kappan, 72,* 582–585.

Fitzgerald, J., Morrow, L., Gambrell, L., Calfee, R., Venezky, R., Woo, D., & Dromsky, A. (2000). *Federal policy and program evaluation and research: The America Reads example.* Manuscript submitted for publication.

Gambrell, L. B., & Heathington, B. S. (1981). Adult disabled readers' metacognitive awareness about reading tasks and strategies. *Journal of Reading Behavior, 13,* 215–222.

Handerhahn, W. (1990). Reading instruction as defined by successful teachers and their first grade students within an early intervention program. *Dissertation Abstracts International,* No. AAC910512.

Haynes, M. C., & Jenkins, J. R. (1986). Reading instruction in special education resource rooms. *American Educational Research Journal, 23,* 161–190.

Hiebert, E. H. (1994). Reading recovery in the United States: What difference does it make to an age cohort? *Educational Research, 23,* 15–25.

Invernizzi, M., Juel, C., & Rosemary, C. (1996–1997). A community volunteer tutorial that works. *The Reading Teacher, 50,* 304–311.

Invernizzi, M., Rosemary, C., Juel, C., & Richards, H. (1997). At-risk readers and community volunteers: A 3-year perspective. *Scientific Studies of Reading, 1,* 277–300.

Iverson, S., & Tunmer, W. (1993). Phonological processing skills and the Reading Recovery program. *Journal of Educational Psychology, 85,* 112–126.

Johnston, P. H., & Allington, R. L. (1991). Remediation. In R. Barr, M. L. Kamil, P. B. Mosenthal, & P. D. Pearson (Eds.), *Handbook of reading research* (Vol. 2, pp. 984–1012). New York: Longman.

Johnston, P. H., Allington, R. L., & Afflerbach, P. (1985). The congruence of classroom and remedial reading instruction. *Elementary School Journal, 85,* 465–477.

Kennedy, M. M., Birman, B. F., & Demaline, R. E. (1986). *The effectiveness of Chapter I services.* Washington, DC: U.S. Department of Education, Office of Educational Research and Improvement.

LeTendre, M. J. (1991). Improving Chapter I programs: We can do better. *Phi Delta Kappan, 72,* 577–580.

Lyons, C. A. (1989). Reading Recovery: A preventative for mislabeling young "at-risk" learners. *Urban Education, 24,* 125–139.

Lyons, C. A. (1991a). A comparative study of the teaching effectiveness of teachers participating in a year-long or two-week inservice program. *National Reading Conference Yearbook, 40,* 367–375.

Lyons, C. A. (1991b). Reading Recovery: A viable prevention for learning disability. *Reading Horizons, 31,* 384–408.

Lyons, C. A. (1998). Reading Recovery in the United States: More than a decade of data. *Literacy Teaching and Learning: An International Journal of Early Reading and Writing, 3,* 77–92.

Madden, N. A., Slavin, R. E., Karweit, N. L., Dolan, L., & Wasik, B. A. (1991). Success for All. *Phi Delta Kappan, 72,* 593–599.

McGill-Franzen, A., & Allington, R. L. (1990). Comprehension and coherence: Neglected elements of literacy instruction in remedial and resource rooms. *Journal of Reading, Writing, and Learning Disabilities, 6,* 149–181.

Minarik, E. (1957). *Little Bear.* New York: Harper Trophy.

Morris, D. (1993). First steps: An early intervention program. Unpublished manuscript.

Morris, D., Shaw, R., & Perney, J. (1990). Helping low readers in grades 2 and 3: An after-school volunteer tutoring program. *Elementary School Journal, 91,* 133–150.

Morris, D., Tyner, B., & Perney, J. (2000, December). Early Steps: Replicating the effects of a first grade reading intervention program. *Journal of Educational Psychology, 92*(4), 681–693.

O'Sullivan, P. J., Ysseldyke, J. E., Christenson, S. L., & Thurlow, M. L. (1990). Mildly handicapped elementary students' opportunity to learn during reading instruction in mainstream and special education settings. *Reading Research Quarterly, 25,* 131–146.

Pikulski, J. (1994). Preventing reading failure: A review of five effective programs. *The Reading Teacher, 48,* 30–39.

Pinnell, G. S. (1989). Reading Recovery: Helping at-risk children learn to read. *Elementary School Journal, 90,* 159–181.

Pinnell, G. S., DeFord, D., & Lyons, C. A. (1988). *Reading Recovery: Early intervention for at-risk first graders.* Arlington, VA: Educational Research Service.

Pinnell, G. S., Lyons, C. A., DeFord, D. E., Bryk, A., & Seltzer, M. (1994). Comparing models for the literacy education of high-risk first graders. *Reading Research Quarterly, 29,* 8–39.

Rasinski, T. (1995). On the effects of Reading Recovery: A response to Pinnell, Lyons, DeFord, Bryk, and Seltzer. *Reading Research Quarterly, 30,* 264–270.

Ross, S. M., Smith, L. J., Casey, J., & Slavin, R. E. (1995). Increasing the academic success of disadvantaged children: An examination of alternative early intervention programs. *American Educational Research Journal, 32,* 773–800.

Rowan, G., & Guthrie, L. F. (1989). The quality of Chapter I instruction: Results from a study of twenty-four schools. In R. E. Slavin, N. L. Karweit, & N. A. Madden (Eds.), *Effective programs for schools at risk* (pp. 195–219). Boston: Allyn and Bacon.

Santa, C. M., & Høien, T. (1999). An assessment of Early Steps: A program for early intervention of reading problems. *Reading Research Quarterly, 34,* 54–79.

Sarason, S. B. (1990). *The predictable failure of educational reform: Can we change course before it's too late?* San Francisco: Jossey-Bass.

Scott-Jones, D. (1992). Family and community interventions affecting the development of cognitive skills in children. In T. G. Sticht, M. J. Beeler, & B. A. McDonald (Eds.), *The intergenerational transfer of cognitive skills: Vol. 1. Programs, policy, and research issues* (pp. 84–108). Norwood, NJ: Ablex.

Shanahan, T. (1998). On the effectiveness and limitations of tutoring in reading. *Review of Research in Education, 23,* 217–234.

Shanahan, T., & Barr, R. (1995). Reading Recovery: An independent evaluation of the effects of an early instructional intervention for at-risk learners. *Reading Research Quarterly, 30,* 958–996.

Share, D. L., & Stanovich, K. E. (1995). Cognitive processes in early reading development: Accommodating individual differences into a model of acquisition. *Issues in education: Contributions from educational psychology, 1,* 1–57.

Slavin, R. E. (1987). Making Chapter I make a difference. *Phi Delta Kappan, 69,* 110–119.

Slavin, R. E., Madden, N. A., Dolan, L. J., & Wasik, B. A. (1996a). *Every child, every school: Success for All.* Thousand Oaks, CA: Corwin Press.

Slavin, R. E., Madden., N. A., Dolan, L. J., Wasik, B. A., Ross, S. M., Smith, L. J., & Dianda, M. (1996b). Success for All: A summary of research. *Journal of Education for Students Placed at Risk, 1,* 41–76.

Stanovich, K. E. (1986). Matthew effects in reading: Some consequences of individual differences in the acquisition of literacy. *Reading Research Quarterly, 21,* 360–407.

Taylor, B. M., Hanson, B. E., Justice-Swanson, K., & Watts, S. M. (1997). Helping struggling readers: Linking small-group intervention with cross-age tutoring. *The Reading Teacher, 51,* 196–209.

Taylor, B. M., Short, R. A., Frye, B. J., & Shearer, B. A. (1992). Classroom teachers prevent reading failure among low-achieving first grade students. *The Reading Teacher, 45,* 592–597.

Taylor, B. M., Strait, J., & Medo, M. A. (1994). Early intervention in reading: Supplemental instruction for groups of low-achieving students provided by first grade teachers. In E. H. Hiebert & B. M. Taylor (Eds.), *Getting reading right from the start: Effective early literacy intervention* (pp. 107–121). Needham, MA: Allyn and Bacon.

U.S. Department of Education (1993). *Reinventing Chapter I: The current Chapter I program and new directions. Final report of the national assessment of the Chapter I program. Executive summary.* Washington, DC: Office of Policy and Planning.

Venezky, R. L. (1994). *An evaluation of Success for All: Final report to the France and Merrick Foundations.* Newark DE: University of Delaware, Department of Educational Studies.

Wasik, B. A. (1998a). Using volunteers as reading tutors: Guidelines for successful practices. *The Reading Teacher, 51,* 562–570.

Wasik, B. A. (1998b). *Volunteer tutoring programs: A review of research on achievement outcomes* (Report No. 14). Baltimore, MD: Johns Hopkins University.

Wasik, B. A., & Slavin, R. E. (1993). Preventing early reading failure with one-to-one tutoring: A review of five programs. *Reading Research Quarterly, 28,* 179–200.

Weiler, J. (1998, December). Success for All: A summary of evaluations. *Clearinghouse on Urban Education Digest, 139.*

Ysseldyke, J. E., Christenson, S. L., Thurlow, M. L., & Bakewell, D. (1989). Are different kinds of instructional tasks used by different categories of students in different settings? *School Psychology Review, 18,* 98–111.

ABOUT THE CONTRIBUTORS

Kathryn H. Au is a professor of education at the University of Hawaii. She has taught at grade levels K–2. Her research interest is the school literacy development of students of diverse cultural and linguistic backgrounds, and she has published numerous articles on this topic. She serves on the board of directors of the International Reading Association and has been president of the National Reading Conference. She has received the Oscar S. Causey Award for outstanding contributions to reading research and is a member of the Reading Hall of Fame.

Rita M. Bean, a professor of education at the University of Pittsburgh, has taught elementary school and served as a reading specialist and reading supervisor. Her publications focus on the role of the reading specialist, instructional procedures for teaching students with reading problems, and comprehension instruction. She has served on editorial advisory boards including those for *Reading Research and Instruction, The Reading Professor,* and *Reading and Writing Quarterly* and has served as chair of the Commission on the Role of the Reading Specialist for the International Reading Association. She currently directs a multiyear professional development project designed to enhance literacy instruction in the primary grades.

Karen Bromley is a professor in the School of Education and Human Development, State University of New York at Binghamton, where she recently received the Chancellor's Award and University Award for Excellence in Teaching. She teaches courses in literacy, language arts, and children's literature and coordinates the Ameri-

ca Reads program. A former third grade teacher and reading specialist, she is the author of *Language Arts: Exploring Connections* (3rd ed.), *Webbing With Literature* (2nd ed.), *Journaling: Engagements in Reading, Writing, and Thinking,* and is co-author of *Graphic Organizers: Visual Strategies for Active Learning* and *50 Graphic Organizers for Reading, Writing, and More.* She consults in area schools, has written for *The Reading Teacher* and *Family Life,* and teaches a doctoral course in writing for publication.

Douglas Fisher, an assistant professor of reading and language in the Department of Teacher Education at San Diego State University (SDSU), is the director of professional development for the City Heights Educational Pilot—a university and school partnership between SDSU and Rosa Parks Elementary, Monroe Clark Middle, and Hoover High Schools. His responsibilities include co-directing a field-based pre-service program and coordinating the schoolwide literacy plans at each of the three schools. He has co-authored and edited many articles, columns, texts, and materials on reading and language arts instruction for diverse student populations. He is co-editor of *The California Reader.*

James Flood, a professor of reading and language development at San Diego State University (SDSU), has taught at the pre-school, elementary, and secondary levels and has been a language arts supervisor and vice principal. He was a Fulbright scholar at the University of Lisbon in Portugal and the president of the National Reading Conference. Currently, he teaches pre-service and graduate courses at SDSU. He is co-editor of *The California Reader* and has co-authored and edited many articles, columns, texts, handbooks, and children's materials on reading and language arts issues, including two books developed with Diane Lapp: *Content Area Reading and Learning* (2nd ed.) and *The Handbook of Research on Teaching Literacy Through the Communicative and Visual Arts.* He was named Outstanding Teacher Educator in the Department of Teacher Education at SDSU and the Distinguished Research Lecturer from SDSU's Graduate Division of Research, and he is a member of the California Reading Hall of Fame.

Anthony D. Fredericks is a professor of education and chair of the Education Department at York College, York, Pennsylvania. A former classroom teacher and reading specialist, he is known for his energetic and practical presentations for strengthening reading instruction. He has authored or co-authored more than 50 teacher resource books, including the best-selling *The Complete Phonemic Awareness Handbook.* Additionally, he has written two dozen children's books on animals and the environment (e.g., *Cannibal Animals, Exploring the Rainforest*). He maintains a website (www.afredericks.com) for elementary educators and administrators.

Kelly Goss-Moore is a first grade teacher at Oak Park School in San Diego, where she teaches culturally and linguistically diverse populations of children; she has also taught in the intermediate grades. She is a doctoral student at San Diego State University. She was the featured teacher in a series of instructionally related films that were made for the state of California. She is interested in issues related to the literacy development of less fluent readers.

Bill Harp is a professor of language arts and literacy in the Graduate School of Education at the University of Massachusetts, Lowell. His elementary school teaching experience ranges from Head Start through sixth grade, and he has served as an elementary school principal and director of programs for the gifted. His university experience includes positions at the University of Delaware, Oregon State University, and Northern Arizona University. His most recent publication is the second edition of *The Handbook of Literacy Assessment and Evaluation* published by Christopher-Gordon, where he also serves as editor of *The Bill Harp Professional Teacher's Library.*

Barbara A. Kapinus, a senior policy analyst and education consultant at the National Education Association, has served as the director of the Curriculum and Instructional Improvement Program at the Council of Chief State School Officers. She was the specialist for reading and communication skills at the Maryland State Department of Education and was a classroom teacher, reading specialist, and curriculum specialist in Prince George's County Public Schools. She directed the development of the current framework for the NAEP in Reading and worked on the International Literacy Study (IEA) and the Program for International Student Assessment (PISA). She served as president of her state reading council, served on the editorial boards of *The Reading Teacher* and *Journal of Reading,* and co-edited the assessment column of *The Reading Teacher.*

Diane Lapp is a professor of reading and language in the Department of Teacher Education at San Diego State University (SDSU). She has taught in elementary and middle schools, co-directs and teaches field-based pre-service and graduate courses, and spent her recent sabbatical team teaching in a public school first grade classroom. She has co-authored and edited many articles, columns, texts, handbooks, and children's materials on reading and language arts issues. Two books co-developed with James Flood are *Teaching Reading to Every Child* (4th ed.) and *The Handbook of Research in Teaching the English Language Arts* (2nd ed.). She was named Outstanding Teacher Educator and Faculty Member in the Department of Teacher Education at SDSU and the Distinguished Research Lecturer from SDSU's Graduate Division of Research. She is a member of the California Reading Hall of Fame and was the International Reading Association's

1996 Outstanding Teacher Educator of the Year. She is co-editor of *The California Reader.*

Christine A. McKeon, an assistant professor of education at Walsh University in North Canton, Ohio, is a former elementary teacher, Title I teacher, and high school reading teacher. She has published in *The Reading Teacher* as well as other literacy journals and publications. Her areas of interest include technology and literacy as well as adolescent and adult literacy.

Juel Ann Moore has been an elementary school principal for 15 years and is currently the principal of Oak Park Music Conservatory with Enriched Studies Magnet School in San Diego. She has also worked as an elementary school teacher, reading specialist, community college and university instructor. She was selected as a coaching principal in her district. She is on the editorial advisory board of *The California Reader* and the Advisory Board for Teacher Education at San Diego State University.

Maryann Mraz is a doctoral student and teaching fellow in the Department of Teaching, Leadership, and Curriculum Studies at Kent State University. Her academic interests include literacy, literacy policy, and the professional development of teachers. She has worked as a teacher, administrator, and adjunct instructor. Currently, she serves as a literacy consultant for several Ohio school districts and as an Education Advisory Committee member for the Playhouse Square Foundation in Cleveland.

Diana J. Quatroche, an assistant professor in the Department of Elementary and Early Childhood Education at Indiana State University in Terre Haute, teaches undergraduate and graduate courses in reading and language arts. She previously taught at Southeast Missouri State University and Kent State University. In addition, she has experience teaching elementary school, supervising school reading programs, and coordinating Title I reading programs. Her research interests include the role of reading specialists, school reading programs, and profes-

sional development school initiatives. She regularly presents at national reading conferences and has written articles that have appeared in *Teaching and Change, Educational Horizons,* and the *Journal of Clinical Reading.*

Lucinda C. Ray is the director of curriculum development at IntelliTools, Inc., in Petaluma, California. She was the group product marketing manager at The Learning Company's School Division, the education product manager at Broderbund Software, and an English teacher and drama director at the middle school, high school, and college levels in Massachusetts, Vermont, and Iowa. Her research interests include multimedia in literacy development and instructional design in electronic learning tools. She has managed the development of software products such as Intellitools®: Reading: Balanced Literacy, Kid Pix Studio® Deluxe, and Kid Pix® Activity Kits. Her publications include teacher's guides for software published by Grolier, Maxis, and Broderbund, and chapters in *Linking Literacy and Technology: A Guide for K–8 Classrooms, Educational Computing in the Schools,* and *Reclaiming the Classroom.*

Dixie Lee Spiegel, a professor of literacy studies at the University of North Carolina at Chapel Hill, teaches graduate and undergraduate courses. She is also the associate dean for students at the School of Education and the director of graduate studies. She has published in a variety of literacy journals, including *The Reading Teacher, Language Arts,* and the *Journal of Reading Behavior.* Her most recent publications focus on balanced literacy instruction and literature response groups.

Dorothy S. Strickland is the State of New Jersey Professor of Reading at Rutgers University. A former classroom teacher and reading specialist, she is a past president of the International Reading Association and its Reading Hall of Fame. Her awards include IRA's Outstanding Teacher Educator of Reading, NCTE's Outstanding Educator in the Language Arts, and the NCTE Rewey Belle Inglis Award as Outstanding

Woman in the Teaching of English. Her publications include *Families: Poems Celebrating the African American Experience; Emerging Literacy; Language, Literacy, and the Child; Teaching Phonics Today;* and *Beginning Reading and Writing.*

William Teale, a professor of education at the University of Illinois at Chicago, also serves as director of the Reading Clinic and chair of the Department of Curriculum and Instruction. The former editor of *Language Arts,* he is best known for his work in the area of early literacy development. He has published in a wide variety of professional journals. His book *Emergent Literacy: Writing and Reading,* which he co-edited with Elizabeth Sulzby, is regarded as a standard reference in the field.

JoAnne L. Vacca is a professor and former chair of the Department of Teaching, Leadership, and Curriculum Studies at Kent State University. She has co-authored two multiple-edition books in the field of literacy education. Her most recent publications include *Reading and Learning to Read* (4th ed.) with Richard T. Vacca and Mary Gove, and *Content Area Reading* (6th ed.) with Richard T. Vacca.

Richard T. Vacca has taught reading and English at the middle school and high school levels. He is a co-author of *Content Area Reading* (6th ed.), *Reading and Learning to Read, Whole Language in Middle and Secondary Classrooms,* and *Case Studies in Whole Language.* He has written numerous articles and chapters on the literacy needs of adolescent learners, conducted staff development workshops throughout North America, and served as project director for the Cleveland Writing Project, a collaborative effort between Kent State University and Cleveland Public Schools. He is the recipient of the College Reading Association's A. B. Herr Award for Outstanding Contributions to Reading Education. He served as a member of the board of directors and as president of the International Reading Association.

Arlene D. Wartenberg was an associate professor at the Center for Education, Widener University, Chester, Pennsylvania. A former classroom teacher and reading specialist, she designed a reading and study skills course for adults at Beaver College, where she was associate director of Continuing Education. At Widener University, she was director of the Academic Skills Center, coordinated and taught reading and study skills, and taught master's and doctoral-level reading courses. A focus of her research is postsecondary reading instruction.

Shelley B. Wepner is a professor of education, director of the Center for Education, and associate dean of the School of Human Service Professions at Widener University, Chester, Pennsylvania. Previously, she was a supervisor of curriculum and instruction and reading specialist in New Jersey. Her research interests include the use of technology for literacy development and teacher education, and leadership qualities of reading specialists and education deans. Her publications include three award-winning software packages: Reading Realities, Reading Realities Elementary Series, and Read-A-Logo. Her latest book is *Linking Literacy and Technology: A Guide for K–8 Classrooms.*

Junko Yokota teaches reading and language arts and children's literature in the Department of Reading and Language, National College of Education, at National–Louis University, Evanston, Illinois. She was an elementary classroom teacher and an elementary school librarian. She is co-author of *Children's Books in Children's Hands* (2nd ed.) and editor of *Kaleidoscope: A Multicultural Booklist for Grades K–8.* Her research interests center on issues regarding multicultural literature and literacy development for multicultural populations.

INDEX

Abbott, J. A., 86
Access issues
  in adolescent programs, 63, 64
  in elementary programs, 53
  to technology, 146–147
    in disabilities, 147
Access, Microsoft [software], 144
Accommodation model of teaching and
  learning, 62
Action research, 112–113, 113f
Ada, F., 161
Adams, M., 8, 187, 188
Administrators
  in material selection, 83–85
  in pre-elementary programs, 39–40
  in professional development pro-
    grams, 108–109
  in writing programs, 133–134
Adolescent literacy programs, 59–70
  access to materials in, 63, 64
  assessment in, 63, 65–66
  changing paradigms of, 62–63
  computer technology in, 65
  content-area reading and writing in,
    61–62
  curriculum in, 61, 69
  diversity of students in, 66–68
  future trends in, 68–70
  historical aspects of, 60–62
  instructional strategies and activities
    in, 63, 64–65
  magazines in, 93
  parent and community involvement
    in, 63, 68
    outreach programs for, 172–174
  reading specialists in, 63, 66
  responsive environment in, 67
  shared responsibilities in, 66
  teachers in
    as models, 63, 64–65
    observation and evaluation of, 103
    understanding of adolescent char-
      acteristics, 63, 66–68
  writing activities in, 60–62, 133

Afflerbach, P., 10, 31, 128, 180, 186, 187
Alliance for Technology Access, 147
Allington, R., 9, 10, 31, 44, 52, 54, 160,
  164, 179, 180, 181, 186, 187, 188
Alphabet knowledge
  in elementary programs, 54
  in pre-elementary programs, 35
  in special needs programs, 188
Alvarado, A., 13
Alvermann, D. E., 67
America Reads, 171–172, 185
American Association of Colleges for
  Teacher Education, 150
American Federation of Teachers, 21
Anderson, R. C., 7, 8, 44, 53, 54, 186
Anderson, R. H., 8
Andrejko, L., 97
Antommarchi, C., 73
Applebee, A. N., 160, 161
Apprenticeship programs in profession-
  al development, 111–112
Archambault, F. X., 18
Armbruster, B. B., 8, 75, 89
Armstrong, A., 151
Arter, J., 11
Asam, C. L., 54
Aschbacher, P. R., 127
Ascher, C., 44
Askew, B. J., 182
Asp, E., 10, 11, 127
Assessment
  of curriculum change, 13
  of professional development pro-
    grams, 116
  of reading programs, 118–127
  of students, 10–11, 118–127
    in adolescent literacy programs, 63,
      65–66
    authenticity of tasks in, 122–123,
      124
    in classroom, 119, 124–126
    competing measures in, 11
    complexity of tasks in, 120–121,
      125

cultural bias in tests affecting, 44
curriculum aligned with, 4
  in diverse populations, 160
  in elementary programs, 46–52,
    55–56
  as instruction guide, 10–11, 126–127
  large-scale, 119–124
  in model of effective school pro-
    gram, 4, 5f
  observation checklist in, 38, 38f
  oral language checklist in, 38, 39f
  outcome or goal focus of, 120
  parents as collaborators in, 125–126
  portfolios in, 51, 122, 125
  in pre-elementary programs, 30–31,
    38–39
  in pull-out programs, 179–180,
    181
  role of reading specialist in, 19
  scoring guides and rubrics in, 11,
    121–122
  self-monitoring in, 9, 11, 51–52
  in standards-based education, 4,
    10–11
  teacher involvement in, 123–124
  on writing, 131–132, 134
  of teachers. *See* Teachers, observation
    and evaluation of
Association for Supervision and Curriculum Development, 136
Atwell, N., 134
Au, K., 44, 54, 55, 56, 57, 153, 154, 155,
  156, 157, 158, 163
Authenticity
  in classroom assessment, 124
  in large-scale assessment, 122–123
  in special needs programs, 186
  in teacher observation and evalua-
    tion, 99
  in writing activities, 135

Baker, K., 10, 54
Bakewell, D., 180
Bakhtin, M. M., 54

197